D0116197

BABY CRAFTS
A Treasury of Gifts from the Heart

Marsha Evans Moore

SEDGEWOOD® PRESS
New York, N.Y.

ACKNOWLEDGMENTS

I would like to thank the following people: Dina von Zweck, for challenging me to design these baby crafts and for all her help in putting this book together; Ellen Liberles, for a superb editing job; and Georgianna Demilio, Linda Meek, and Bernice Rubin for lending some photo props. Special thanks to Georgianna Demilio for making the wooden farm animals on page 168.

Credits: High chair (page 182) and crib (page 103) from Ben's for Kids, New York, NY. Background fabrics on pages 74 (floral fabric), 99, 137, 177, and 193; toys on pages 94, 161, and 173; and pillow on page 103, from Marimekko Store, New York, NY. Tiles on page 177 from Ceramica Mia, New York, NY.

Project Director: Dina von Zweck

For Sedgewood® Press:
Director: Elizabeth P. Rice
Editorial Project Manager: Bruce Macomber
Associate Editor: Leslie Gilbert
Project Editor: Sandy Towers
Production Manager: Bill Rose
Book Design: Remo Cosentino
Photography: Thomas Famighetti

Copyright© 1988 by Diamandis Communications Inc. All rights reserved.

Woman's Day® is a registered trademark of Diamandis Communications Inc.

Distributed by Macmillan Publishing Company, a division of Macmillan, Inc.

ISBN: 0-02-496840-4
Library of Congress Catalog Card Number: 86-61602

Printed in the United States of America

10 9 8 7 6 5 4 3 2 1

Contents

Introduction

Baby Crafts is a useful compendium of beautiful projects, and it's full of imaginative ideas. Babies deserve to be cherished and pampered. Whether the baby you have in mind is a child of your own, a grandchild, or the child of an expectant friend, you can create any project in this book as a special gift. The soft, delicate folds on a smocked dress, the snuggly warmth of a hooded sweater, the brightness of a patchwork toy—all are made unique by your needlework skills.

No event is more joyfully anticipated than the birth of a baby. What better way to spend the "waiting months" than to plan the nursery, and the baby clothes and toys? Even if you are an expectant mother busy working, spend a little time each day stitching and dreaming of your baby's life. It's a wonderful way to relax. If it's a friend or family member who's expecting, you'll want to show your love with a special handmade gift. New parents love to receive something made especially for their baby.

Handmade babycrafts give you the opportunity to choose exactly the colors and materials you want. And the simple cotton fabrics, soft acrylic yarn, and dainty eyelets and ribbons you'll use are inexpensive, too. You may even have some in your sewing room now. Your wonderful hand-crafted items will cost a fraction of what you'd spend to buy them in a shop. These days, saving money is a consideration for almost every new family. If you need to stretch your budget even further, save the scraps left over from the major projects. Many of the toys and accessories can be made from these scraps at almost no cost—and they'll coordinate beautifully with what you've already made.

There are projects for every level of skill, from quick-and-easy projects to more ambitious ones—everything from a simple rattle to an elaborate Heirloom Christening Ensemble. If you like, first try some of the projects that look simple, such as the Classic Carriage Ensemble, the Bouncing Babies garland or the Big, Bright Balls. In the how-to chapter, you'll find a lot of helpful information about basic sewing techniques. If you're a beginner, read through this chapter first so you'll be familiar with what's offered there.

Almost all of the clothing patterns are sized 6–18 months. You'll also find a lot of interesting ideas for first and second birthday presents, or Christmas gifts.

I hope you enjoy making the projects in this book to commemorate the arrival of a new little one.

HOW-TO:

TECHNIQUES

How-To: Techniques

BASIC TOOLS AND MATERIALS

Here are the basic tools and materials you should have on hand to do the projects in this book.

Tracing or Wrapping Paper, for enlarging patterns. Tracing paper is best because you can see through it and trace patterns directly from the book.

Graph or Quadrille Paper, for enlarging patterns or planning cross-stitch names.

Pencils and Pens, for drawing patterns and marking fabric.

Dressmaker's Carbon, for transferring designs or marking fabric.

Ruler, for enlarging patterns and measuring fabric.

Tape Measure, for measuring lengths that are not flat or for fitting clothes.

Compass or Circle Templates, for drawing circles.

Sewing Machine, for sewing most projects together.

Dressmaker's Shears, sharp, for cutting fabric.

Paper Scissors, for cutting paper, so you don't dull shears.

Embroidery Scissors, with sharp, pointed tips, for cutting small pieces of fabric and trimming sewing and embroidery threads.

Seam Ripper, for pulling out stitches if necessary.

Pins, for holding patterns in place while cutting and holding fabric pieces together while sewing.

T-Pins, for holding stuffed animals together.

Needles, for hand-sewing. You'll need an assortment of different-size needles for sewing different weights of fabric and embroidering with different weights of floss; you'll also need a blunt tapestry needle for sewing knit and crochet projects, and a long needle for sewing stuffed animals together.

Dowel or Chopstick, for turning fabric tubes and pushing in stuffing.

Embroidery Hoop, for holding fabric taut as you embroider.

Other tools and materials you'll need are listed at the beginning of each project.

FABRICS

The fabrics listed for each project were used to make the project photographed. Therefore, the lists are, in most cases, very specific. Use your judgment or, if you are a beginner, ask a knowledgeable salesperson to substitute a similar, available fabric. If you can't find the colors or kinds of prints used in a project, pick a new main fabric for the project. Then coordinate all the other fabrics and the ribbon, lace, embroidery floss, and so forth to match.

Even though we try to treat boy babies and girl babies alike so far as playthings and activities are concerned, when it comes to dressing them or decorating the nursery, many of us still feel that pink is for girls and blue is for boys. If you want to make a project specifically for a boy or a girl, pick the appropriate main color and coordinate the other materials. For example, you may want to use a stripe for a boy and a floral print for a girl; a plain eyelet for a boy and a delicate lace for a girl. You will soon be able to visualize the photographed projects in different fabrics and trims. When you do, you will be ready to create your own very special project.

HOW TO ENLARGE PATTERNS

When a pattern or design for a project is too large to fit on the book's pages, it is shown reduced on a grid.

Find a piece of tracing or wrapping paper large enough to accommodate the final design, piece two sheets of paper together if necessary. With a pencil and ruler, draw a grid on the tracing or wrapping paper, spacing the lines ½-inch apart, 1 inch apart, or whatever measurement is indicated on the pattern. Be sure to draw the right number of squares for a given project. Copy the pattern square by square, first marking dots on your grid where the pattern lines intersect corresponding lines on the reduced grid given with the pattern. Then sketch in the lines between the dots. Use a ruler to draw any straight lines, and a French curve, if desired, to draw curved lines. Include any other pattern markings. Cut out the enlarged patterns.

Instead of drawing a grid, you can use a large sheet of printed blue graph (quadrille) paper. It can be purchased in pads and comes in several sizes. Some sewing supply stores carry special grid paper marked with 1-inch squares for enlarging patterns.

If you are planning to enlarge several patterns using grids of the same scale, it saves time to make a master grid on heavy paper or on a sheet of graph paper. Tape a layer of tracing or tissue paper over the grid and draw the pattern as you would on the grid itself. When the pattern is complete, remove the paper from the grid and save the grid to use again.

Patterns on grids can also be photostated or photocopied to the scale given for the pattern, although these processes are somewhat expensive.

HOW TO CUT OUT PATTERNS

Be sure to check the care directions for the fabrics you choose. Look for fabrics that can be washed and dried easily. Preshrink all fabrics, following the manufacturer's directions *before* marking or cutting. Then press the fabric, making sure the grain is straight.

Work on a large, smooth surface, such as a table or floor, on which the fabric can be laid out flat. Pin all pieces to the fabric as closely together as possible. Also, check for square, rectangular or circular pieces that are needed but do not appear on the reduced grid. The dimensions for these pieces are given in the written instructions. Place all edges labeled *Place on Fold* on the middle fold of the fabric to get one symmetrical piece. Place arrows along the straight grain. For fabrics with nap, cut pieces so the nap runs down and feels smooth from the top to the bottom of the piece.

Cut out all pieces accurately, using sharp dressmaker's scissors. If only one fabric piece is needed, cut that from a single layer of fabric. If two sym-metrical fabric pieces are needed—the right and left sides of a teddy bear's front, for example—fold the fabric in half, right sides together, with the selvage edges lined up. Pin each pattern piece onto both layers of fabric at once. When you cut around the pattern through the two layers of fabric, you will have both fabric pieces you need, and they will be perfectly symmetrical.

HOW TO TRANSFER DESIGNS AND MARKINGS ONTO FABRIC

Trace the design from the book or use the pattern piece you have enlarged. Decide whether the marking or design should appear on the right or wrong side of the fabric. In general, embroidery designs, placement markings, and facial features should be marked on the right side. Darts, dots, and other markings that indicate how seams should be sewn should be marked on the wrong side. Often it is not necessary to transfer placement markings for stuffed animals or appliqué designs. Simply note the marking on the pattern piece in relation to the fabric piece. Then use your judgment and your eye to determine where the other pattern pieces should be placed or attached. Then use one of the following transfer methods.

■ For most fabrics, insert dressmaker's carbon between the pattern piece and the fabric, shiny side facedown on the fabric. Trace over the design with a pencil or tracing wheel.

■ To mark dots, darts, and other placement markings, pin the pattern piece to the fabric and insert a pin at marking. Lift up edge of pattern and mark fabric with lead or pastel pencil.

■ For smooth, light-colored fabrics, turn your traced design over and retrace the lines on the wrong side of the paper with a soft lead pencil. Place the pattern piece right-side-up on the fabric and trace over the lines again. The pencil lines on the wrong side will come off on your fabric.

■ Trace the design, using a marker or dark lead pencil. Place the fabric over the paper. Tape it in place, either against a window during daylight hours or on a lightbox. Trace the lines on the fabric.

■ For fur fabrics or other napped fabrics, mark the wrong side using a lead or pastel pencil. If you need to mark something on the right side, mark on the back. Then sew tailor's tacks to show dots and lines of basting stitches to show lines on right side.

Transfer pens and papers are available at art supply, sewing, or craft shops. Be sure to follow the manufacturer's directions exactly.

HOW TO PRESS FABRIC

Use a steam iron. Always press seams, darts, pleats, and so forth before joining them to other seams. Press napped fabrics on the wrong side, or face the fabric right-side-up, cover it with a clean terrycloth towel, and press carefully. Test a scrap piece first to be sure you can press the fabric without crushing it. You do not need to press seams when making animals or other stuffed items, because the stuffing holds the seams in place. Finger-pressing is exactly that, pressing with your fingers. It is used on fabrics that cannot be ironed such as fur fabric or when you need to hold something open temporarily. Place the fabric piece on your working surface and run your finger along the dart or seam pressing down as hard as you can. Or run the fabric between thumb and forefinger pressing them together. Repeat the motion until the fabric stays in the desired position.

HOW TO TRIM, GRADE, AND CLIP SEAM ALLOWANCES

Trim seam allowances when less bulk is desired. Trim diagonally at corners if the piece will be turned right-side-out (A).

When the seam allowance is bulky or when more than two layers of fabric are sewn together, you will want to grade the seam allowance. To do this, trim each layer of the seam allowance to a different width so that the layers lie flat and no ridge shows along the seam allowance on the right side (B).

Clip curved seams after stitching, trimming, or grading so that they lie flat and do not pucker or pull. Clip *almost* to the stitching at regular intervals of ¼ inch to ¾ inch, depending on the sharpness of the curve. The sharper the curve, the more closely spaced the clips should be. Outer curves should be notched by cutting out a small wedge of

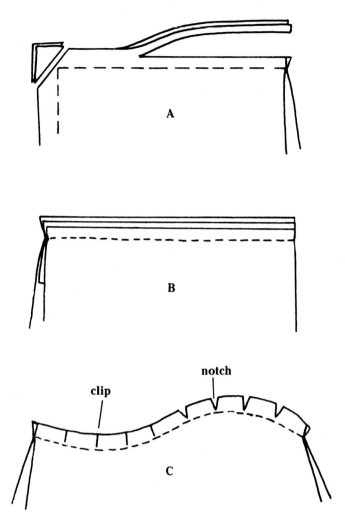

A

B

clip   notch

C

fabric. Outer curves of stuffed animals usually do not need notches; just clip them (C).

HOW TO STUFF PROJECTS

For a large item, such as a pillow or animal body, insert stuffing in large handfuls. Distribute the stuffing evenly so that it does not lump together and the outside of the project is smooth. For small sections, such as ears, insert small bits of stuffing no larger than cottonballs. For long, narrow areas, such as legs, use a dowel or chopstick to push the stuffing into the bottom of the shape. Check the shape carefully from the outside as you go to be sure it is smooth, soft, and evenly stuffed.

HOW TO MAKE A NARROW HEM

Turn the fabric under ⅜ inch from the edge and press. Fold top (or outer) edge of hem down toward the crease. Press. Slipstitch the folded-over top edge of hem in place. You may find it helpful to pin the edge in place before you stitch.

HOW TO STITCH DARTS

Fold the fabric along the center of dart, matching stitching lines. Beginning at the widest part at the outer edge of the fabric piece, stitch to point of dart. Backstitch to knot the thread (A). For thin fabrics, press the dart to one side (B). For heavy fabrics and fur, slash along the center of the dart to within ½ inch or 1 inch of the point; press or finger-press the dart open (C).

Hem

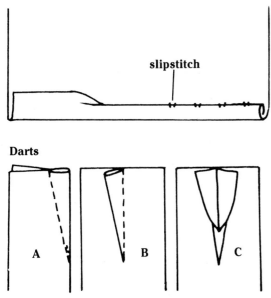

slipstitch

Darts

A   B   C

HOW TO GATHER FABRIC

Sew a row of stitches along the seam line and a second row of stitches about halfway between the seam line and the edge of your fabric. If you are using a sewing machine, sew long, straight stitches about six stitches per inch. Pull the thread ends to gather the fabric and then secure the ends in a figure eight, around pins placed at the side edges of the gathered fabric (A). If you are sewing by

Gathers

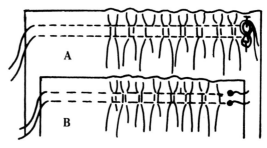

A

B

hand, knot one end of your thread. (For heavy fabrics use thread doubled and ends knotted together.) Sew a row of small ⅛-inch- to ¼-inch-long running stitches along the seam line. Cut the thread. Sew a second row halfway between the seam line and the fabric edge. Pull unknotted ends to gather fabric and secure the loose thread ends around a pin as described above (B).

HOW TO CUT AND JOIN BIAS STRIPS

To make bias strips, which are strips cut diagonally across the grain of the fabric, cut your fabric at a 45° angle to the grain, as follows: Spread out a large piece of fabric on a flat surface with the grain of the fabric running up and down. Fold the fabric diagonally from one corner so that the corner touches the long edge opposite. Press along the fold. Open the fabric out and cut along the fold. Parallel to the diagonal, measure and mark strips the width indicated in the instructions. Cut the strips from the fabric.

When possible, cut one strip of fabric the desired length for the project. If you must piece strips together to get the desired length, cut the number

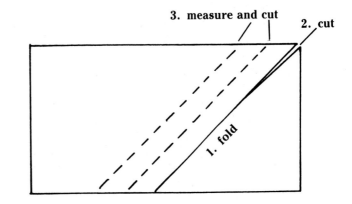

3. measure and cut   2. cut

1. fold

of strips to equal the needed length *plus* ¼-inch seam allowance on each end of each strip. Right sides together, and with the two strips at right angles to each other, stitch across the seam lines. Press the seams open.

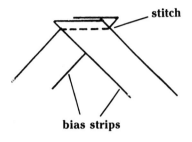

stitch

bias strips

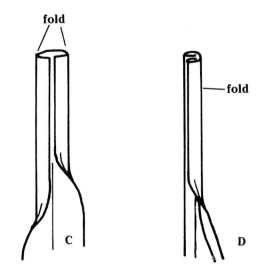

fold

fold

C

D

HOW TO MAKE BIAS TAPE

Press a bias strip, stretching it slightly to make the fabric more stable (A). Fold the strip in half lengthwise, wrong sides together. Again, press lightly (B).

Open the fold and press lightly once more, leaving a visible crease at the center. To make single-fold bias tape, fold the long side edges toward the center, crease, and press (C).

To make double-fold bias tape, refold the strip at the center (or better, slightly to one side) and press (D).

HOW TO MAKE BINDING

To apply binding in one step, place purchased or handmade double-fold bias tape over the fabric edge being bound with the wider half of the tape underneath. Pin in place. Then, from the top, stitch along the inner edge of the tape. The extra width underneath will ensure that the edge of the tape underneath is caught by the stitching. You may find it helpful to baste the tape in place by hand before stitching (A).

fold and press

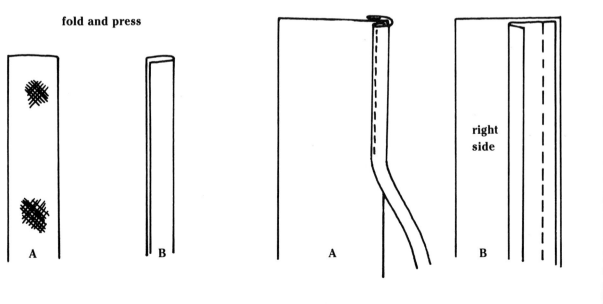

A

B

right side

A

B

The slipstitch method of binding an edge requires single-fold bias tape or just a bias-binding strip. Open out one fold of the tape or strip. Place it on the right side of the fabric near or along the fabric edge. Line up seam lines. Stitch (B). Then turn the bias tape or strip over the seam allowance to the wrong side of the fabric, so that the fold of the free edge of the tape or strip is along the seam line on the wrong side. On plain bias strips, turn under the free edge along the seam line. Pin the tape or strip edge in place. Slipstitch the strip or tape to the fabric over the seam line (C).

The topstitch method of binding an edge also requires single-fold bias tape or a bias-binding strip. Open out one fold of the tape or strip. Place it on the wrong side (or the lining or backing side) of the fabric near or along the fabric edge. Line up seam lines. Stitch (D). Then turn the bias tape or strip over the seam allowance to the right side of the fabric so that the fold of the free edge of the tape or strip is along the seam line on the right side. On plain bias strips, turn under the free edge along the seam line. Pin or baste the tape or strip edge in place. Topstitch along the inner edge of the binding (E).

HOW TO MAKE PIPING

Cut the bias strip or strips needed for the project. Piece strips together if necessary to make a strip of the desired length. Then fold the strip in half lengthwise, wrong sides together. Place cotton cording inside the fold. Using a zipper foot, machine-baste along the edge of the cording (A). Right sides together, baste the piping to one piece of fabric along the seam line. Right sides together, place second piece of fabric over fabric with piping. Stitch the seam just inside the line of basting stitches, holding piping to fabric (B).

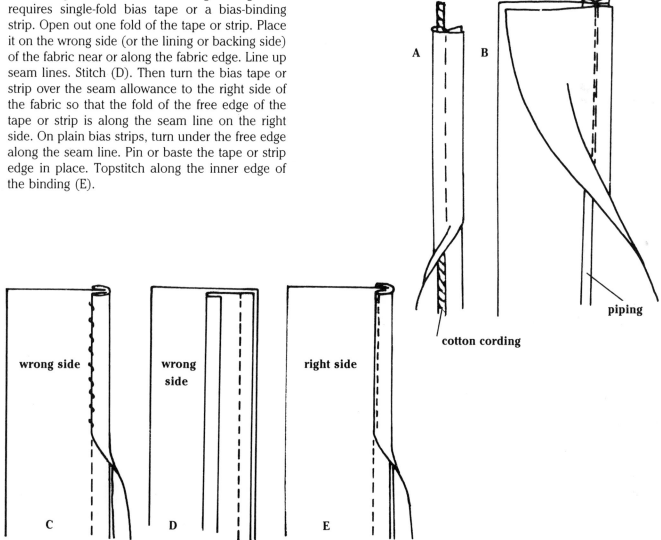

HOW TO MITER BINDING

Right sides together, pin and stitch bias binding strip to one edge of the project, backstitching at corner (A). Fold the binding strip diagonally to bring it around corner; pin it in place. Pin the binding along the adjacent edge. Beginning at backstitched corner, stitch to next corner (B). Continue around all edges.

Forming a miter—a diagonal fold—with the binding on the right side around one corner, fold binding over edge to wrong side (C). Turn the raw edge of the binding under along the seam line, forming a miter on wrong side of binding by making a fold in the opposite direction to the fold on the right side. Pin the turned-under edge in place. Slipstitch the binding to the wrong side, and then slipstitch edges of miter together (D).

For the topstitch method of binding, follow the directions above but reverse right and wrong sides of project. Topstitch binding in place on right side.

HOW TO MITER LACE

Right sides up, pin the lace around the corner, folding the lace diagonally at the corner to form a miter. Finger-press the foldline to mark it (A).

Unpin lace from corner. Pin the miter in, leaving the extra fold of lace on the wrong side. Stitch along fold of the miter by hand or machine (B).

Trim the seam allowance close to the stitching. Overcast or zigzag-stitch the seam allowance to keep the trimmed edge from fraying.

Repin lace to edge of project. Stitch (C).

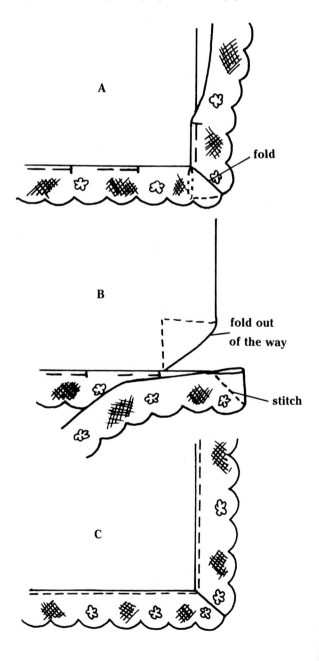

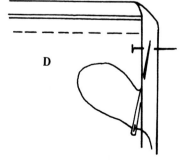

HOW TO STITCH SEAMS

FRENCH SEAM

This kind of seam encloses the raw edges of the seam allowance. Pin the edges of fabric with wrong sides together; stitch ⅜ inch from raw edges. Press the seam allowance to one side and trim it to ⅛ inch (A). Fold the fabric forward over the seam allowance so that the right sides are together and encase the seam allowance. Press along the fold. Now, the wrong sides of the fabric are out. Stitch ¼ inch from the edge—the first stitch line (B). The encased seam allowance will be on the wrong side.

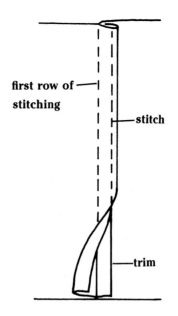

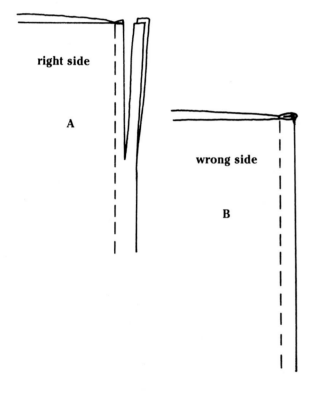

FLAT-FELLED SEAM

With wrong sides of the fabric together, stitch along the seamline. Working on the right side of the fabric, press the seam allowance to one side. Trim the lower seam allowance to ¼ inch. Fold the upper seam allowance in half over the trimmed edge of the lower seam allowance. Pin the seam allowance to the fabric. Topstitch through all layers close to the turned edge.

HOW TO HAND-STITCH

BACKSTITCH

Used for sewing strong seams or for attaching trims by hand. Bring needle up from the underside of the fabric and insert it about ⅛ inch to the right of the point where it came out. Bring the needle out again about ⅛ inch to the left of the starting point. Continue in the same manner.

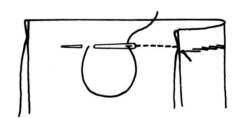

WHIPSTITCH

Used to join two edges or to attach a trim or appliqué. Bring the needle through the fabric to the front. Insert the needle again, moving from back to front, close to the edge and at a diagonal angle. Repeat, making stitches close together.

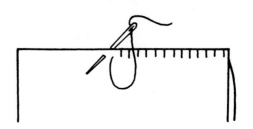

OVERCAST STITCH

Used to finish raw edges. Make diagonal stitches over the edge of the fabric, inserting needle straight instead of at an angle.

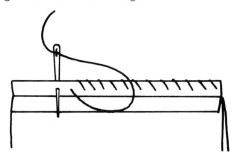

RUNNING STITCH

Used to sew seams by hand, to baste, to gather fabric, and to quilt. Working in a straight line, weave needle in and out of the fabric two or three times. Pull the thread through. Keep your stitches small and even.

BASTING STITCH

Used to hold layers of fabric together or to hold trim or lace securely in place while being stitched by machine. By hand, make running stitches, ¼ inch long or longer.

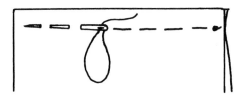

TACK

Used to hold fabric, trims, and ribbons in place. Make several small straight stitches in the same spot or one directly under another.

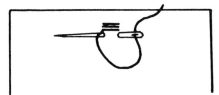

SLIPSTITCH

Used to join two folded edges of fabrics, such as openings for turning and stuffing. Make ⅛-inch stitches, moving from one folded edge to the other, just catching the edge. Your stitches should be even.

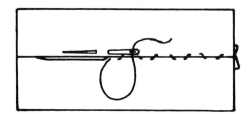

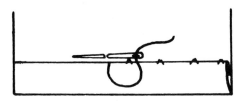

Use uneven slipstitches to make a hem. Slip needle through the folded hem edge without piercing the fabric for ¼ inch or ½ inch. Bring the needle out at the folded hem edge, and then take a small stitch under one or two threads of the fabric beneath the hem. Repeat around or for the length of the hem.

HOW TO WORK EMBROIDERY STITCHES

BACKSTITCH

Bring the needle up from the underside of fabric and insert it one stitch length away to the right. Bring it out again one stitch length ahead, to the left. Repeat, keeping stitch lengths even.

FRENCH KNOT

Hold the needle in your right hand. With your left hand, wrap thread around needle two or more times, depending on the size of knot you want to make. Be sure the needle points away from the fabric when you wrap the thread around it, and wrap close to where the thread comes through the fabric. Insert needle close to where it came out. Holding knot in place, pull the needle to the wrong side to secure the knot.

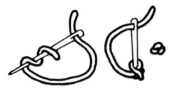

LAZY-DAISY STITCH

Bring thread from wrong side of fabric at the inner edge of the petal. Insert needle where the thread came out, making a short loop. Bring needle through the fabric at outer edge of the petal and catch the loop under the needle's point. Insert needle again just outside the loop to hold it in place. To embroider flower, bring needle up right next to the inner point of the first petal and begin the next stitch. Make as many petals as you wish, keeping them concentric by beginning close to the inner point of the first petal.

LONG-AND-SHORT STITCH

Work parallel straight stitches close together to fill in a shape. Vary the length of the stitches so that they are staggered for a textured effect.

STEM STITCH

Working from left to right along the line of a design, make stitches of equal length, keeping the thread on the same side of the needle. Bring the needle out each time where the last stitch went in.

SATIN STITCH

Work parallel straight stitches close together across the entire area to fill in a shape.

STRAIGHT STITCH

This stitch is used for occasional single stitches scattered in a design. It may also be used to form letters, or (grouped in a ring) to form flowers. Each stitch is separated from the next one.

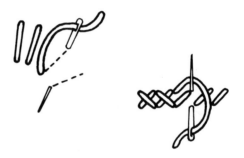

CROSS-STITCH

This stitch is usually worked on even weave fabric—fabric that has threads crossing each other at right angles and that can be counted easily. Starting at the lower left corner of a stitch and working from left to right, make a diagonal stitch to the upper right corner. Bring the needle to the front again directly under where it was inserted and even with the lower left corner of the last stitch. Continue across, making a row of parallel slanting stitches. Each should cover the same number of threads. Work back over these stitches from lower right to upper left, to "cross" them. You can work each cross-stitch individually and in any direction, but be sure to cross all your stitches in the same direction.

BLANKET STITCH

Working from left to right, bring needle out on a design line or close to a raw or hem edge. Take an upright stitch to the right with the needle pointed down. Catch the thread under the point of the needle as you come out on the line or edge. Repeat for desired length.

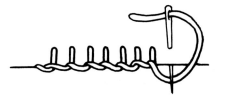

FLY STITCH

To make a V-shaped stitch, bring the needle to the front of the fabric and insert it again even with where it came out. Pull through, leaving stitch slack. Bring the needle up again at center of the **V**. Catch the stitch under the point of the needle and insert the needle back into the fabric on the other side of the loop. If the thread is not pulled tightly, it will make a curved stitch rather than a V-shaped stitch and can be used for a mouth.

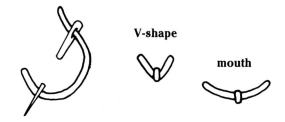

V-shape

mouth

HOW TO MAKE RIBBON ROSES

For each rose, you will need 18 inches of ⅜-inch-wide ribbon, 1 yard of 1-inch-wide ribbon, or 60 inches of 1½-inch-wide ribbon. Use single-faced satin ribbon only.

Fold your ribbon in half diagonally at center of ribbon length (A). Fold the right side of the ribbon back under fold (B). Fold the left side of the ribbon back under right (C).

Continue to fold first the right side and then the left side of the ribbon under one another in the same manner until you are almost at the end of the ribbon (D).

With one hand, grasp ends firmly together where they last cross (E). Release the folded por-

tion. With your other hand, hold one side of the ribbon against itself one fold above the last cross so that a loop is formed around the other end of the ribbon (F). Pull the other ribbon end, holding the loop carefully under the folded portion. You have pulled enough when ribbon looks like a rose with first fold of ribbon at rose's center (G).

Carefully holding the rose together, turn it over and trim the ends about ½ to 1 inch from the bottom of the rose, depending on width of ribbon. Turn the ends under twice against the rose's bottom. Tack the ends in place (H).

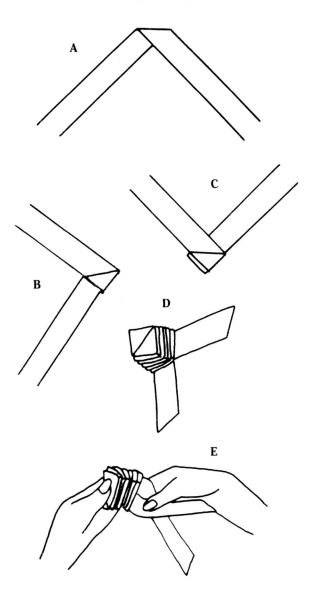

A

C

B

D

E

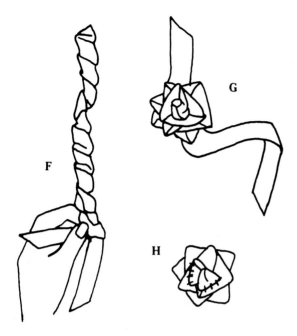

HOW TO SMOCK

Smocking, a decorative and functional kind of embroidery, secures tiny, gathered pleats across a piece of fabric, making the fabric softly elastic. The dainty stitches allow the garment to expand a little as the child grows.

To make the required number of pleats, you will have to make detailed marks on your fabric. Then the marks will have to be gathered in accordion pleats.

Sewing-supply stores carry hot-iron dot transfers. To use a hot-iron transfer, cut the paper transfer to fit the width of the area to be smocked and the number of rows indicated in the pattern. It's a good idea to test a scrap of transfer on a scrap of your fabric first. Place the transfer on the wrong side of the fabric, as indicated in the instructions. The top auxiliary row of dots falls in the seam allowance, and the next row of dots falls just below the seam line. Pin the fabric and transfer in place on ironing board.

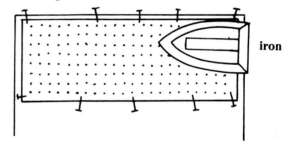

iron

With the iron on a medium heat setting, press the iron on the fabric for about ten seconds. Lift the iron and check one corner of fabric to see if dots are transferred. If not, press longer. Lift the iron off the surface to move it. Do *not* iron back and forth or the dots will smear. Press the entire transfer. Remove the fabric from ironing board and discard the used transfer.

To use graph paper to mark your dots, cut the paper the width of the fabric to be smocked and the length needed to accommodate the number of rows for the design. Use eight squares to the inch if you wish dots to be ⅜ inch apart; eight or four squares to the inch if dots are to be ¼ inch or ½ inch apart. Following the squares on the paper, pierce holes at the desired intervals with a large needle.

Position the graph paper on the wrong side of

HOW TO MAKE POMPONS

Draw two circles on cardboard to the measurement given in the pattern. Then draw a smaller circle in the center of each. Cut out the outer circles and then the center holes.

Set aside a 12-inch length of yarn from the yarn required for the pompon. Cut the remaining yarn into 2-yard lengths. Thread a large needle with one end of a 2-yard length so yarn is doubled. Hold cardboard circles together and wrap the length of yarn around them (A). Continue with the rest of the yarn. The cardboard will be covered.

Slide a scissor blade under the yarn and between cardboard circles. Cut around the outside edge. Pull the circles apart slightly and tie the 12-inch length of yarn *tightly* around the center of the cut yarn (B). Remove the cardboard circles. Fluff the yarn and trim the short ends evenly. Use the ends of the center-tie to sew the pompon onto the project.

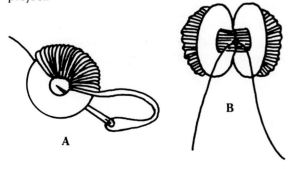

your fabric, as indicated in the instructions. The top auxiliary row of dots falls in the seam allowance, and the next row falls just below the seam line. Mark the dots lightly but clearly with a soft lead pencil through each hole.

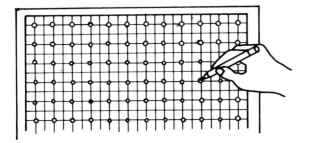

To mark a curved area using transfer dots or graph paper, slash the paper between the rows of dots from the bottom to the top row. Align the top edge with the upper edge of the curve. Pin or tape the paper in place along the curve and mark or transfer dots.

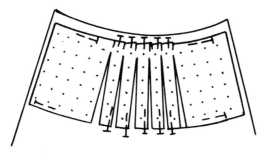

To gather fabric, use a color of thread that contrasts with the color of the fabric. Thread a needle with enough thread to complete one row of stitching across the width of the fabric. Knot one end. Make a tiny, ⅛ inch running stitch at each dot. Leave loose thread end hanging at the side edge. Complete all rows. Note: you'll have one less pleat than you have dots in a row.

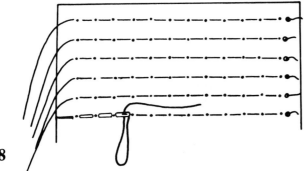

Pull the threads together from the edge to gather the fabric in parallel, uniform pleats. The pleats should be stable but with a little space left between them in which to work embroidery. Generally, gather the fabric to 1 inch narrower than the desired finished width of the smocking. Tie the gathering threads together in pairs, knotting them securely. The rows of stitches will serve as a guide for the placement of the smocking stitches. Do not remove the gathering threads until the smocking is complete.

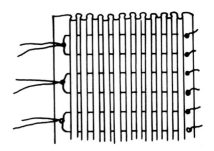

If you have never done smocking, it is a good idea to practice on a sampler before you begin your project. Cut an 8-inch × 12-inch piece of scrap fabric. With fabric held horizontally, begin rows of dots 1 inch from top and bottom and ½ inch from sides. Following instructions, gather fabric to about 3½ inches wide. Then practice the embroidery stitches with three or four strands of embroidery floss plied together. Cut the floss into 18-inch lengths for ease in stitching.

HOW TO WORK
SMOCKING STITCHES
CABLE STITCH

Bring the needle up to the left of the first pleat. Holding the thread above the needle, stitch through the second pleat from right to left to make an "up" cable (A). Holding the thread below the needle, stitch through pleat three from right to left to make a "down" cable (B). Alternate "up" and "down" cables across the row (C).

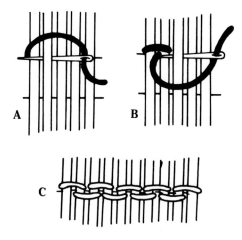

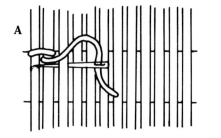

TRELLIS STITCH

This stitch is worked over two rows. Bring the needle up to the left of the first pleat of the upper row. Work an "up" cable through the second pleat. Holding the thread above the needle, work a tiny wave stitch one-quarter of the way toward the lower row through third pleat (A).

Make three more wave stitches, each another quarter of the way down to the next row. Work a "down" cable at the lower row over sixth and seventh pleats (B).

Holding the thread below the needle, wave up to the top row in four even wave stitches. Work an "up" cable at the upper row, as before (C). Trellis stitch may be worked with any number of wave stitches between the upper and lower cable stitches.

WAVE STITCH

This stitch is worked over two rows. Bring the needle up to the left of the first pleat along the lower row. Work a "down" cable, bringing the needle up to the left of the second pleat. Bring the needle up to the upper row. Holding the thread below the needle, stitch through the third pleat from right to left to make an "up" wave (A). Work an "up" cable through fourth pleat (B). Bring the needle down to the lower row. Holding the thread above the needle, stitch through fifth pleat from right to left, making a "down" wave (C). Then stitch through the sixth pleat, making a "down" cable (D).

Repeat these stitches across the row.

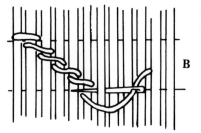

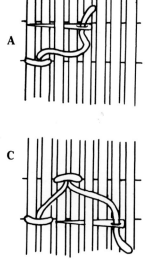

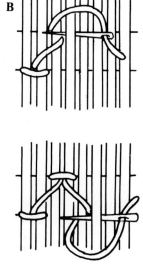

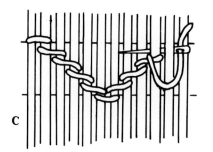

19

HOW TO MACHINE APPLIQUÉ

From your enlarged design, make patterns for all appliqué pieces by tracing the shape onto tracing paper. Look at the design and notice which shapes seem to overlap other shapes. Extend the shape that appears to go under the other by ⅛ inch to ¼ inch so that they both can be finished with a single row of zigzag stitching.

Since it is easier to work with large shapes, you may wish to simplify shapes that seem interrupted by other shapes. To do this, connect any lines in the design that seem to be part of one piece, make one pattern, and cut as one piece. For example, for a scene, make the entire sky one piece and position clouds, trees, and so forth on top of the sky piece.

Cut the appliqué pieces from fabric. Back each piece with fusible webbing: Place a sheet of scrap paper on your ironing board and place a piece of fusible webbing on it. Arrange the fabric pieces right-side-up on the webbing. Turn off the steam on your iron and, for a second only, touch the very tip on the iron to the pieces in a few places to tack them to the webbing. Gently pull the fabric and the webbing away from the scrap paper. Then cut out the shapes. You may also trace appliqué pieces onto fabric and cut roughly around them (leaving a margin of fabric around the drawn lines). Apply the webbing as described above. Then trim the excess fabric and excess webbing from the piece at the same time.

When all the pieces have been cut out and backed, arrange them webbing-side-down on the background fabric. Turn on the steam on your iron and fuse the pieces in place. Zigzag-stitch around each shape, using matching thread unless otherwise indicated in the instructions. Draw or transfer additional lines in the design for machine or hand embroidery. For machine embroidery, zigzag-stitch along lines, using the color thread indicated. Hand-embroider small details and features using the color and embroidery stitch suggested in the instructions.

HOW TO BLOCK KNITTED AND CROCHETED PROJECTS

Block each piece of a knitted or crocheted item before the seams are sewn. For acrylic and acrylic-blend yarns, dampen each piece by wrapping it in a wet towel or by misting pieces with a spray bottle. Place the pieces on a flat, padded surface right-side-up. Carefully stretch each piece into the correct shape and size, following the measurements given in the instructions. Using rustproof pins, pin edges to surface at 1-inch intervals so edges are not scalloped. Allow pieces to dry thoroughly. For 100% wool yarn, pin pieces wrong-side-up on a padded surface, same as above, without dampening them. Place a wet press cloth over the pieces and steam lightly with an iron. Do not place the weight of the iron on the fabric. Allow pieces to dry thoroughly.

BABY'S

WORLD

Quilt and Coordinating Accessories

elcome Baby with a wonderful quilt and coordinating accessories. The cozy quilt features a country cottage surrounded by baby animals, and a "Welcome" greeting. The cuddly fleece lamb is a perfect first toy. The teddy bear wreath is surprisingly simple to make.

WELCOME-TO-THE-WORLD QUILT

FINISHED SIZE: 34″ × 41″, including ruffle

MATERIALS:

45″-wide cotton fabric:

1 yard print with white background for quilt top

1¼ yards pale yellow for border and backing

¾ yard white or off-white to underline heart-shaped appliqué

½ yard light blue with white dots

⅜ yard light green

Scraps of pink; light brown with white dots; white; yellow; pink-and-white print; blue; off-white; green-and-white print; brown; beige; and gray

33″ × 40″ piece bonded polyester quilt batting

½ yard 18″-wide fusible webbing

2 yards each dark brown, pink, yellow, and light orange six-strand embroidery floss.

4¼ yards 1¼″-wide white eyelet ruffling

Sewing thread to match fabrics

Quilting thread for hand quilting, if desired

Enlarge patterns for heart-shaped appliqué scene and other appliqué pieces, following instructions in the how-to chapter. Add ½-inch seam allowance to outer edge of heart and cut it out from white underlining fabric. Following instructions for machine appliqué in the how-to chapter, make patterns for the following pieces and cut them from fabrics indicated: Sky from blue with white dots; ground from light green; sun from yellow; clouds from white; tree trunk from brown; tree top from green-and-white print; path from light brown with white dots; house from pink-and-white print; door and flowers from pink; heart on door from off-white; leaves from green; duck from white; cat from gray; pond from blue with white dots; bear from beige; bunny from brown; bunny's tail from white; turtle from green; and curtains from yellow.

Place sky and ground pieces on heart-shaped piece of fabric; baste in place along edges. Arrange remaining pieces in the scene a few at a time and fuse them in place. Zigzag-stitch windows and doors using light brown thread, and all other shapes using matching thread. At the same time, zigzag-stitch around detail lines of each shape, using yellow for sun rays, pink for rabbit's ear, green for flower stems, beige for turtle-shell lines, and matching thread for all other details. Hand-embroider centers of flowers with yellow French knots, eyes and noses of animals with brown satin stitch, mouths with pink backstitches, beaks with light orange satin stitch or straight stitch, and bear's bow with yellow backstitch.

Cut a 29″ × 36″ piece of print fabric with white background. Trim seam allowance from heart pattern and cut heart shape out of center of background fabric. Baste heart-shaped center hole around heart-shaped appliqué scene; then zigzag-stitch along edge with white thread.

Make patterns for the other appliqué pieces and cut them from fabric as follows: two birds from blue; two beaks from yellow; two lamb bodies from white (if background print shows through white fabric, cut two pieces for each lamb and baste them together along outer edges); face and legs from light brown with white dots; one bow from pink-and-white print and another bow from blue with white dots; and *WELCOME BABY* from different pastel prints and solids.

Arrange a bird in each upper corner about 1¾

inches in from top and side edges; fuse each in place. Between birds' beaks, draw a string to hold greeting letters and arrange letters of the word *WELCOME* on string; fuse in place. Zigzag-stitch all pieces in place, using matching thread. Machine-embroider string with light brown zigzag stitch. Hand-embroider eyes with brown satin stitch.

Arrange one lamb in each lower corner about 1¾ inches from bottom and side edges; fuse each in place. Fuse blue bow to left lamb and pink bow to right lamb. Draw a string between lambs' mouths, and arrange letters of the word *BABY* on string; fuse in place. Zigzag-stitch left lamb's body with pink, right lamb's body with blue, and the other shapes using matching thread. Machine-embroider string with light brown zigzag-stitch. Hand-embroider eyes and nose with brown satin stitch, and mouths with pink backstitch.

From yellow fabric, cut 33″ × 40″ backing, two 29″ × 3½″ top and bottom borders, and two 36″ × 3½″ side borders. Cut four 3½-inch squares from white print, and four pink hearts. Fuse a heart to center of each square and zigzag-stitch along edges. Use ½-inch seams to attach quilt borders. Right sides together, stitch heart squares to each end of top and bottom borders. Stitch side borders to quilt. Stitch top and bottom borders with heart squares to quilt, matching seams.

Place batting between top and backing with right sides out. Pin the three layers together.

To prepare for hand-quilting, baste edges together, and then baste from quilt center to each corner and from center to midpoint of each side. Insert quilt "sandwich" in quilting hoop or frame.

To prepare for machine-quilting, first baste edges together by hand. Then baste by machine along seam line between quilt's center panel and its borders, and around all shapes listed below. Use 8 to 10 stitches per inch, and match top thread to background. Use yellow thread on your bobbin.

Quilt, by hand or machine, around heart-shaped scene, inner seam of borders, large birds and lambs, ground top, house, path, clouds, sun, and tree. Remove basting from outer edge. Baste top to batting alone. Right sides together, stitch a ruffle binding to quilt top, ½ inch in from edges, making small pleats in corners for extra fullness. See Diagram 1. Turn seam allowance to wrong side. Turn under ½ inch on backing and slipstitch folded edge in place over line of stitching.

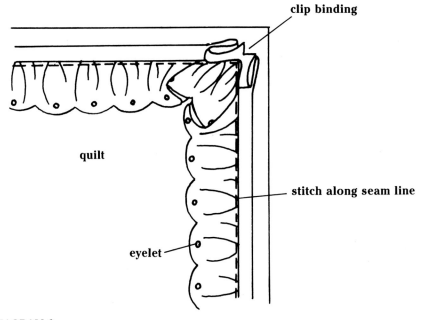

DIAGRAM 1

1 square = 1 inch

1 square = 1 inch

26

FLEECY LAMB

MATERIALS:

¼ yard or a 12″ × 18″ piece off-white fleece-fur fabric

⅛ yard or scraps of cotton print fabric

3″ × 5″ piece pink cotton fabric

¼ pound polyester stuffing

3″ × 5″ piece thin quilt batting

1 yard each brown and pink six-strand embroidery floss

Off-white sewing thread

¾ yard ⅝″-wide light blue ribbon

Enlarge lamb pattern pieces, following instructions in the how-to chapter. Place fur fabric wrong-side-up on a flat surface and pin pattern pieces on wrong side, matching arrows to direction of nap. Cut one body, one head, one tail, and one under-body. Reverse patterns (turn them over) and cut another body, head, and tail. From cotton print, cut face top, two face sides, two ears, and eight legs. Cut two ears each from pink fabric and quilt batting. Transfer all dots to wrong side of fabric pieces. Mark facial features and placement lines on right side.

Sew all pieces together with right sides together, using ¼-inch seam allowance, as follows:

Stitch body pieces together along front and back edges, leaving neck edge, lower edge, and tail area open. See Diagram 1. Matching dots, stitch underbody to lower edge of sides. See Diagram 2. Stitch tail pieces together along curved edge. Clip and trim seam allowance; turn right-side-out. Stuff tail with a little bit of stuffing. Stuff body firmly. Insert tail in place, turning under seam allowances on body; slipstitch it firmly in place. See Diagram 3. Make a row of gathering stitches by hand around neck edge.

Stitch face sides together along center curved edge. Stitch face top to face sides, matching nose center to seam. See Diagram 4. Clip seam allowance; turn face right-side-out. Stitch both darts for each side of head. Clip along all dart centers and finger-press darts open. Stitch two head pieces together along upper curve and across point at inner corners. See Diagram 5. Make a row of gathering stitches along front edge. With right sides together, pin face to head, gathering head fabric to fit edge of face and matching center top dots and bottom

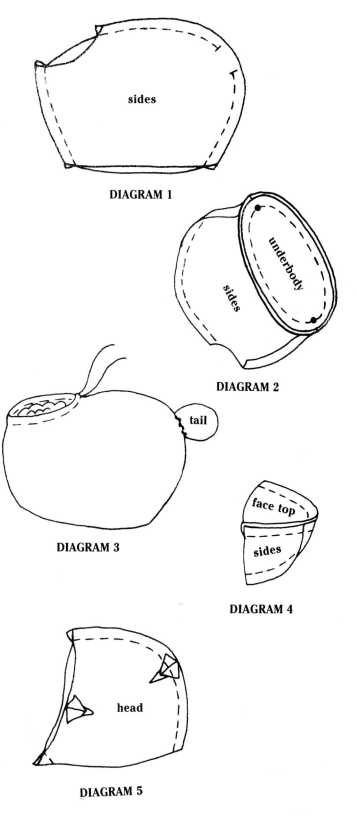

DIAGRAM 1

DIAGRAM 2

DIAGRAM 3

DIAGRAM 4

DIAGRAM 5

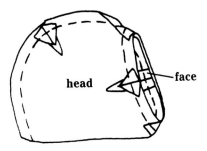

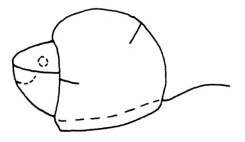

DIAGRAM 6

seams. See Diagram 6. Stitch over gathering stitches. Turn assembled head right-side-out. Turn lower edge of head under and baste it in place. See Diagram 7. Stuff face and head. Pin and slipstitch head to body. See Diagram 8.

Baste quilt batting to wrong side of print fabric ears. Trim batting seam allowance close to stitching. With fabric sides together, stitch print ears to pink ears, leaving straight edge open. Trim and clip seam allowance; turn ears right-side-out. Turn seam allowance under along straight edge; slipstitch edge to head. Tack underside to head so that ears lie close to head. See Diagram 9.

Sew four legs together from pairs of fabric pieces, leaving straight edge open. Clip all seam allowances along stitching; turn legs right-side-out. Turn edge seam allowances under and baste them in place. Stuff legs. Pin and then slipstitch legs to under body—one on each side of front and one on each side of back. See Diagram 10.

Embroider eyes and nose in satin stitch, using four strands of brown floss. Embroider mouth with backstitch, using four strands of pink floss. Tie ribbon around lamb's neck and make a bow.

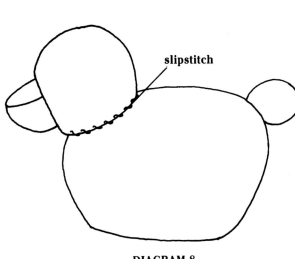

DIAGRAM 7

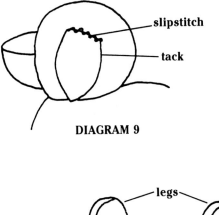

DIAGRAM 9

DIAGRAM 8

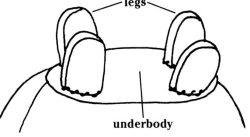

DIAGRAM 10

28

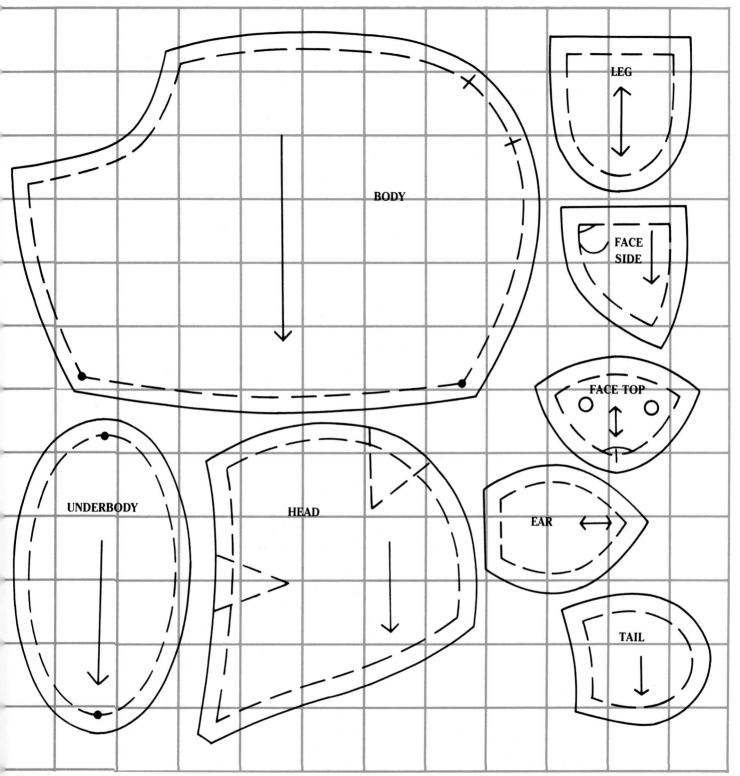

LEG

FACE SIDE

BODY

FACE TOP

UNDERBODY

HEAD

EAR

TAIL

1 square = 1 inch

29

TEDDY BEAR WREATH

MATERIALS:

Cotton fabrics:
   7½″ × 44″ piece green-and-white print
   28″ × 4″ piece print with white background
   5″ × 8″ piece pink
   8″ × 10″ piece blue
   5″ × 10″ piece light brown
About 3 handfuls of polyester stuffing
1 yard each brown and pink six-strand embroidery floss
½ yard light brown and blue six-strand embroidery floss
Sewing thread to match fabrics
½ yard ¼″-wide yellow satin ribbon
22″ piece of wire or part of a coathanger

Using pliers, bend wire into a circle 7 inches in diameter, overlapping ends but not fastening them. Press under ¼ inch on ends of green-and-white-print fabric. Fold it in half lengthwise, with right sides together; stitch ¼ inch away from raw edges. Turn right-side-out and press so that seam is to one side. Stitch 1 inch from folded edge and again slightly more than ¼ inch from first line of stitching to form a casing. Insert wire circle into casing, tucking in wire ends. Slipstitch ends of fabric together.

Fold your print fabric in half lengthwise. Trim ends diagonally. Stitch ¼-inch from edge and ends, leaving an opening for turning near center of long side. Trim corners from seam allowance. Turn right-side-out and press. Tie into a 5½-inch-wide bow.

To make the teddy bear, trace around same-size pattern piece onto wrong side of one half of light brown fabric. Then fold fabric in half with right sides together and pin the two layers together along outline. Stitch along line, leaving an opening between dots. Trim and clip seam allowance. Carefully turn bear right-side-out. Stuff, and then slipstitch edges of opening together. Using two strands of light brown floss, quilt along broken lines. Em-broider eyes and nose, using three strands of brown floss and satin stitch. Embroider mouth and heart, using three strands of pink floss and backstitch. Make a row of tiny running stitches with pink along inner lines of ears. Tie a piece of yellow ribbon around bear's neck and make a little bow.

To make the birds, trace two birds and two wings onto wrong side of one half of the blue fabric, allowing ¼-inch seam allowance around each piece. With right sides together, fold fabric in half; pin layers of each shape together and cut them from fabric at least ¼ inch from outlines. Stitch around each bird, leaving an opening between dots. Clip and trim seam allowance. Turn birds right-side-out. Stuff the bodies, and then slipstitch opening closed. Next, stitch all around each wing. Trim and clip seam allowance. Pull apart the two layers of fabric that you have sewn together for each wing and make a ⅝-inch slash on one layer. Be sure to make a left wing and a right wing. Turn each wing right-side-out through its slash. Stuff slightly. Sew edges of each slash together. By hand, quilt along broken lines on wing. Slipstitch a wing to each bird, slashed side under. Embroider eyes, using three strands of brown yarn and satin stitch. For each beak, make a tuck in a 1-inch piece of ribbon to form a triangular point. Sew beak to wrong side of bird's head so that just a small point shows.

Trace three hearts on wrong side of one half of your pink fabric, with ¼-inch seam allowance around each shape. Fold fabric in half with right sides together, and pin layers along heart outlines. Cut out hearts. Stitch around hearts, leaving an opening between dots. Trim and clip seam allowances. Turn each heart right-side-out. Stuff, and then slipstitch openings. Arrange and pin bow, bear, hearts, and birds to wreath. Using a doubled thread, sew each piece securely to the wreath. Cut a 4-inch piece of ribbon. Make a hanging loop by folding it in half and sewing ends to back of wreath top at casing.

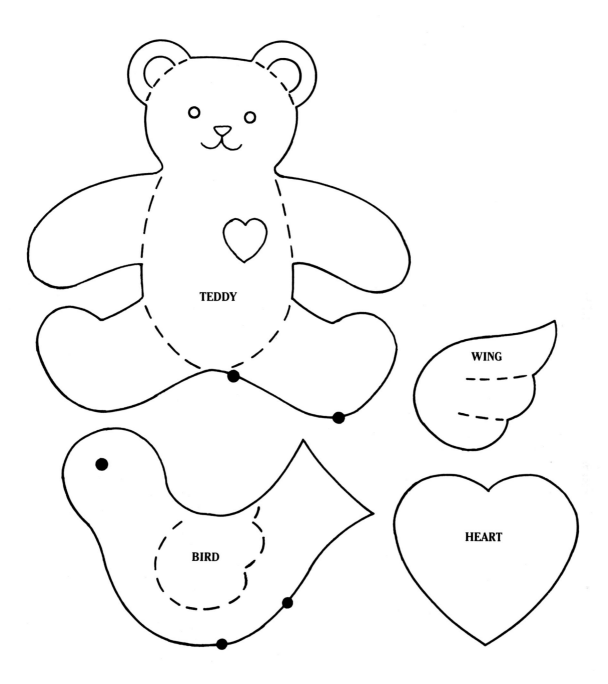

TEDDY

WING

BIRD

HEART

Under-the-Rainbow Mobile

Stitch and stuff these brightly colored, easy-to-make birds and rainbow . . . and arrange them over Baby's crib. Babies love to focus their eyes on bright, cheerful colors.

MATERIALS:
Cotton fabrics:
   12″ square off-white
   5″ × 10″ piece white
   5″ × 10″ piece yellow
   6″ square of printed or dotted fabrics with backgrounds of light green, bright pink, yellow, blue, and light purple
   3″ × 5″ piece light pink
2″ square bright yellow felt
12″ × 18″ piece thin quilt batting
A few handfuls of polyester stuffing
8″ × 10″ piece cardboard
1 yard brown six-strand embroidery floss
Single-fold bias tape:
   1 yard bright pink
   ¾ yard each orange and yellow
   ⅝ yard each light green and blue
   ½ yard light purple
Sewing thread to match fabrics and bias tape
Several yards off-white quilting thread or other heavy thread to string mobile

Enlarge pattern pieces, following the instructions in the how-to chapter.

Trace two suns on your solid yellow fabric. Cut out, adding ¼-inch seam allowance all around. Pin suns to quilt batting and cut out batting around sun edges. Baste suns to their batting pieces along solid lines; trim batting close to stitching. Zigzag-stitch on broken lines. Trace a sun on cardboard; cut out ⅛ inch *inside* the line so that cardboard sun is smaller. Place cardboard between fabric suns right-sides-out and line up ray points. Hand-baste along solid line. Zigzag-stitch along outer line, using moderately spaced stitches. Trim fabric close to stitching and zigzag-stitch around sun shape again to finish the edge neatly.

Trace two rainbows including broken lines onto off-white fabric. Cut two bias tape pieces from each color in the following lengths: bright pink, 14 inches; orange, 13 inches; yellow, 12 inches; green, 11 inches; blue, 10 inches; purple, 9 inches. For each side of rainbow, lightly press open both folds of bright pink bias tape so that crease is still visible. Stretch and press bias tape into the shape of the curve of the upper section of the rainbow. Center bias tape over upper stripe and baste it along the creases. Press open one edge of orange bias tape. With fold at top, press it into curve of second rainbow stripe, overlapping bright pink tape. Stitch along upper edge of orange bias tape using matching thread. Continue in the same manner with yellow, green, blue, and light purple stripes.

When both your rainbows are complete, pin each one to quilt batting and trim around edge. Baste along outer seam line and trim batting close to stitching. Trace rainbow shape on cardboard and cut it out ⅛ inch inside the line so that it will be smaller than fabric rainbows. Baste, stitch, and zigzag-stitch the layers together the same way as for sun.

With cloud pattern pieces facing up, trace one of each cloud on white fabric; mark all dots lightly outside tracing line. Reverse patterns (turn them over) and trace one of each again. Cut out clouds, adding ¼-inch seam allowances all around. Pin clouds right-side-up on batting and trim batting even. Baste along lines and trim batting close to stitching. Clip seam allowances almost to stitching at dots and along curves between dots. Baste under seam allowance between dots. Zigzag-stitch along turned-in edge between dots. Baste clouds together right-sides-out, leaving opening between dots. Finish remaining edge the same way as for sun. Stuff the clouds lightly. Place clouds on rainbow, matching dots. Sew in place by hand with white thread and whipstitches that will blend in with zigzag stitching.

Trace one bird and two wings to half of each light green, bright pink, yellow, blue and light purple printed or dotted fabric. Fold fabric in half and pin inside the shapes; cut out the shapes, adding ¼-inch seam allowance all around. Stitch along lines, leaving an opening for turning between dots. Trim and clip all seam allowances. Turn birds right-side-out. Stuff birds and wings firmly. Turn seam allowance under along opening and slipstitch the edges together. Pin a wing to each side where indicated on the pattern; slipstitch in place. Draw and embroider eyes, using brown floss and satin stitch. Cut two beak pieces for each bird from yellow felt. Pin curved edges of beaks to each head just above and below the line shown on pattern. Whipstitch beaks to heads.

Trace heart on half of your pink fabric; fold fabric in half and pin the layers together. Stitch along the line, leaving an opening between dots.

Clip and trim seam allowance. Turn heart right-side-out. Stuff it firmly. Turn seam allowance under along opening and slipstitch edges together.

Join mobile pieces together with quilting or heavy thread at connection points indicated by small x's. To connect the pieces, take several tiny stitches through each piece and knot thread securely. Take one final stitch, bringing needle out away from connecting point and trim thread close to fabric to bury end. If desired, use felt-tipped pens to color the thread stitches on each piece to match fabrics.

There should be about 3 to 4 inches between sun and rainbow, 3 inches between rainbow and heart, 8 inches between heart and center bird, 9 inches between rainbow and side birds, and 5 inches between rainbow and remaining birds. Attach a long thread to the top of sun and hang it from a hook in the ceiling over your baby's crib.

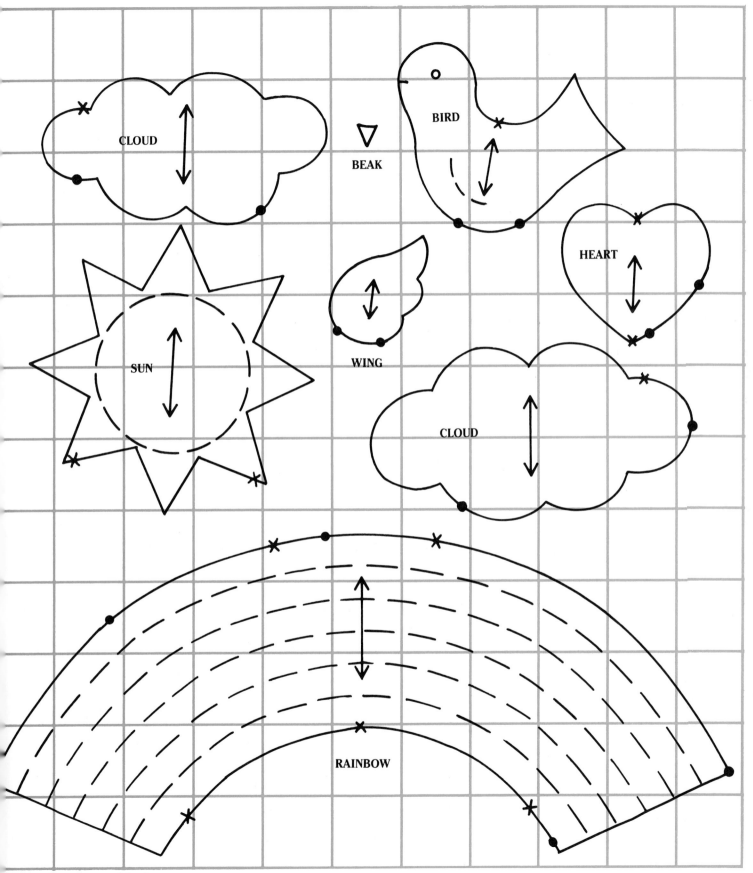

CLOUD

BEAK

BIRD

HEART

SUN

WING

CLOUD

RAINBOW

1 square = 1 inch

"Be Quiet As a Mouse"

What better way to announce to friends and family that Baby is sound asleep? Naptime won't be interrupted. And mouse—dressed in a flannel nightshirt—can dream sweet dreams in the crib alongside Baby. This project would make a wonderful gift from Grandma.

DOOR SIGN

MATERIALS:
9″ × 10″ piece off-white linen
¼ yard red fabric with white dots
A few handfuls of polyester stuffing
Six-strand embroidery floss:
   5 yards brown; 3 yards each blue, beige, and gray; 2 yards each light blue and red; 1 yard each green, black, light gray and peach
¾ yard ¾″-wide lace ruffling
Red and blue sewing thread
1 yard ¼″-wide blue ribbon
Embroidery hoop

The design is shown full size—you do not have to enlarge it. Trace heavy lines from pattern onto tracing or lightweight paper. Transfer design to center of linen piece, leaving about 2 inches all around the rectangle. See instructions for transferring designs and markings in the how-to chapter. Insert fabric in embroidery hoop and stitch, using three strands of floss except where otherwise indicated.

Embroider words in blue backstitch, dotting *i*'s with French knots. On cradle, embroider heavy lines in brown stem stitch and broken lines in brown running stitch. Fill in between stem-stitch lines as follows: Cradle edge in beige satin stitch, rockers in beige long-and-short stitch, and pegs of rocker in brown satin stitch.

On mouse, embroider inner ear in peach satin stitch; tip of nose in light gray satin stitch; ears, face, and arms in gray long-and-short stitches; eyes with two strands of black floss and straight stitches; nose with two strands of black floss and satin stitch; mouth with two strands of peach floss and backstitch; tiny claws with one strand of black floss and straight stitch; and whiskers with one strand of light-gray floss and straight stitch.

Embroider bow in red satin stitch. On pillow and coverlet, work heavy lines with light blue backstitch, tiny lines with light blue straight stitch, and dots with red French knots. Work leaves with two strands of green floss and lazy-daisy stitch.

Steam-press embroidery lightly from wrong side. Trim linen to ½ inch outside broken outer line. From red fabric with white dots, cut a 5½″ × 7″ piece for back and two 3″ × 25½″ pieces for ruffle. Right sides together, baste lace ruffling around line on embroidered front, making tiny pleats at corners for extra fullness. (See the diagram on page 24.) Right sides together, sew ends of lace together; trim edge ¼ inch from stitching and zigzag-finish edge. Sew ends of fabric strips together, using ¼ inch seams. Right sides out, fold dotted fabric strip for ruffle lengthwise and press. Make two rows of gathering stitches ¼ inch and ½ inch from raw edges. Gather ruffle to size of linen front over lace, matching cut edges of ruffle and embroidered linen; baste ruffle in place along inner row of gathering stitches. Right sides together and with ruffles between layers, sew back to front, leaving an opening for turning on lower edge. Turn right-side-out. Stuff as you would a small pillow. Slipstitch edges of opening together over seam of ruffle.

Cut a 9½-inch length of ribbon. Turn under ¼ inch on each end and sew to upper corners of back so that ribbon slants diagonally to center above top. Make a small bow and sew it to center of lower edge of sign.

BABY'S SLEEPING

BE QUIET AS A MOUSE

MOUSE

MATERIALS:

¼ yard or 7″ × 22″ piece gray knit fabric (can be cut from a T-shirt)

3″ × 5″ piece light peach knit

9″ × 12″ piece red-and-white cotton flannel

A few handfuls of polyester stuffing

1 yard each black and peach six-strand embroidery floss

⅝ yard ¼″-wide lace edging

Gray and white sewing thread

⅜ yard ⅜″-wide red ribbon

Enlarge pattern, following instructions in the how-to chapter. From gray knit, cut two bodies, one head front, one head back, and two ears. Remember to place folds and arrows on lengthwise grain or rib of knit fabric. Cut a 1″ × 6½″ strip for tail, placed crosswise on the knit fabric. Transfer fea-

tures to right side of head front. Cut two ears from light peach knit.

Stitch all seams right sides together, using ¼-inch seam allowance unless otherwise indicated. Fold head front in half, right sides together; stitch seam below nose. Stitch outer curves of head front to head back. See Diagram 1. Turn right-side-out. Stuff head. Sew a row of gathering stitches around neck by hand; gather slightly and knot thread.

Stitch body pieces together, leaving neck edge open. Clip seam allowance along curves. Turn right-side-out. Turn seam allowance on neck edge under and baste it in place. Stuff body. Insert head in neck edge, matching center front and back; slipstitch head securely in place. See Diagram 2.

Sew each light-peach ear to a gray ear along outer curve, right sides together. Trim seam allowance along stitching. Turn right-side-out. Turn seam allowance under at lower edge. Slipstitch

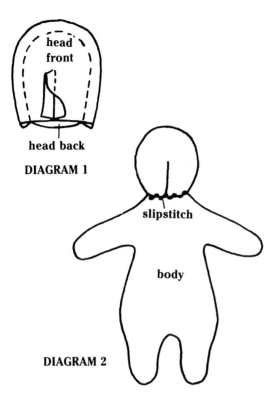

DIAGRAM 1

DIAGRAM 2

fabric, placing appropriate pattern edges on fabric folds, and cut out. Mark dots. Remove pattern and open crosswise fold. Slash solid line from center dot to shoulder for neck opening. Open fabric completely and slash from center dot to front dot for front opening. Press under along broken lines on neck and front. Make a row of gathering stitches around neck edge and gather so each front neck edge is 1¼ inches and back edge is 2½ inches. Check against mouse's neckline to make sure nightshirt fits with fronts overlapping about ¼ inch. Stitch along neck and front placket. See Diagram 3.

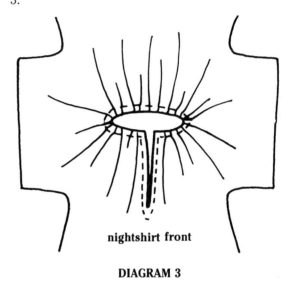

nightshirt front

DIAGRAM 3

edges together; then pull thread to gather each ear to ⅞ inch wide, and knot thread securely. Sew ears to seam of head securely with peach-side facing front.

Fold tail in half, right sides together, and stitch a scant ¼ inch from raw edges. Using a small safety pin to push fabric through, turn tail right-side-out. Turn ends of tail under ¼ inch and slipstitch edges together. Sew one end of tail securely to center back body at position marked X.

Using three strands of black floss, embroider long line of eyes with backstitch, and lashes with straight stitches. Embroider nose in black satin stitch. Embroider tiny claws on front of feet and back of hands. Using three strands of peach doubled in needle, embroider mouth. Insert needle from the top in nose area and bring it up at center seam just below nose. Insert needle on right-hand side of mouth and bring it up at center seam ½ inch below nose. Insert needle on left-hand side of mouth and bring it out again on top of nose. Knot thread securely.

For nightshirt, fold flannel fabric in half lengthwise, then crosswise in quarters. Place pattern on

On the right side, fold front of nightshirt from center front dot to short line just to the left of the dot to form pleat; sew across pleat from dot to line to hold in place.

Press under ¼ inch at each sleeve edge. Make a row of gathering stitches ⅛ inch from edge. Gather sleeve edge to 2¾ inches. Place over lace and stitch through both layers along edge.

Right sides together, fold nightshirt in half along shoulders; stitch side and underarm seams.

Press under ¼ inch along lower edge. Place over lace and stitch through both layers along edge. Sew a 5½-inch length of ribbon to top of each side of front placket, ¼ inch from edge. Place nightshirt on mouse and tie ribbons in a bow.

39

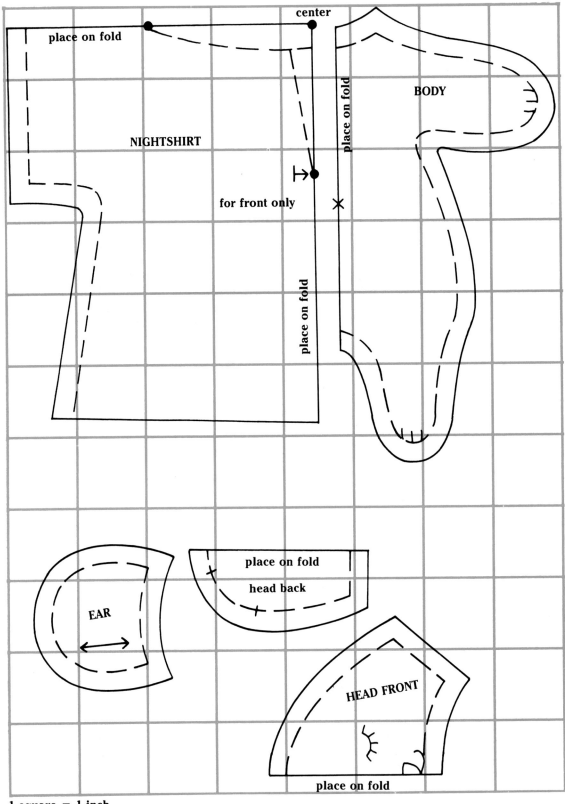

place on fold

center

NIGHTSHIRT

place on fold

for front only

place on fold

BODY

place on fold

EAR

place on fold

head back

HEAD FRONT

place on fold

1 square = 1 inch

40

The "Everything" Tote and Accessories

Y ou'll have everything a baby could need when you take along this quilted and appliquéd tote. The cover flap opens instantly to make a soft, clean area on which to lay Baby down. A changing pad is held in place by Velcro. And there's a matching bottle cozy to keep formula warm or cold, as preferred. To complete the "everything" tote, make the matching bib for meals-on-the-go.

MATERIALS:

1¼ yards 45″-wide blue quilted fabric with reversible fabric side

or

1¼ yards 45″-wide blue cotton twill fabric, matching print fabric, and quilt batting

Scraps of red, white, yellow, and tan cotton fabric for appliqués

½ yard white terrycloth

4″ × 15″ piece fusible webbing

½ yard each dark brown and red six-strand embroidery floss

Two 3-yard packages ½″-wide tan double-fold bias tape

One 4-yard package ¼″-wide blue double-fold bias tape

Tan, blue, red, yellow, and white sewing thread

¾ yard ¾″-wide white Velcro strip

6″ piece ¾″-wide tan Velcro strip

TOTE

To make your own quilted fabric for the bag and bottle cozy, cut one piece each from solid blue fabric, matching print, and quilt batting, following measurements given in the next paragraph. For shoulder strap, omit lining piece. On right side of each blue piece except shoulder strap, lightly draw first quilting line ½ inch from one vertical side edge (the vertical measurement is given first for each piece). For flap, sides, pockets, and rectangular cozy pieces, draw vertical quilting lines at 2-inch intervals parallel to the first line. For center strip, draw quilting lines ½ inch and 1½ inches from each long edge (center lines are 2 inches apart). With right sides out, pin pieces together along outer edge and quilting lines. By machine, with bobbin thread to match lining fabric and blue thread as the top thread, stitch along quilting lines and ½ inch from top and bottom edge. Cut circles for cozy from fabrics and batting and baste the layers together ¼ inch from the edge. Baste batting to wrong side of shoulder strap ½ inch from edges and along lengthwise center.

Cut each of the following pieces from quilted fabric, centering quilted lines across pieces (vertical measurement of each piece is given first): Cut two bag sides 12½″ × 17″; changing flap, 30½″ × 17″; center strip, 42″ × 5″; pocket, 8½″ × 17″; strap, 48″ × 5½″; two top flaps, 3½″ × 17″; cozy bottom, 6″ × 11″; cozy top, 2½″ × 11″; bottom circle, 3 inches in diameter; and top circle, 3¼ inches in diameter (to fit a standard baby bottle). Check your bottles to make sure they will fit. If necessary, enlarge patterns so bottom is slightly larger than bottle. Make pattern for top circle ¼ inch larger than bottom. Add ¼-inch seam allowance to top and bottom circles.

On sides and pocket, trim ¼ inch from side edges (vertical measurements). On top flaps, trim 1 inch from each side edge (vertical measurement). To stitch bag, use ½-inch seam allowances and stitch right sides together, unless otherwise indicated. Bind one long edge of pocket with tan bias tape, following the instructions given in the how-to chapter. Topstitch binding along inner edge on right side. Matching raw edges, with right sides up, baste pocket to one bag side along side and lower edge. See Diagram 1. Stitch along center quilting line. Pin one long edge of center strip to pocket side along 12½-inch sides and bottom; clip center strip almost to stitching at corners. See Diagram 2. Trim ends of center strip even with top of bag. Stitch seam. Stitch remaining side to center strip in same manner. Zigzag-finish edge. Sew binding to top edge of bag. Right sides out, fold bag along seams and topstitch ⅛ inch from seam. See Diagram 3.

For top flaps, round corners on either side of one long edge. Bind two short and one long edge so round corners are bound. Right sides up, place 1 inch of unfinished edge of flap under top edge of sides. Stitch layers together along top edge of binding on sides. On lining side, turn under ⅜ inch on lower edge of flap; slipstitch in place. Cut tan Velcro into three 2-inch pieces. Sew hook side of Velcro pieces to right side of one flap along top edge. Sew fuzzy side of Velcro to lining side of other flap along top edge so Velcro pieces match.

For changing flap, trim ¼ inch from each long and one short edge. Turn ¼ inch, then 1 inch to lining side on trimmed short edge. Stitch along inner edge of hem. Round corners on other end of flap. Sew binding to raw edges of flap, turning under ends along hem. See Diagram 4.

Enlarge pattern for appliqué, following instructions in the how-to chapter. Trace design lightly to right side of flap with carriage centered ¾ inch above binding. Following instructions for machine appliqué given in the how-to chapter, make patterns for carriage, wheel, bear, balloon and bow. Cut carriage and balloon from red, bear from tan,

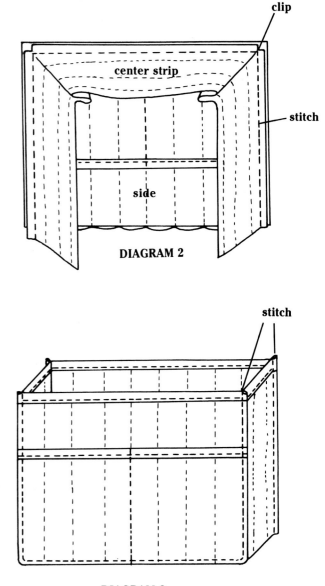

DIAGRAM 2

DIAGRAM 3

and wheels and bow from yellow. Trace features on bear's face. Arrange pieces on flap. Make a little clip between bear's arm and body so arm can overlap carriage and lower edge of body is tucked under carriage. Fuse all pieces in place. Zigzag-stitch around shapes with matching thread. At the same time, zigzag-embroider spokes of wheel and balloon string with tan, and handle and *Good-bye!* with yellow. Hand-embroider eyes and nose with satin stitch, using three strands of brown floss. Backstitch along lines of mouth, using two strands of red floss.

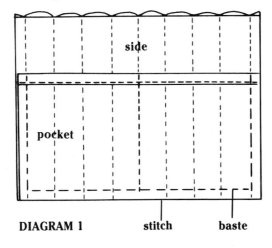

DIAGRAM 1

turn under end

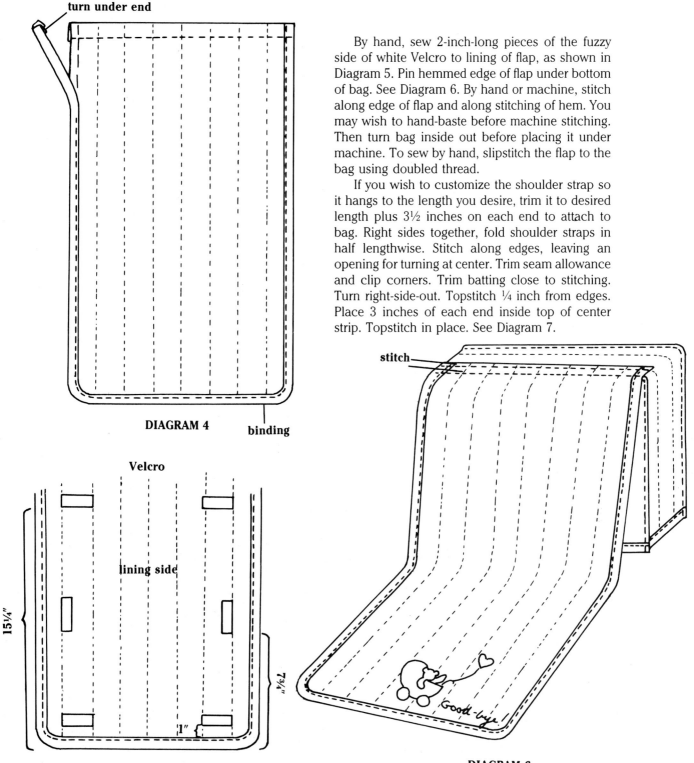

By hand, sew 2-inch-long pieces of the fuzzy side of white Velcro to lining of flap, as shown in Diagram 5. Pin hemmed edge of flap under bottom of bag. See Diagram 6. By hand or machine, stitch along edge of flap and along stitching of hem. You may wish to hand-baste before machine stitching. Then turn bag inside out before placing it under machine. To sew by hand, slipstitch the flap to the bag using doubled thread.

If you wish to customize the shoulder strap so it hangs to the length you desire, trim it to desired length plus 3½ inches on each end to attach to bag. Right sides together, fold shoulder straps in half lengthwise. Stitch along edges, leaving an opening for turning at center. Trim seam allowance and clip corners. Trim batting close to stitching. Turn right-side-out. Topstitch ¼ inch from edges. Place 3 inches of each end inside top of center strip. Topstitch in place. See Diagram 7.

stitch

DIAGRAM 4   binding

Velcro

lining side

15¼"

7¾"

1"

you will see wrong side of appliqué stitching

DIAGRAM 5

Good-bye

DIAGRAM 6

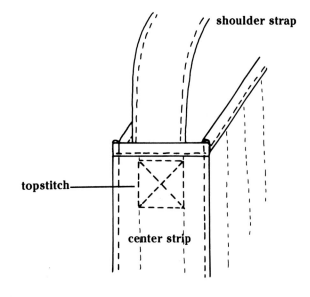

shoulder strap

topstitch—

center strip

DIAGRAM 7

BOTTLE COZY

For bottle cozy, enlarge appliqué pattern, following instructions in the how-to chapter. Following instructions for machine appliqué in the how-to chapter, make pattern for bear, bib, bow, bottle, and bottle top. Cut bear from tan, bottle and bib from white, and bottle top and bow from yellow. Trace features on bear's face. Arrange pieces centered on cozy bottom 1 inch from lower edge; fuse pieces in place. Using matching thread, stitch along edges of pieces and inner lines of design. Stitch lower edge of bib, using red. Embroider face same as bear in carriage. Sew all seams with right sides together, using ¼-inch seams. Measure the circumference of the seamline of bottom circle and add ¾ inch (¼ inch on each end for seam allowance and ¼ inch for ease). Trim the cozy bottom to this measurement so the appliqué is still centered. Remove the stitching parallel to the lower edge if you quilted your own fabric. Stitch 6-inch edges together. Trim batting from seam allowance

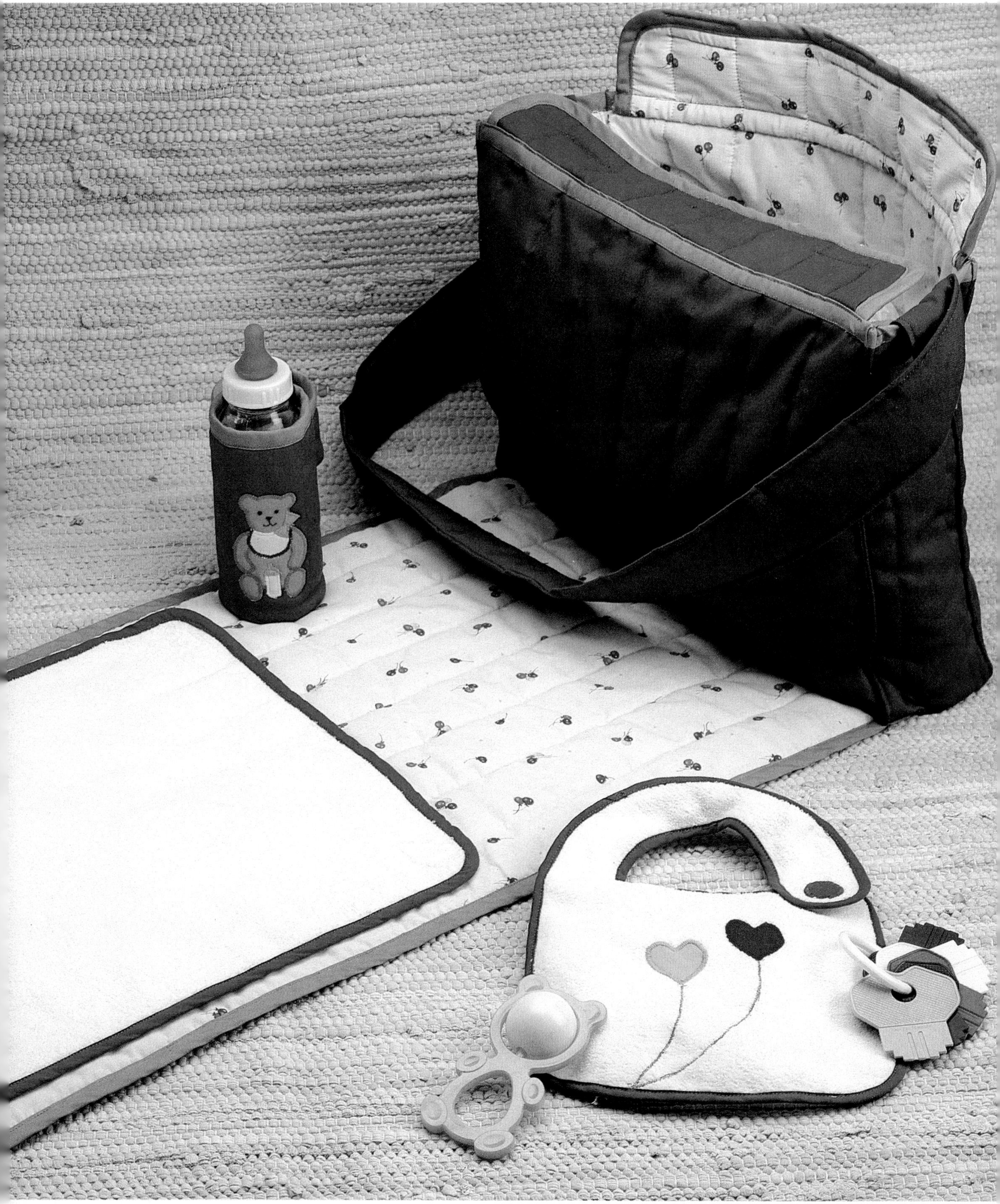

and zigzag-finish edge. Sew binding to top edge. Stitch ¼ inch from lower edge. Clip seam allowance to stitching at ½-inch intervals. Stitch cozy to circle. See Diagram 8. Finish seam allowance same as before. Turn right-side-out. Sew cozy top to top circle in same manner. Place top on bottom, overlapping 1 inch or to fit bottle. Slipstitch together at back seams. See Diagram 9. Sew a small piece of Velcro to front of cozy bottom at top edge and inside edge of top.

BIB

Enlarge pattern for bib, following instructions in the how-to chapter. To make a bib for a small baby,

follow the broken line for the bottom edge and redraw the balloon strings. Make pattern for balloons (or use balloon pattern from bag). Cut one yellow and one red balloon, and a 1-inch-diameter circle from blue. Fuse or baste the pieces in place. Zigzag-stitch around balloons and circle with matching thread. Zigzag along strings using tan thread. Baste a 3½-inch strip of the fuzzy side of the Velcro diagonally to the wrong side of the neck tab. See Diagram 10. Sew blue binding over edges of bib, beginning and ending at neck edge. Using white thread, stitch around blue circle to hold Velcro strip. Sew a 1-inch piece of the hook side of Velcro to right side of bib at top.

bottom circle

DIAGRAM 8

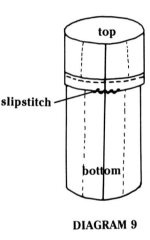

DIAGRAM 9

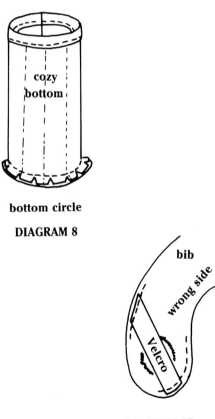

DIAGRAM 10

Good-bye!

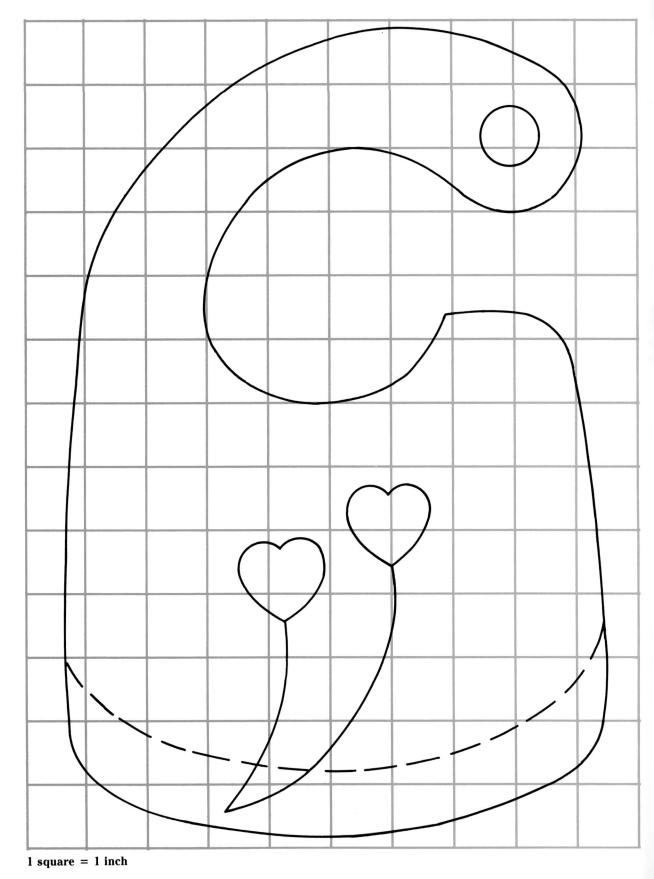

48

1 square = 1 inch

Classic Carriage Ensemble, with Matching Rattles

Believe it or not, this classic carriage ensemble is easy to make. An eyelet ruffle with a ribbon woven through the eyelet beading edge creates interesting detail. The lining is a contrasting-color fabric.

Plain, inexpensive plastic rattles become extra-special when you cover them with appliquéd bear and baby faces in pastel tones.

MATERIALS:
1 yard 45″-wide eyelet embroidered fabric
1 yard solid pastel fabric
4 yards eyelet beading with attached ruffle
White sewing thread
6 yards ⅜″-wide pastel ribbon to match fabric

CARRIAGE COVERLET

For carriage coverlet, cut one 20″ × 24½″ piece each from eyelet and pastel fabrics. Right sides together, sew eyelet to pastel fabric ¼ inch from edges, leaving several inches open on one side for turning. Press seams open and trim corners. Turn right-side-out. Turn under ¼ inch along opening and slipstitch edges together. Weave ribbon through 2½ yards of beading. Beginning at one corner, pin beading portion of trim around edge of eyelet side so ruffle extends past edge. Miter at corners so edge of eyelet ruffle turns corners smoothly. Pin in miter on wrong side. Remove trim from corners and stitch along miter. Trim corner ¼ inch from seam; zigzag over edge. Join ends of trim in similar manner. Repin corners to coverlet and stitch along inner and outer edges of beading. Cut two 11-inch pieces of ribbon. On top corners, place ribbon diagonally over beading portion of trim and sew across ribbon; tie a bow.

PILLOW SHAM

For pillow sham, cut front 12″ × 15″ and two backs 12″ × 9¼″ from both eyelet and pastel fabric. Right sides up, baste eyelet front to pastel front ¼ inch from edge. Right sides together, sew an eyelet back to each pastel back ¼ inch from one 9¼-inch edge. Press seam; turn right-side-out, folding along seam so edges match. Topstitch ⅛ inch from seam. Baste remaining edges of each piece together. Eyelet-side-up, overlap finished edges so back is 15 inches wide; baste along top and bottom edges. Eyelet sides in, stitch front to back around edges. Trim corners; turn right-side-out. Weave ribbon through 1½ yards of beading. Pin eyelet trim to edge of sham and miter corners same as on coverlet. Stitch along outer edge of beading by machine. Sew inner edge of beading to front only by hand, using tiny running stitches. Sew 11-inch lengths of ribbon to top corners and tie bows same as on coverlet.

BABYFACE RATTLE

MATERIALS:
1 inexpensive baby rattle with 2″-diameter flat circular top
5″ square flesh-colored fabric
5″ square eyelet fabric
5″ square pastel fabric
Scraps of light pink and blue cotton fabric
9″ × 5″ piece thin quilt batting
1 handful polyester stuffing
2″ scrap fusible webbing
2 yards yellow embroidery floss
21″ length 1¼″-wide eyelet edging
Blue, light pink, pink, and white sewing thread
13″ piece ⅜″-wide pastel ribbon

Cut face from flesh-colored fabric; lightly trace or transfer features to right side. Using face pattern, cut pieces for bonnet-back from pastel and eyelet

fabrics, and two pieces from quilt batting. Make pattern for rosy cheeks and cut two from pink. Make pattern for eyes and cut two from blue. Cut pieces from fusible webbing and fuse eyes and cheeks to face. Zigzag-stitch around pieces, using matching thread. Zigzag-embroider nose with light pink and mouth with pink thread. Using three strands of yellow floss, embroider lashes with straight stitches. Baste quilt batting to wrong side of face. Right-sides-up, place eyelet on pastel fabric and baste both to quilt batting. Trim batting close to stitching on face and bonnet-back. Right sides together, sew ends of eyelet edging together; zig-zag-finish ends. Make two rows of gathering stitches along raw edge of eyelet edging. Right sides together, with edges matching, gather eyelet around face and baste along seam line. Right sides together, stitch bonnet-back to face, leaving lower edge open between dots and being careful to catch only basted edge of eyelet edging in seam. Clip seam allowance; turn right-side-out. Place head over rattle. Fill out head with bits of stuffing. Turn seam allowance under along opening and pin edges together so face is centered on rattle; slip-stitch edges together. Tie ribbon in a bow and sew it to center of lower edge of face.

BABY BEAR RATTLE

MATERIALS:

1 inexpensive baby rattle with 2″-diameter flat cir-
 cular top
5″ × 10″ piece pastel cotton fabric
Small scraps of pink, blue, and light brown cotton
 fabric
5″ × 10″ piece thin quilt batting
1 handful polyester stuffing
2″ scrap fusible webbing
½ yard light brown embroidery floss (or use a cou-
 ple of strands of sewing thread)
3″ scrap ¾″-wide eyelet ruffling
Blue, light brown, white, and pink thread, plus
 thread to match pastel fabric
15″ length ⅜″-wide white satin ribbon

Cut two heads each from pastel fabric and quilt batting. Lightly trace or transfer features to one head piece for front. Make pattern for ear piece, eye, and nose. Cut ear piece from light pink, eyes from blue, and nose from light brown. Cut appliqué

pieces from fusible webbing. Fuse pieces to head front and zigzag-stitch around each, using match-ing thread. Zigzag-embroider muzzle with white thread and mouth with pink. Embroider eyelashes with light brown straight stitches, using three strands of floss or thread. Baste quilt batting to wrong side of head pieces along seam line. Trim batting close to stitching. Right sides together, stitch front to back, leaving lower edge open be-tween dots. Clip seam allowance; turn right-side-out. Place bear over rattle; fill out head with bits of stuffing but do not push it up into ears. Turn seam allowance under along opening and pin edges to-gether so head is centered on rattle. Slipstitch edges together. Using pastel thread, doubled, quilt along lower edge of ears. Wrap eyelet ruffling around top of handle, turning under top end on center back. Slipstitch ends together and then slip-stitch top edge to lower edge of bear. Tie ribbon around top of eyelet and make a bow; tack bow in place securely.

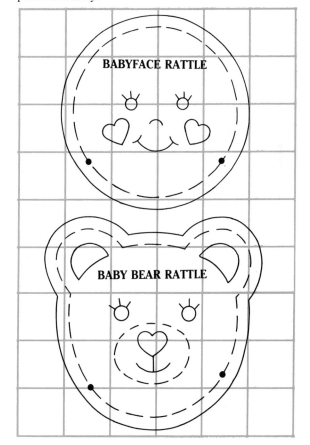

BABYFACE RATTLE

BABY BEAR RATTLE

1 square = 1 inch

Growth Chart

Decorative as well as practical, this bright hanging of playful bears will record your child's growth for many years. What better way to document all those healthy and happy inches? Just stand your child against the appliquéd tape measure and mark her or his height and age, and the date.

MATERIALS:
29″ × 66″ piece off-white cotton or cotton-blend canvas
½ yard blue cotton fabric
Scraps of bright red, green, yellow, and beige cotton fabric
14″ × 66″ piece quilt batting
½ yard 18″-wide fusible webbing
1 yellow fabric tape measure, 60″ long
2 yards ⅜″-wide red grosgrain ribbon
Sewing thread to match fabrics, except off-white
Six-strand embroidery floss: 2 yards black; 1 yard each red and white
Four ½″-diameter plastic rings

Cut off-white canvas in half lengthwise. With one canvas rectangle held lengthwise, pin tape measure in place, 2¾ inches from left edge, beginning exactly at lower edge. Cut five 14-inch pieces of red ribbon. Place pieces horizontally across canvas so a top edge of ribbon is even with 12″, 24″, 36″, 48″, and 60″ marks on tape measure. Stitch ribbons and tape measure in place on canvas.

Enlarge patterns for bears, bear accessories, numbers, and letters, following instructions in the how-to chapter. Make patterns for bears, front and back paw pads, inner ears, bows, and heart. Draw and cut patterns for simple block letters approximately 2⅛ inches high and 1¼ inches to 1½ inches wide to spell Baby's name. Cut bears from light brown dotted fabric, and front and back paw pads and inner ears from beige. Cut letters, numbers, bears' bows and heart from red, yellow, green and blue fabrics. Cut letters, numbers, bears, bears' bows, heart, inner ears, and front and back paw pads from fusible webbing.

Allowing 1 inch on all edges of canvas for binding, place numbers above ribbon to left side of tape measure with *ft* next to *5*; fuse them in place. Center name at top of canvas, spacing letters evenly; fuse in place. Arrange pieces of one bear with bows and so forth in the lower right corner of each block. Fuse bears in place. Zigzag-stitch around each fused piece, using matching thread.

Use four strands of floss for embroidering features. Embroider eyes with black and white satin stitch, noses with black satin stitch, and mouths with red backstitch. Using two strands of black floss, embroider claws with tiny black straight stitches.

Place batting between canvas pieces with design facing up and pin layers together. Stitch around chart 1 inch from edge. Hand-baste next to edges of tape measure and top edge of ribbons, and around bears. Machine-quilt along basted lines.

Cut 3¾-inch-wide bias strips of blue fabric. Piece a strip 164 inches long to make a 1-inch-wide binding and apply it to the chart, following the instructions given in the how-to chapter. Miter binding at corners. Sew rings to wrong side at upper and lower corners. Hang chart from hooks on wall so bottom edge is even with floor.

At regular intervals of time, measure the baby or child against the chart (for a small baby, lay the chart on the floor). Mark the height to the right of the tape measure and write the date and the age next to it. Use a permanent marker, or write with pencil and then embroider the date and/or age using backstitch.

54

"Our Little Star" Photo Album

Here's a special keepsake for the baby photos every parent is so proud of. You can make it by covering a purchased photo album with fabric decorated with patchwork, embroidery, and shadow appliqué . . . and you'll be able to show off your needlework skills along with your snapshots.

MATERIALS:

Loose-leaf photo album with cover 11¼″ wide × 10¾″ high × 2¼″ thick

Cotton fabrics:
  1 yard 45″-wide white
  ⅜ yard 45″ wide sheer white voile or organdy
  5″ × 7″ piece yellow
  5″ square peach
  Scraps of blue, green, and peach prints
13″ × 26″ piece quilt batting
1¼ yards 1″-wide lace edging
¾ yard ⅝″-wide lace edging
Six-strand embroidery floss: 4 yards each yellow, white, peach, and blue; 1 yard light green
White sewing thread
5″ × 7″ piece fusible webbing

Make patterns for large star, small star, and heart from embroidery diagrams. Make patterns for patchwork strips, following corner diagram; add ¼-inch seam allowance to all edges. From both white fabric and sheer fabric, cut album cover 15½″ × 12¾″, side border 2″ × 12¾″, a top and a bottom border each 2⅝″ × 8¾″, center square 5¼″ × 5¼″. Cut two facings from white fabric 12¾″ × 11″.

Cut large star from yellow fabric and fusible webbing. Lightly trace star and embroidery onto center of sheer fabric square. Place webbing and star in center of heavier fabric square, lining them up with tracings on center of sheer fabric. Remove sheer fabric and fuse star in place. Replace the sheer fabric and baste around the edges of the

square. Using four strands of yellow floss, back-stitch around star, sewing through all layers. Using four strands of blue floss, embroider words with backstitch. Using three strands of floss, embroider flowers, making peach lazy-daisy petals, light green lazy-daisy leaves, and yellow French-knot centers.

For corners, cut four of each patchwork section. Make each section a different print. Right sides together, stitch the corner units together one at a time, using ¼ inch seams. Follow the corner diagram to assemble each unit. Stitch a patchwork corner to each edge of the center square, starting and stopping ¼ inch from ends of seam. Stitch seams on end of the longest patchwork strip to join corner sections. Trace four hearts onto peach fabric and cut out, adding ¼-inch seam allowance on each piece. Stitch along seam line of each heart, using matching thread. Clip seam allowance to stitching and press to wrong side. Place a heart in each corner, ¾ inch from edges. Slipstitch heart to patchwork. Using three strands of white floss, work blanket stitch around heart.

To make pattern for embroidery on album spine, draw a straight line on a piece of tracing or tissue paper. Trace the words *Our Little Star* so they are next to each other on the line. Trace the small star to the right and to the left of the lettering. See Diagram 1. Trace this design onto the sheer fabric album cover so the lower edge of the lettering is 3⅛ inches from one 12¾-inch edge. Cut the small stars from yellow fabric and fusible webbing. Place the webbing and the stars on the heavier fabric and line them up with the stars on the sheer fabric. Remove the sheer fabric and fuse stars in place. Replace the sheer fabric and baste around edges. Work embroidery, using same colors and stitches as on the front.

Baste sheer border pieces to corresponding heavier fabric border pieces. Stitch all seams, right sides together, using ¼-inch seam allowance.

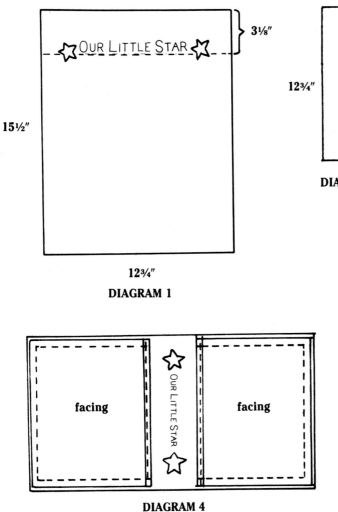

15½"

3⅛"

⭐ Our Little Star ⭐

12¾"

DIAGRAM 1

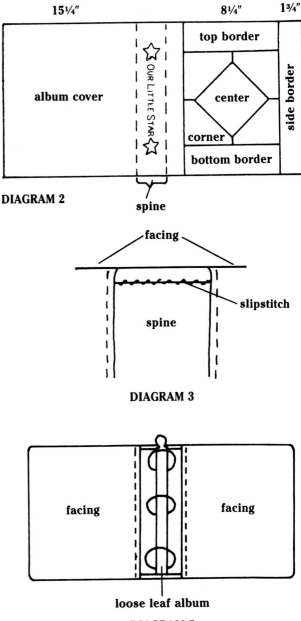

15¼"   8¼"   1¾"

top border

album cover

Our Little Star

center

side border

corner

bottom border

DIAGRAM 2

spine

facing

slipstitch

spine

DIAGRAM 3

facing

⭐
Our Little Star
⭐

facing

DIAGRAM 4

facing

facing

loose leaf album

DIAGRAM 5

Stitch top and bottom borders to patchwork square. See Diagram 2. Stitch side border to right-hand side and embroidered edge of cover to left side. Place batting between cover and backing; baste ½ inch from edge. Machine-quilt around outer edges of patchwork square and white square. Place 1¼-inch-wide lace around inner edge of border, mitering corners of lace as instructed in the how-to chapter. Sew inner edge of lace in place, using three strands of blue floss and tiny running stitches. Place ⅝-inch-wide lace around inner edges of patchwork. Sew in place along inner edge, using three strands of peach floss and tiny running stitches. Sew outer edge of lace invisibly to cover, using white sewing thread.

Turn under ¼ inch on one long edge of each facing piece; topstitch along fold. Pin unsewn edges of facings to sides of album cover with right sides together. See Diagram 3. Stitch in place, using a ½-inch seam. Trim seam allowances to ¼ inch along facing edges only. Turn right-side-out. Turn under ¼ inch twice on cover spine between facings; slipstitch. See Diagram 4. Slip cover onto photo album. See Diagram 5.

EMBROIDERY DIAGRAM

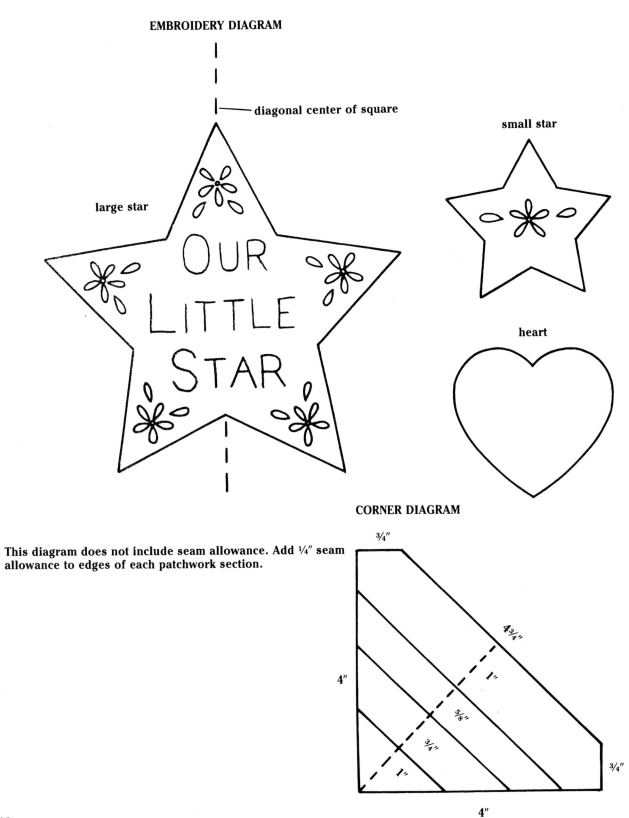

diagonal center of square

large star

OUR LITTLE STAR

small star

heart

CORNER DIAGRAM

This diagram does not include seam allowance. Add ¼″ seam allowance to edges of each patchwork section.

¾″

4¾″

4″

1″

5/8″

¾″

1″

¾″

4″

58

Pastel Plaid Blanket

A relaxing make-ahead project for an expectant mother . . . or for a grandmother to make and give as a gift. This blanket is very simple to crochet, and you can make it in white and pastel colors. Soft and warm for a baby girl or boy.

SIZE: About 34″ × 34″.

MATERIALS:

Acrylic sport-weight yarn, 6 (50 gr—1¾ oz) skeins white (Main Color—MC); 1 skein each of yellow (color A), light blue (B), peach (C), and mint (D)

Aluminum crochet hook, size G (4.50 mm), or size that gives you the correct gauge

GAUGE: In pattern, 11 mesh = 4″.

Note: See page 214 for Crochet Abbreviations and Terms.

Center Panel: With Main Color (MC), ch 169.

Row 1: Sc in 3rd ch from hook, * ch 1, skip 1 sc, sc in next ch (mesh made); repeat from * across. Ch 2, turn.

Row 2: Sc in first ch-1 space, * ch 1, sc in next ch-1 space; repeat from * across, ending with ch 1, sc over turning ch-2. Ch 2, turn. Repeat row 2 for pattern. (*Note:* To change colors at end of row, ch 1 for turning ch, break off old color, attach new color, and ch 1 to complete turning ch-2. Work over ends of yarn on next row.) Work colors as follows: Work until 8 rows MC are completed. Then work * 1 row D, 2 rows MC, 1 row C, 2 rows MC, 1 row B, 2 rows MC, 1 row A, 22 rows MC; repeat from * until 5th A row is completed. Work 9 rows MC. Break off.

Vertical Stripes: Stripes are rows of ch sts crocheted over mesh. On first row of panel, mark 5th ch-1 space from left side. Make slipknot loop of D on hook and insert hook into marked ch-1 space. With yarn held under blanket, make ch over starting ch. See Diagram 1. Make another ch over sc by inserting hook into next space directly above space last worked. See Diagram 2. Continue in this manner, working chain straight to top of blanket and

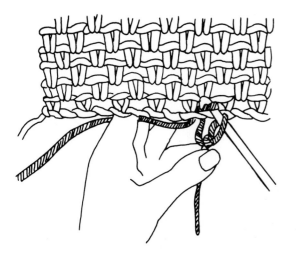

DIAGRAM 1

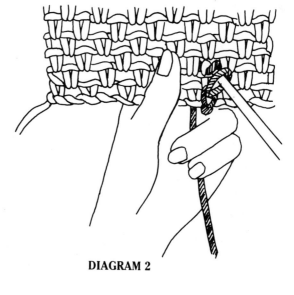

DIAGRAM 2

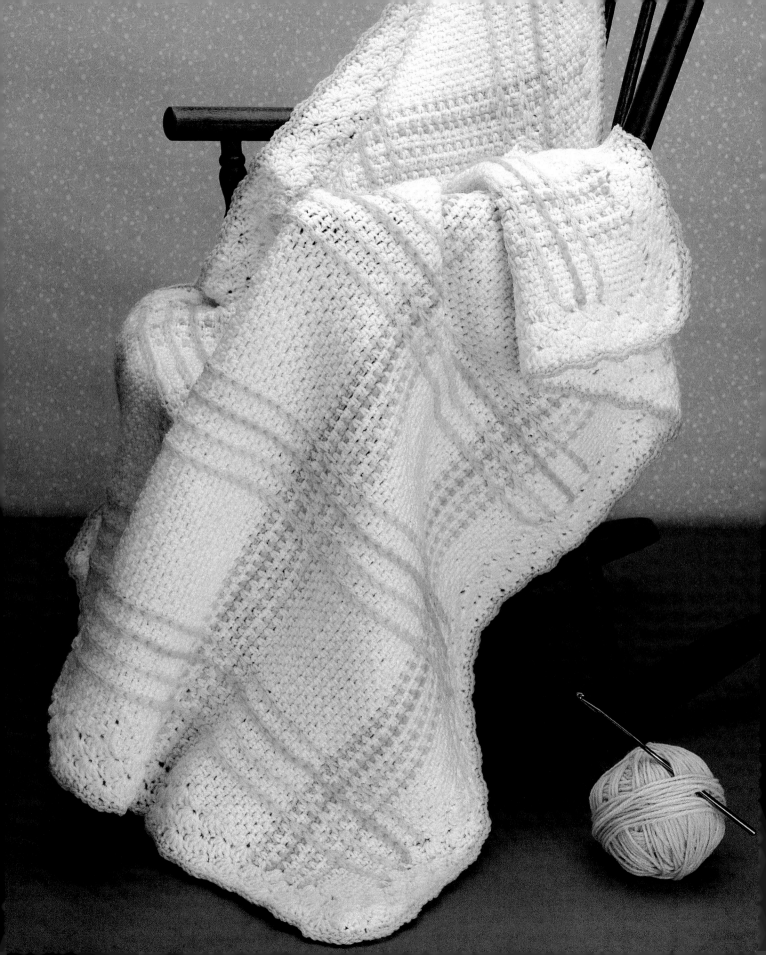

maintaining correct tension so chain lies flat without puckering. Break off. Work remaining vertical stripes as follows: * Skip next ch-1 space to right of D ch, work C ch in next space; skip 1 space, work B ch; skip 1 space, work A ch; skip 10 spaces, work D ch; repeat from * across blanket, ending with 5th A stripe.

Border: Attach MC to upper right corner space of panel. With right side of work facing you, work across top edge as follows:

Rnd 1: Ch 3 (count as first dc), work 2 more dc in same space, skip next space, sc in next space, * skip next space, work 4-dc shell in next space, skip next space, sc in next space. Repeat from * across top edge, working 3 dc, ch 1, and 3 dc at corner, then working into ends of rows and spacing 4-dc shells along side edge to correspond to top edge, work sc and 4-dc shells along side edge; work 3 dc, ch 1 and 3 dc at corner, work across lower edge as for top, work corner and remaining side edge as before, ending with 3 dc, ch 1, sl st in top of ch-3.

Rnd 2: Ch 3, work 2 dc in same place as sl st, * sc in next dc, work 4-dc shell in next sc, sc in top of next 4-dc shell between 3rd and 4th dc, repeat from * to first corner, ending with sc in top of first 3-dc shell, work 3 dc, ch 1, and 3 dc in ch-1 space at corner; repeat from * around, ending 3 dc, ch 1 and sl st in top of ch-3.

Rnd 3: Repeat rnd 2.

Rnd 4: Ch 3, ** work 5 dc in top of first sc, sc in top of next 4-dc shell, * 4 dc in next sc, sc in top of next shell; repeat from * to top of last shell before next corner, 5 dc in next sc, sc in ch-1 space at corner; repeat from ** around, ending with sc in last corner space; join to ch-3. Break off.

Rnd 5: Attach D (or other contrasting color) to first sc of one side, ch 1, * sc in next st, 2 sc in next st (center of 4-st shell), sc in next st, skip 1 st, sc in next sc; repeat from * to first 5-dc shell at next corner, sc in each st to corner sc, 3 sc in corner sc, sc in next 6 sts; repeat from * 3 times more. Sl st to first sc. Break off.

Finishing: Weave in any ends and block blanket, following instructions for acrylic yarn on page 20.

Choo-Choo Train Wall Organizer

Keep baby supplies within your easy reach and away from Baby's. Functional and decorative, the wall organizer is the perfect solution to keeping Baby's changing area neat and tidy. Later, it can be hung lower on the wall. Then your toddler can use it to stow toys in.

MATERIALS:

For background fabric:
¾ yard 40″-wide striped ticking fabric
30″ × 38″ piece quilt batting
⅝ yard muslin or other cotton fabric for backing
or
⅝ yard striped quilted fabric
20″ square quilt batting
Two 3½″ × 17″ pieces cotton fabric for hanging strip
2½″ × 5″ piece muslin

For pockets:
½ yard red print fabric *or* 3½ yards red ½″-wide double-fold bias tape
¼ yard each red, green, blue, and yellow cotton fabrics
8½″ × 17″ piece each blue and white, green and white, and yellow and white print fabrics
36″ × 2″ × ¼″ strip of pine
6″ × 9″ piece light brown fabric with dots for bear
About 2 handfuls polyester stuffing
½ yard each red and dark brown six-strand embroidery floss
Brown, red, green, blue, yellow, and off-white sewing thread
¼ yard ¼″-wide ribbon for bear
3 screw eyes to fit over hooks on wall
1 yard ¼″-wide elastic
Eight ½″-diameter buttons, 2 each of red, blue, green, or yellow

Enlarge pattern for engine, caboose and bear, following instructions in the how-to chapter. Add ¼-inch seam allowance to edges of patterns. Make separate patterns for window, triangular cowcatcher, and smoke stack. Draw a 2½-inch-diameter circle for wheel pattern.

To make your own quilted fabric for the background, cut one 20″ × 38″ piece each from striped ticking, quilt batting, and backing fabric. (If you are not using a striped fabric for the background, draw quilting lines 2 inches apart, parallel to 20-inch edges.) Right sides out, place quilt batting between fabric and backing; pin pieces together along outer edge. On striped ticking fabric, pin and then quilt along edge of every fifth stripe so fabric is quilted at 2-inch to 2¼-inch intervals. Also, quilt ½ inch from edges.

From green fabric, cut engine, engine pocket, 6½″ × 7¾″, four wheels, 1″ × 5″ center roof, and two 1″ × 3¾″ side roofs. From red fabric, cut caboose; caboose pocket, 7¾″ × 11¼″; four wheels; cowcatcher; and smokestack. From yellow, cut car, 10½″ × 11¼″; engine roof, 1″ × 5½″; and four wheels. Cut windows from muslin. From quilt batting, cut engine, caboose, all roof pieces, eight wheels, two 5¼″ × 11¼″ pieces for cars, 3¾″ × 6½″ piece for engine pocket, and 3¾″ × 11″ piece for caboose pocket. If you wish, cut fusible webbing for windows, cowcatcher, and smokestack.

Use ¼-inch seam allowance on train. Fuse or baste windows to engine and caboose. Zigzag-stitch around windows. Baste engine, caboose, and all roof pieces to quilt batting ¼ inch from edges. Trim batting close to stitching. Press or baste seam allowances to wrong side, clipping almost to basting at inner corners. With background fabric horizontal, measure 9 inches from top edge and mark with a row of pins. Line up lower straight edge of engine, cars, and caboose with this line. Pin engine and roof to background 2¼ inches from left side. Fuse or baste smokestack and cowcatcher under edges. Zigzag-stitch around red pieces. Stitch engine and roof in place along edges. Quilt around windows.

Pin caboose and roof pieces on background, 1¾ inches from right side. Stitch in place along edges. Quilt around window.

To make pockets and box cars, baste quilt batting to one half of wrong side of fabric pieces. See Diagram 1. Right sides together, fold fabric in half along the top edge of batting. Stitch along edges, leaving an opening for turning on lower edge. See Diagram 2. Trim batting close to stitching. Turn right-side-out. Slipstitch edges of opening together. To make pleat along sides of engine pockets, fold 1 inch to wrong side. Stitch ⅛ inch from fold. See Diagram 3. Fold pleat in half and stitch ⅛ inch from fold. See Diagram 4. To make pleat on box cars and caboose pocket, fold 1½ inches on side edges to wrong side; stitch ⅛ inch from fold. Fold pleat in half; stitch ⅛ inch from fold. Pin side and lower edge of pockets to engine and caboose. Pin box cars between engine and caboose. Stitch side edges of pleat in place. See Diagram 5. Then stitch across entire lower edge catching pleats in stitching at each side. See Diagram 6.

To make each wheel, baste quilt batting to one fabric piece. Trim batting close to stitching. Right sides together, stitch around wheel ¼ inch from edge. Trim and clip seam allowance. On side without batting, separate one layer of fabric; cut a 1-inch slit for turning. See Diagram 7. Carefully turn wheel right-side-out. Whipstitch edges of slash together loosely without distorting wheel shape. Pin wheels to lower edge of train with a contrasting-color button on each wheel. Stitch buttons in place through wheels and background.

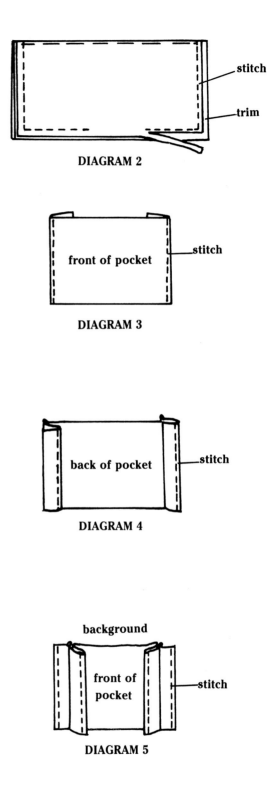

DIAGRAM 2

stitch

front of pocket

DIAGRAM 3

stitch

back of pocket

DIAGRAM 4

background

front of pocket

stitch

DIAGRAM 5

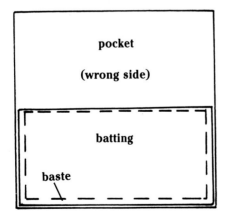

pocket

(wrong side)

batting

baste

DIAGRAM 1

For pockets, press under ½ inch on all edges of 8½″ × 17″ pieces. Press under 1 inch on one long edge. Stitch ⅝ inch and 1 inch from edge to make a casing. See Diagram 8. Insert a 10½-inch piece of elastic in casing and stitch across ends. Make a row of gathering stitches ⅛ inch from other long edge. Gather lower edge to 10½ inches wide. Pin pockets, evenly spaced, across background, 1½ inches from lower edge. Stitch along side and lower edges.

For hanging strip, cut two 3½″ × 17″ pieces of ticking or any other fabric you wish to use. Press under ½ inch on short ends; stitch along fold. Stitch to wrong side of top edge, 1½ inches from sides. See Diagram 9. Turn under ½ inch at lower edge; slipstitch securely to back of organizer.

For fabric binding, cut 2-inch-wide bias strips to make a binding 120 inches long, following the instructions in the how-to chapter. Or bind the edges with bias tape (also discussed in the how-to chapter).

Insert wooden strip in casing on wrong side, adding screw eyes in top edge of wood at sides and center. See Diagram 10.

To make bear to ride in Baby's train, cut two bear pieces from light brown fabric. Trace seam line to wrong side of one bear piece. Right sides together, stitch along edges, leaving an opening between dots. Trim and clip seam allowance. Turn right-side-out. Stuff bear. Slipstitch edges of opening together. Quilt along lines between head and ear. Embroider eyes and nose with brown satin stitch and mouth with red backstitch. Tie a bow with ribbon around bear's neck.

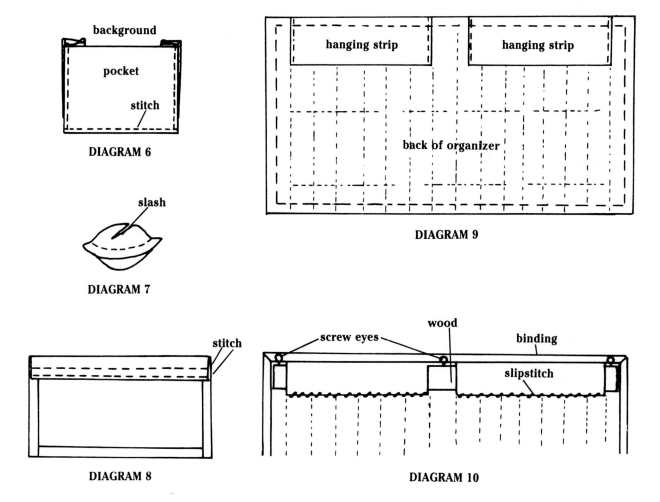

DIAGRAM 6

DIAGRAM 7

DIAGRAM 9

DIAGRAM 8

DIAGRAM 10

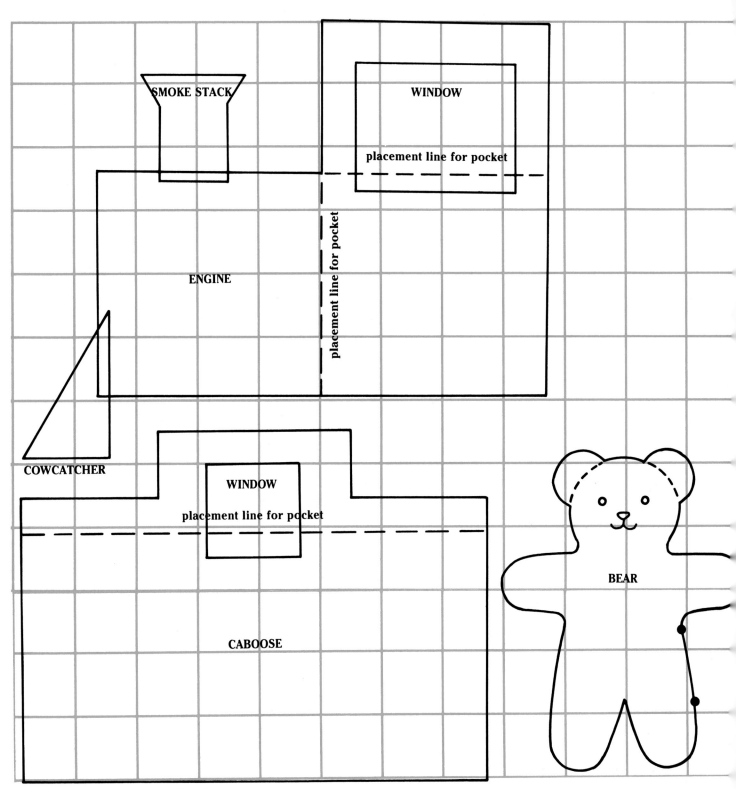

SMOKE STACK

WINDOW

placement line for pocket

placement line for pocket

ENGINE

WINDOW

placement line for pocket

COWCATCHER

CABOOSE

BEAR

1 square = 1 inch

66

BABY'S

TOYS

67

Terry Teddy Bear

Soft, cuddly, and completely washable—a wonderful first teddy bear! Make it in light brown velour terrycloth with sewn-on eyes, nose, mouth, and even a heart. Add a pastel-colored satin ribbon—and Teddy's ready for a hug and lots of kisses.

MATERIALS:
⅜ **yard 45″-wide light brown velour terrycloth**
or
21″ × 40″ **velour bath towel**
Scraps of dark brown, white, and pink felt
⅓ **pound polyester stuffing**
½ **yard each dark brown, white, and pink six-strand embroidery floss**
Light brown sewing thread
¾ **yard ⅝″-wide light green ribbon**

Enlarge the pattern, following the instructions in the how-to chapter. Place towel or fabric on your work table, velour-side-up. Pin pattern pieces in place with arrows on straight grain pointing in the same direction as the nap. Cut out one body back, one body front, one head back, one head side, one head center, two arms, two legs, and two ears. Reverse the patterns (turn them over), and cut out all pieces again *except* the head center. Cut the heart from pink felt, the nose and two small eye pieces from dark brown, and the large eye pieces from white felt.

Sew all seams right sides together, using ¼-inch seam allowance. Clip seam allowance along curves, before turning pieces right-side-out. Sew together as follows:

Stitch head sides together along center front. Stitch head center to top edge of head sides, matching center of nose to seam. See Diagram 1.

Stitch ears together in pairs along outer curve. Trim seam allowance to a generous ⅛ inch, then clip along seam. Turn right-side-out. Stuff ears a little; baste lower edges together. Baste ears to head front between dots. See Diagram 2.

Stitch head backs together along center seam. Stitch front to back, leaving lower edge open. Make a row of tiny gathering stitches along lower edge. Stuff head firmly.

Stitch darts in body back. Clip darts open along center line, following the instructions in the how-to chapter; finger-press open. Stitch body fronts and backs together along center seams. Stitch fronts to backs along sides, leaving an opening between two upper dots. Turn under seam allowance along remaining edges; baste along edges. See Diagram 3. Stuff body.

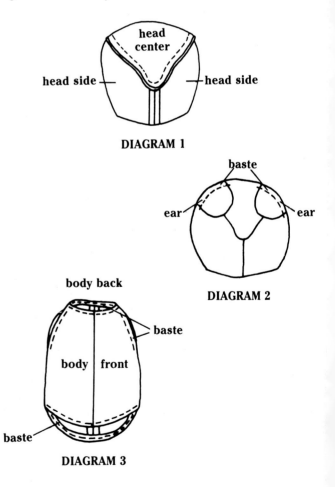

DIAGRAM 1

DIAGRAM 2

DIAGRAM 3

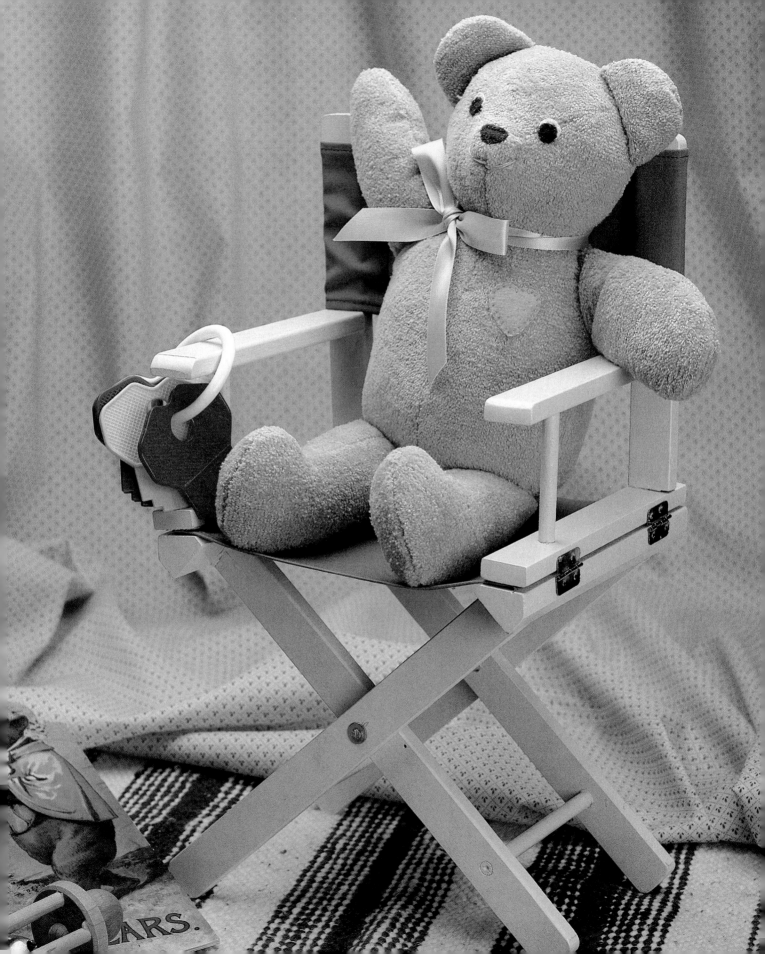

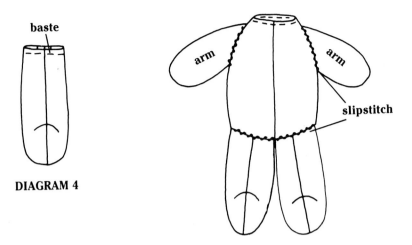

baste

DIAGRAM 4

DIAGRAM 5

slipstitch

arm **arm**

Stitch arms together, leaving end open between dots. Turn right-side-out and stuff arms so top portion remains flat. Baste ends together along seam line.

Stitch legs together in pairs, leaving straight end open. Turn right-side-out and stuff so top remains flat. Fold top ends in half, matching seams at center, and baste along seam line. See Diagram 4.

Insert arms in side openings of body, matching dots. Insert legs in lower opening between center and side. Slipstitch securely in place, using doubled thread. See Diagram 5. Push in any extra stuffing to fill out body before finishing seam.

Insert head in top of body, gathering lower edge to fit and matching front, back, and side seams. Slipstitch three-quarters of head to body, using doubled thread. Push in extra stuffing for a firm neck. See Diagram 6. Finish slipstitching neck seam.

For mouth, use all six strands of pink floss, doubled, in a large embroidery needle. Insert needle from the top in nose area and bring it up at center seam just below nose. Insert needle on right-hand side of mouth and bring it up at center seam ½ inch below nose. See Diagram 7. Insert needle on left-hand side of mouth and bring it out again on top of nose. See Diagram 8. Knot thread securely.

Pin heart to bear's left front side, and eyes and nose to head. Sew pieces to body, using blanket stitch and three strands of matching embroidery floss. Place ribbon around neck and tie a bow.

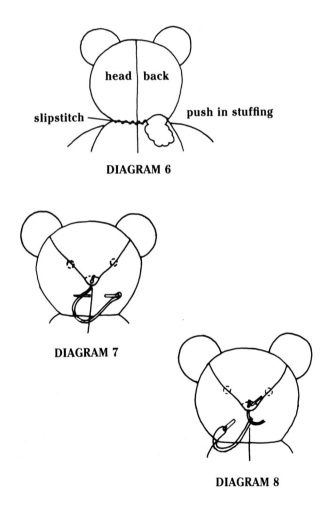

head **back**

slipstitch **push in stuffing**

DIAGRAM 6

DIAGRAM 7

DIAGRAM 8

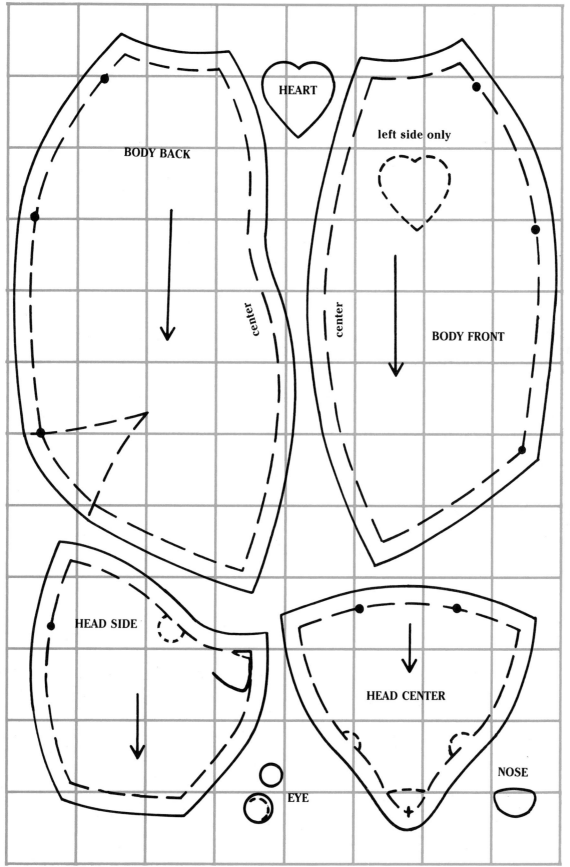

HEART

BODY BACK

left side only

BODY FRONT

center

center

HEAD SIDE

HEAD CENTER

EYE

NOSE

71

1 square = 1 inch

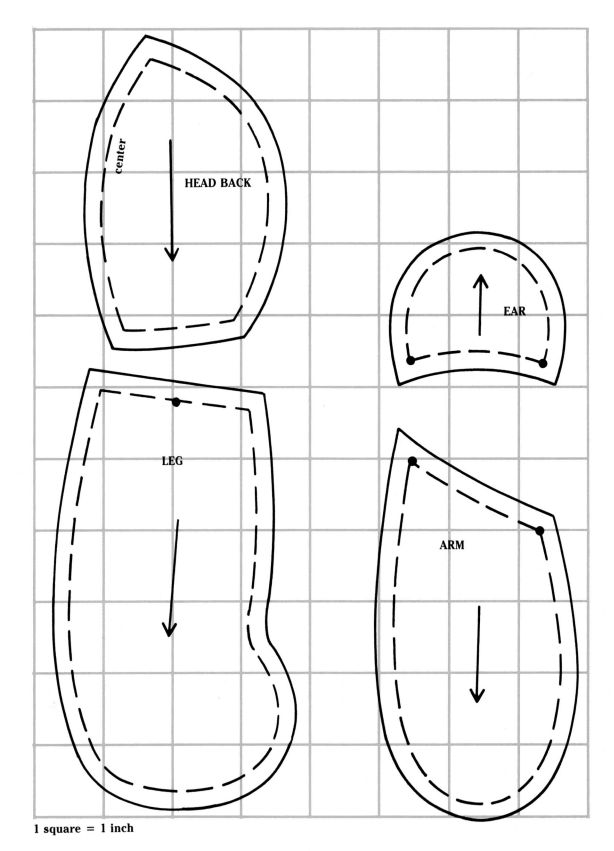

center

HEAD BACK

EAR

LEG

ARM

72 1 square = 1 inch

Sunshine Sue and Cheerful Charlie

Here's a smiling twosome ready to be Baby's first friends. Their simple shapes are just right for small hands to hold. Bright cotton fabric and yarn (and a little bit of love) are all you need to create these charming toys.

MATERIALS:

For dolls:
⅜ yard flesh-colored cotton twill fabric
4″ square each of red and blue fabric for shoes
½ pound polyester stuffing
six-strand embroidery floss: 1 yard each light blue, brown, white, and beige, 2 yards red
Two 15-meter skeins each yellow and brown #3 pearl cotton
Thread to match fabrics and yarn

For Sue's clothes:
¼ yard white cotton fabric
6″ × 20″ piece yellow heart-print fabric
¼ yard ⅜″-wide eyelet ruffling
White sewing thread
¼ yard ⅛″-wide red grosgrain ribbon
⅝ yard ¼″-wide elastic

For Charlie's clothes:
6″ × 20″ piece red-and-white striped cotton fabric
7″ × 20″ piece blue cotton fabric with white dots
1 yard bright yellow six-strand embroidery floss
Blue and white sewing thread
¼ yard ⅛″-wide white grosgrain ribbon
3″ piece ¼″-wide elastic

Enlarge patterns for dolls and clothes, following the instructions in the how-to chapter. For dolls, fold flesh-colored fabric in half, wrong sides out. For each doll, cut two body pieces. Trace outline of body to wrong side of each piece. Trace the features to the right side of the front. Trace markings for shoes and socks to the right side of the legs,

omitting sock line on Charlie. For Charlie, cut four shoe pieces from red fabric. For Sue, cut four shoe pieces from blue (two fronts and two backs) and four 2½-inch-long pieces of eyelet edging for socks.

Right sides up, place Sue's sock pieces on front and back, top edge even with sock line on legs. Baste along sides and lower edge. For both dolls, place shoes on front and back. Baste along seam line and upper edge. Using matching thread, zig-zag-stitch along top edge of shoes. With right sides together, stitch body fronts to backs, leaving an opening between dots. Clip seam allowance along curves. Trim seam allowance of ears to ⅛ inch. Turn right-side-out. Stuff body firmly. Slip-stitch opening closed. Using doubled thread, quilt along broken line at the ears with tiny running stitches.

Using three strands of embroidery floss, work satin stitch on lower section of eye with blue, upper section of eye with white, and rosy heart-cheeks with red. With light brown, backstitch around eye. With beige, backstitch line of nose. Using four strands of red, embroider mouth with backstitch.

To make hair, cut two 2″ × 11″ strips of paper for each doll. Fold each strip in half lengthwise. Wrap pearl cotton yarn around each strip to form tightly spaced 1-inch loops. See Diagram 1. Using matching thread, machine-stitch about 3/16 inch from one long edge of paper. Tear paper carefully from loops along perforations caused by stitching. Beginning at left side of head back, wrap and pin one strip of hair across back, up over ear, across front just below head seam, and down over other ear. See Diagram 2. Continue to pin hair so that stitching line is about ¼ inch above previous row, as indicated by broken lines on Diagram 3. Using matching thread, sew hair in place using back-stitches.

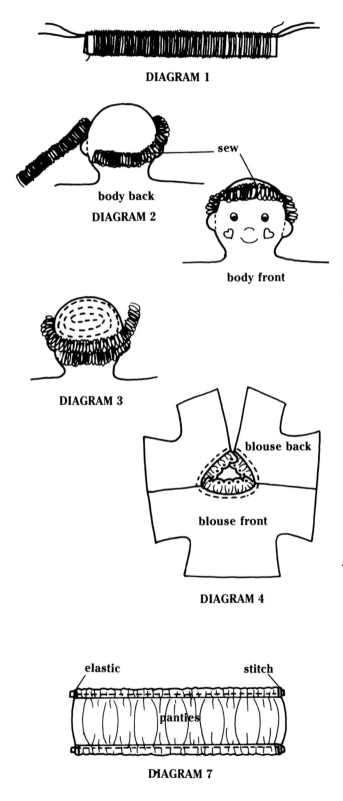

DIAGRAM 1

sew

body back

DIAGRAM 2

body front

DIAGRAM 3

blouse back

blouse front

DIAGRAM 4

Sue's Clothes

From white fabric, cut one blouse front and two blouse backs. Stitch backs to front along shoulder seams. Stitch along seam line all around neck edge. Clip seam allowance along neck and press edge under along stitching. Cut a 6½-inch piece of eyelet ruffling. Place eyelet under neck edge; stitch ⅛ inch from neck edge. See Diagram 4. Press under ¼ inch along center back edges; stitch in place. Make a row of gathering stitches ¼ inch from sleeve ends. Cut two 5-inch pieces of eyelet ruffling. Gather sleeves evenly to 5 inches wide and stitch eyelet to ends of sleeve. See Diagram 5. Press seam allowances toward sleeves. Stitch front to backs along underarm seam. Clip seam allowance along curves. Press under ¼ inch on lower edge of blouse. Stitch ⅛ inch from edge. Place blouse on doll, over lapping back edges. Slipstitch backs together at center. See Diagram 6.

From white fabric, cut panties, 12″ × 3½″. Along each long edge, press under ⅛ inch, then ⅜ inch; stitch along inner folded edge to form a casing on each long side. Insert a 9½-inch piece of elastic in each casing; stitch in place along side edges. See Diagram 7. Stitch short ends together. Turn right-side-out. Match seam to center of lower edge. Tack lower edges together at center. See Diagram 8. Slip on doll.

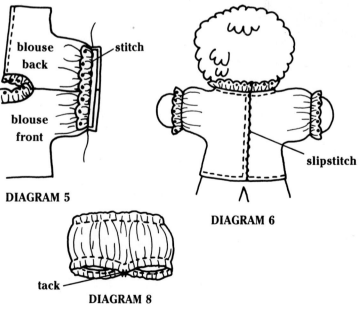

blouse back

stitch

blouse front

DIAGRAM 5

slipstitch

DIAGRAM 6

elastic

stitch

panties

DIAGRAM 7

tack

DIAGRAM 8

For jumper, from yellow heart print, cut two skirts, two yoke fronts, and four yoke backs. Slash skirt back along center to dot. Press under ¼ inch along short diagonal edges of skirt front and back, and edges of center back opening. Stitch close to folds. Make a row of gathering stitches ¼ inch from top edge. Gather skirt front to fit front yoke between dots; stitch seam. Gather skirt back to fit back yokes between dots; stitch seams. See Diagram 9.

Stitch back yokes to front yoke at shoulders. Stitch remaining yokes together in same manner for facing. Press under armhole edges of yoke and facing. Press under lower edge of facing. Stitch yoke facing to wrong side of yoke along center back and along neck edge. Clip seam allowance. See Diagram 10. Turn facing to wrong side of yoke.

Topstitch ⅛ inch from neck, arm, and waist edges. Stitch back to front along side seams of skirt. Turn under ½ inch twice along lower edge; stitch hem in place. Place jumper on doll, overlapping back edges; slipstitch back edges together. Make two small bows with red ribbon. Sew one to blouse at center front of neckline and one to hair at side.

Charlie's Clothes

From red-and-white striped fabric, cut one shirt front and two shirt backs. Stitch backs to fronts along shoulder seams. Stitch along seam line all around neck edge. Clip seam allowance along neck and press edge under along stitching. Press seam allowance under along center back and sleeve edges. Stitch ⅛ inch from fold. See Diagram 11. Stitch backs to front along underarm seam. Press

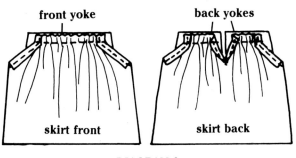

DIAGRAM 9

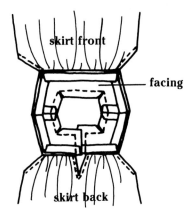

DIAGRAM 10

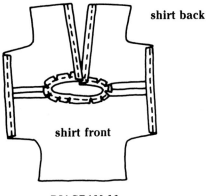

DIAGRAM 11

DIAGRAM 12

under ¼ inch along lower edge and stitch hem in place. With shirt on doll, overlap center back edges and slipstitch together. See Diagram 12.

For overalls, from blue dotted fabric, cut two fronts, two backs, one bib facing, and two straps 1⅜″ × 6″. Right sides together, stitch fronts together along center seams; stitch backs together in same manner. On top edge of back, press under ⅛ inch, then ⅜ inch; stitch along lower edge of fold to form a casing. Insert elastic through casing; stitch ends in place along sides. See Diagram 13. Press under ¼ inch along lower edge of bib facing. Right sides together, stitch facing to top edge of front. Clip and trim seam allowance. Turn facing to inside. Embroider buttons at corners, using yellow satin stitch. Stitch backs to fronts at side seams,

keeping facing free from stitching. Fold seam to front and fold facing down over seam; tack sides in place. See Diagram 14. Topstitch ⅛ inch from top edge of front. Turn ¼ inch under twice on lower edge of legs; stitch in place. Stitch fronts to backs along inner leg seam. Turn right-side-out. Fold straps in half lengthwise. Stitch ¼ inch from long edge. Turn right-side-out. Press with seam along one edge. Topstitch ⅛ inch from long edges. Place overalls on doll. Pin one end of straps inside upper edge of front. See Diagram 15. Crossing straps in back, insert ends in upper edge of back. Slipstitch straps to upper edge of overalls. See Diagram 16.

Make two small bows from white ribbon. Sew to center front of shoes ¼ inch below top edge.

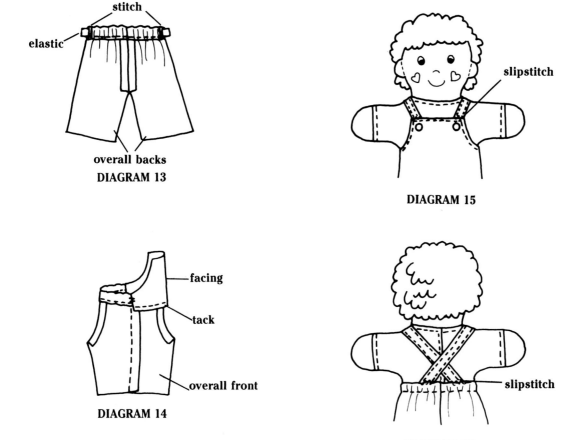

DIAGRAM 13

DIAGRAM 15

DIAGRAM 14

DIAGRAM 16

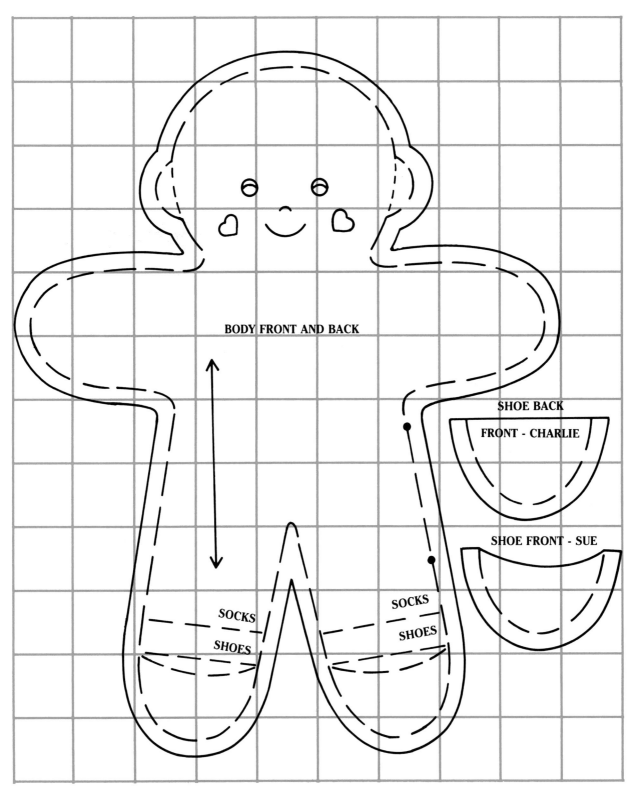

BODY FRONT AND BACK

SHOE BACK

FRONT - CHARLIE

SHOE FRONT - SUE

SOCKS

SOCKS

SHOES

SHOES

1 square = 1 inch

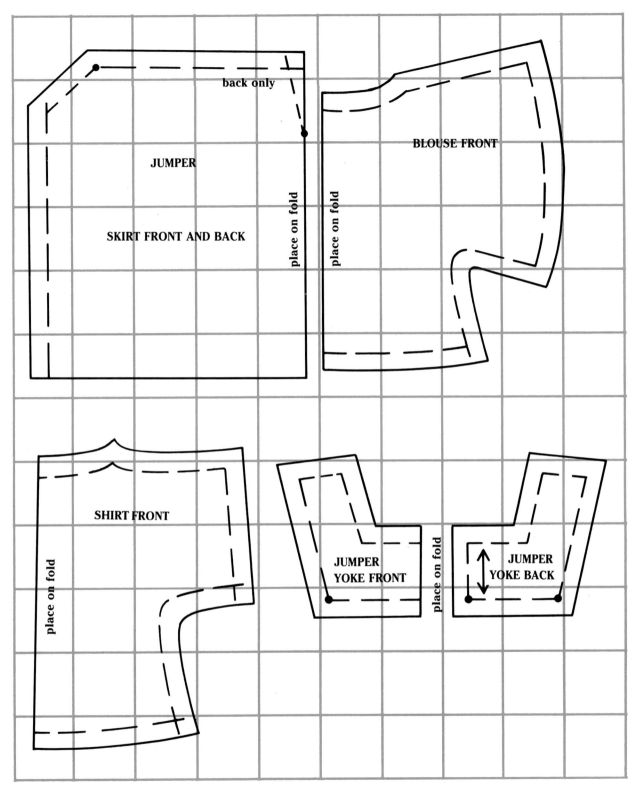

JUMPER

SKIRT FRONT AND BACK

back only

place on fold

place on fold

BLOUSE FRONT

SHIRT FRONT

place on fold

JUMPER
YOKE FRONT

place on fold

JUMPER
YOKE BACK

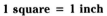

1 square = 1 inch

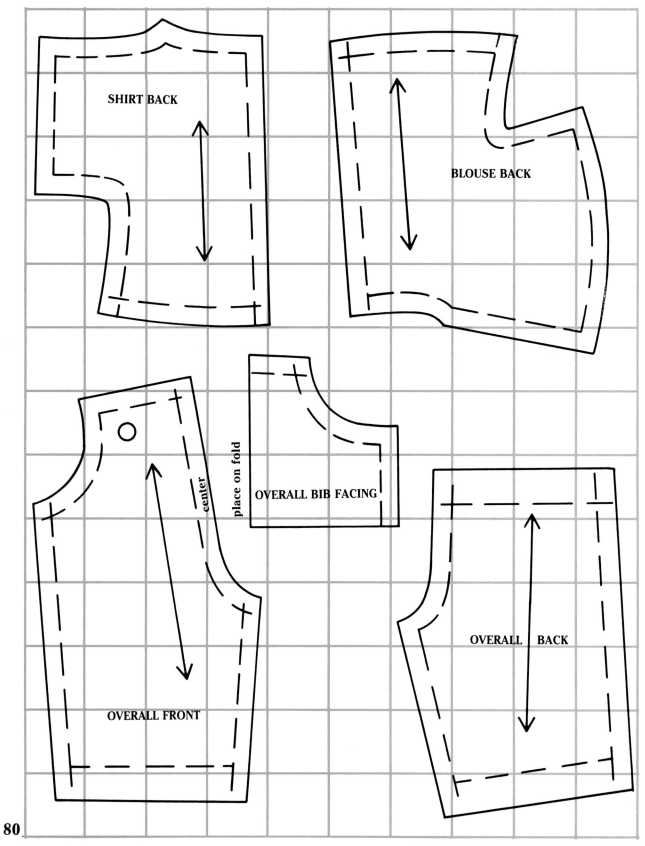

SHIRT BACK

BLOUSE BACK

center

place on fold

OVERALL BIB FACING

OVERALL FRONT

OVERALL BACK

80

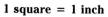

1 square = 1 inch

Hop-About Harry

A sweet bunny for Baby's first Easter... or any day of the year. He's easy to make in soft cotton flannel, with a fluffy, white-yarn tail. His face is embroidered with appliquéd felt eyes and nose. And his arms are opened wide—just waiting to be hugged.

MATERIALS:

⅜ yard white cotton flannel
6″ × 10″ piece pink cotton flannel
Small scraps of brown and pink felt
7″ × 8″ piece quilt batting
¼ pound polyester stuffing
2″ × 4″ piece cardboard
1 yard each pink, blue, brown and white six-strand embroidery floss
15 yards white sportweight yarn
Pink and white sewing thread
¾ yard ⅜″-wide yellow ribbon

Enlarge patterns, following the instructions in the how-to chapter. From white flannel, cut two head backs, two body backs, two body fronts, one head front, four ears, four arms, and four feet. From pink flannel, cut one tummy, two inner ears, two paw pads, and two soles. Transfer markings to wrong side of each piece and transfer placement markings to right side, if desired. Cut two ears and two soles from quilt batting. Make patterns for eyes and nose. Cut eyes from brown felt and nose from pink felt.

For ears, baste inner ears in position on two ear pieces for fronts. Zigzag-stitch along the edge, using pink thread. Baste quilt batting pieces to wrong side of each ear.

Stitch all seams right sides together, using ¼-inch seam allowance as follows:

Stitch ear fronts to remaining ear pieces, leaving bottom end open. Trim and clip seam allowance. Turn right-side-out. Baste lower edges to-gether. Machine-quilt around inner ear. With right sides together, baste ears to head front between marks. See Diagram 1. Make a row of gathering stitches by machine along lower edge of head front between dots. Stitch head backs together along center back. Sew head backs to head front; leaving lower edge open between dots. See Diagram 2. Clip curves. Turn right-side-out and stuff head firmly.

Sew body fronts together and body backs together along center seams. Baste tummy in position on right side of joined front. Zigzag-stitch along edge with pink. Stitch back to front, leaving neck edge open. See Diagram 3. Clip seam allowance.

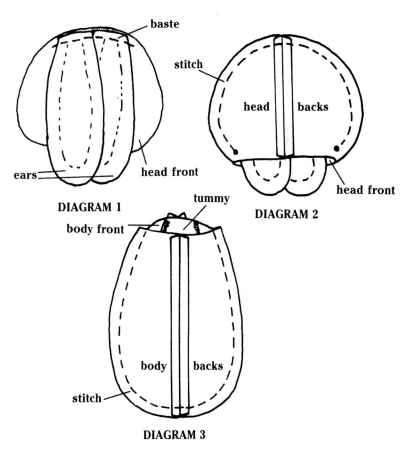

DIAGRAM 1

baste
stitch
head backs
ears
head front

DIAGRAM 2

head front

DIAGRAM 3

tummy
body front
body backs
stitch

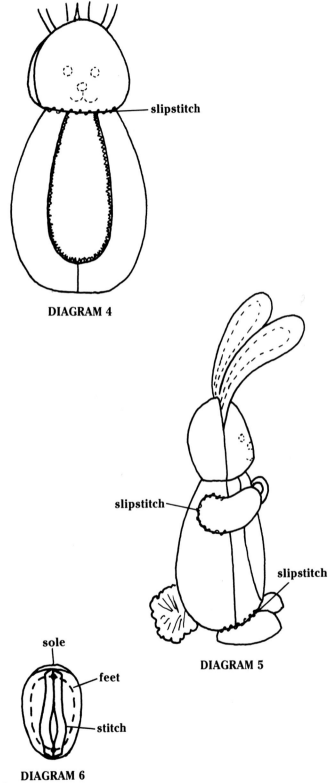

DIAGRAM 4

DIAGRAM 5

DIAGRAM 6

sole

feet

stitch

slipstitch

slipstitch

slipstitch

Turn right-side-out. Stuff firmly. Turn seam allowance on lower edge of head under. Pin head back over top edge of body back, matching seams. Gather lower edge of head front over body front, matching centers. Using doubled thread, slipstitch head to body securely. See Diagram 4.

Baste a paw pad to each of two arm pieces for inner arms (be sure to reverse second pieces so there is both a right and a left arm). Using pink, zigzag-stitch around paw pads. Stitch arms with paw pads to remaining arms, leaving an opening for turning between dots. Clip seam allowance; turn right-side-out. Stuff arms. Turn edges of opening under and slipstitch them together. Pin inner arms to side of backs about ¾ inch below neck seam. See Diagram 5. Slipstitch securely to body, using doubled thread.

Baste quilt batting to wrong side of soles. Stitch feet together in pairs along upper curve, leaving an opening between small dots in center of seam (leave other side open). Sew feet to soles, matching large and small dots. See Diagram 6. Clip seam allowance along curves. Turn right-side-out. Stuff feet firmly. Slipstitch edges of opening together. Pin feet to bottom of body about ¾ inch apart; slipstitch feet securely to body, using doubled thread. See Diagram 5.

Using two strands of matching embroidery floss, sew eyes and nose to face with blanket stitch. Make two or three tiny straight stitches in the center of each eye to highlight them. Embroider mouth in stem stitch, using three strands of pink floss. Using two strands of light blue, embroider whiskers with long straight stitches. Embroider little claws on outer arms and feet with two strands of brown floss, using straight stitch.

Make a pompon for tail using 1½-inch-diameter cardboard circles with ⅜-inch-diameter hole in center, following instructions in the how-to-chapter. Sew pompon in position on center back seam. See Diagram 5. Tie ribbon around neck and make a bow in front.

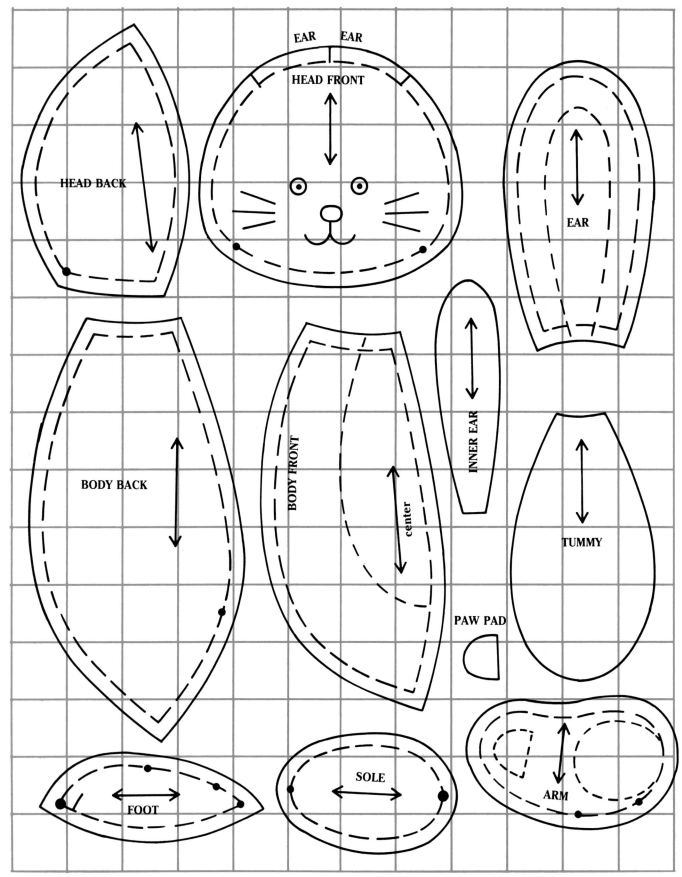

EAR   EAR

HEAD FRONT

HEAD BACK

EAR

BODY BACK

BODY FRONT

center

INNER EAR

TUMMY

PAW PAD

FOOT

SOLE

ARM

1 square = 1 inch

Playful Puppy

Here's a lovable pup made of washable cotton print fabric. His floppy felt ears and friendly face will make him a lively companion for Baby in the playpen or crib.

MATERIALS:
¾ yard beige cotton fabric with brown dots
3″ square dusty pink cotton fabric
8″ × 12″ piece dark brown felt
1″ squares each of red and white felt
6″ square quilt batting
⅓ pound polyester stuffing
Beige, brown, and white sewing thread
¾ yard ⅝″-wide blue satin ribbon
Beige, brown, and white sewing thread

Enlarge the patterns, following instructions in the how-to chapter. From beige fabric with brown dots, cut one upper body, two under bodies, two upper heads, two under heads, and two tails. Cut two mouths from dusty pink. From brown felt, cut four ears, two small eye pieces, and two noses. Cut two large eye pieces from white felt and one tongue from red felt.

Sew all seams right sides together, using ¼-inch seam allowance, as follows:

Stitch tail pieces together, leaving straight end open. Clip seam allowance along curves and trim seam allowance to ⅛ inch near pointed end. Turn right-side-out. Stuff tail. Fold open end so seams meet in the center. Baste along seam line. Matching dots, baste tail to upper body so that it will curve up when extended away from the body.

Stitch curved darts on under bodies; clip almost to stitching. See Diagram 1. Stitch under body pieces together along center seam. Matching edges, stitch under body to upper body, leaving neck end open and catching tail seam between fabric layers. Clip seam allowance along curves. Turn right-side-out. Stuff body.

Stitching along center seam, sew upper-head pieces together. Sew under-head pieces together along center seam. Stitch a mouth to each piece, matching dots. Sew upper heads to lower heads along sides from dots to neck edge. See Diagram 2. Sew straight edge of mouth pieces together. See Diagram 3. Clip seam allowance of all head seams. Turn right-side-out. Turn seam allowance of neck edge under and baste it in place. Stuff head. Place head on body, matching lower center and side seams; slipstitch head securely to body.

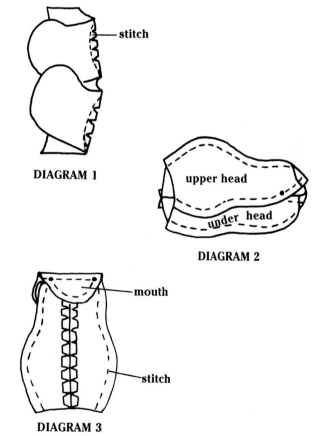

DIAGRAM 1

DIAGRAM 2

DIAGRAM 3

Stitch ears together in pairs, leaving an opening between dots. Clip and trim seam allowance. Turn right-side-out; press ears flat. Cut two ear pieces from quilt batting, omitting seam allowance. Insert batting in each ear and smooth out. Turn under seam allowance along opening and slipstitch edges together. Slipstitch top edge of ears very securely to upper head along placement lines. Stitch nose pieces together, using 1/8-inch seam allowance. Clip almost to stitching along curve at 1/4-inch intervals. Turn right-side-out. Place nose on head with a little stuffing under it. With matching, doubled thread, sew nose in place, using blanket stitch. Sew eye pieces in place, using blanket stitch and matching thread. Place tongue in center of mouth and sew straight end to mouth along seam. See Diagram 4. Place ribbon around neck and tie a bow.

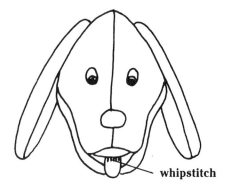

whipstitch

DIAGRAM 4

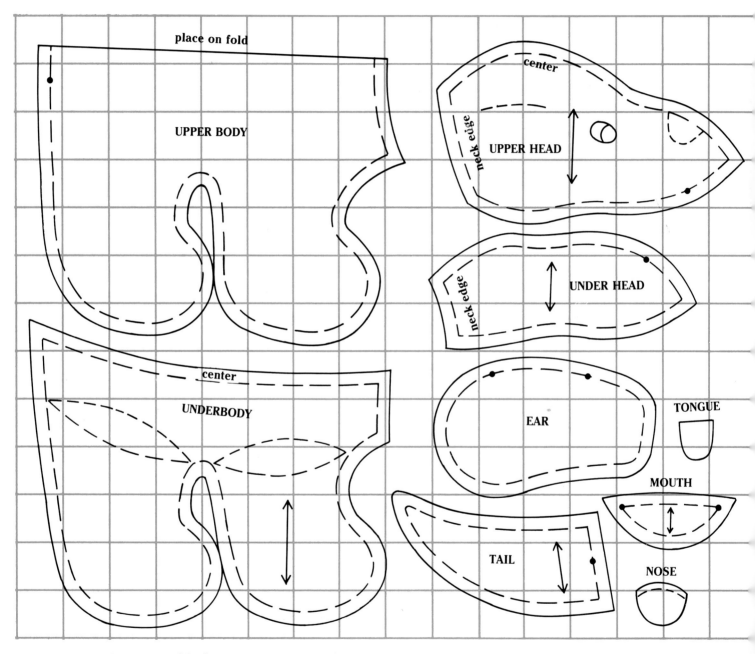

place on fold

UPPER BODY

center

UNDERBODY

center

UPPER HEAD

neck edge

neck edge

UNDER HEAD

EAR

TONGUE

MOUTH

TAIL

NOSE

1 square = 1 inch

Big, Bright Balls

Y ou can make these balls from bright fabric scraps . . . and they come in many sizes. They're stuffed with soft polyester fiber, and Baby can have fun pushing and throwing them. The puzzle balls have wedges that are easy for tiny hands to grasp. The wedges come apart, and they can be put together as a puzzle.

MATERIALS:

Cotton fabrics (see below)
Polyester stuffing
Cardboard for templates
Sewing threads to match fabric

PENTAGONAL BALLS

MATERIALS:

For small pentagonal ball (4″ diameter):
Three 3″ squares each of red, green, yellow and blue print fabric

For large pentagonal ball (6″ diameter):
Three 4½″ squares each of red-and-white stripe, red print, white print with red hearts, and green print with white dots fabric

Trace same size large or small pentagon onto cardboard or heavy paper and cut out along lines to make a template. Using template, trace a pentagon at center of each square on wrong side of fabric. Cut out around the pentagons ¼ inch *outside* the line to add seam allowance. Arrange five pentagons around each of the remaining two. See Diagram 1. Right sides together, stitch each pentagon to one side of the center pentagon along drawn lines. Stitch pentagons together along adjoining sides, with right sides together, stopping stitching just at the end of the line. Position halves of ball so pentagons of the same color do not touch. Right sides together, stitch edges of the halves together so points of the pentagons interlock. Leave one edge open. See Diagram 2. Turn right-side-out through slit. Stuff firmly and smoothly. Slipstitch edges of opening together.

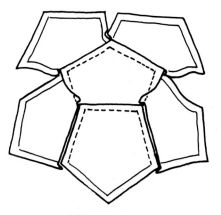

DIAGRAM 1

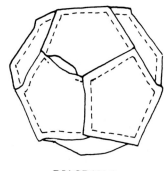

DIAGRAM 2

RAINBOW BALL

MATERIALS (4½″-diameter ball):
½″ × 3″ pieces each of red, orange, yellow, green, blue, and purple dotted or print fabric

Trace shape onto cardboard or heavy paper and cut out to make template. On wrong side of each fabric piece, center the template and trace around it. Cut out each piece ¼ inch *outside* the line to add seam allowance. Stitch all seams with right sides together. Arrange the pieces in rainbow order and, matching the lines, stitch red to orange along one side. See Diagram 1. Join yellow to other side of orange, and then continue until all pieces are joined. Stitch purple piece to the red, leaving a 2-inch opening in the center of the seam. See Diagram 2. Turn right-side-out. Stuff firmly and smoothly. Slipstitch edges of opening together.

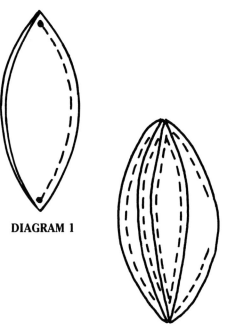

DIAGRAM 1

DIAGRAM 2

PATCHWORK BALL

MATERIALS (8″-diameter ball):
14″ × 16″ piece patchwork print
14″ × 5¼″ piece each of red, blue, and green dot or print fabric

Enlarge pattern piece following instructions in the how-to chapter. Trace shape onto cardboard or heavy paper and cut out to make template. Trace three shapes on patchwork fabric with ¼-inch seam allowance around each piece. Center template on remaining fabric and trace around edge. Cut out pieces ¼ inch *outside* line to add seam allowance. Stitch pieces together on seam lines, alternating patchwork with other fabrics. Leave a 3-inch opening in the center of the last seam. Turn right-side-out. Stuff firmly and smoothly. Slipstitch edges of opening together.

PUZZLE BALL

MATERIALS (5″-diameter ball):
¼ yard 36″-wide blue fabric
Twelve 2¼″ × 4½″ pieces yellow, red, and blue print fabric

Cut twelve sides from solid fabric and twelve tops from print. Mark dots on wrong side of fabric. Right sides together, stitch half of curved edge of a side piece to one side of a top piece, starting and stopping at end of seam line. See Diagram 1. Clip seam allowance of side almost to stitching at dot. Matching edges, stitch other curved edge of side piece to other side of top piece. See Diagram 2. Repeat for all twelve side and top pieces. On each unit, stitch straight edges of folded side together, leaving an opening for turning. Clip seam allowance along curves; turn right-side-out. Stuff each unit. Slipstitch edges of openings closed. See Diagram 3. Place shapes in groups of four with points at center. See Diagram 4.

Join the pieces with a twisted bar stitch about ¼ inch long, using two strands of thread, both doubled. Stitch down at **A**, up at **B**, down at **A**, and up at **B**, keeping pieces ¼ inch apart. See Diagram 5. Wrap thread around stitches until the thread is completely covered. See Diagram 6. Knot thread securely to fabric at one end.

For first group of four, join all outer corners, again using bar stitch. Follow Diagram 7. For second group, join all outer corners. Join pieces together in pairs at center. For third group, join all outer corners and all pieces together at center. Slip group 2 over group 3 so that they are perpendicular to each other. See Diagram 8. Slip group 1 around center of other pieces. See Diagram 9.

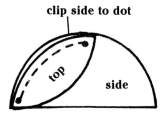

clip side to dot

top

side

DIAGRAM 1

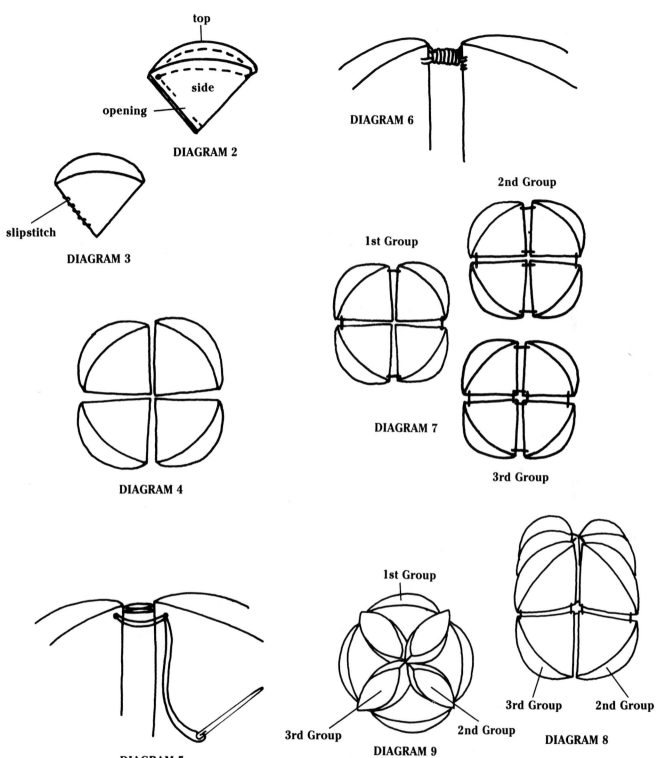

top

side

opening

DIAGRAM 2

slipstitch

DIAGRAM 3

DIAGRAM 6

2nd Group

1st Group

DIAGRAM 4

DIAGRAM 7

3rd Group

DIAGRAM 5

1st Group

3rd Group

2nd Group

DIAGRAM 9

3rd Group

2nd Group

DIAGRAM 8

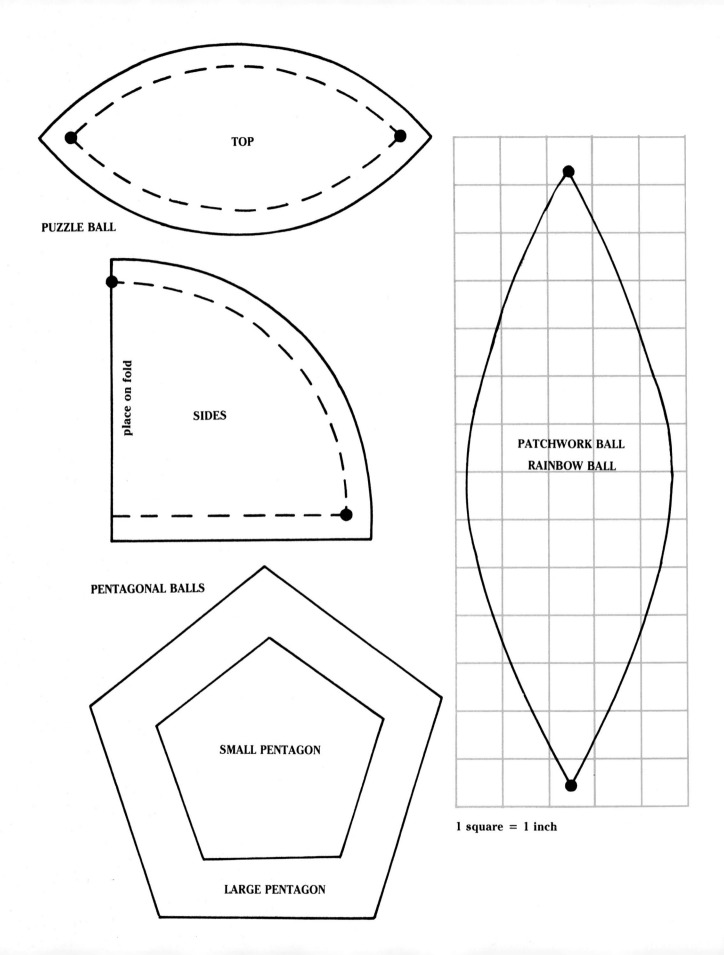

PUZZLE BALL

TOP

place on fold

SIDES

PENTAGONAL BALLS

SMALL PENTAGON

LARGE PENTAGON

PATCHWORK BALL

RAINBOW BALL

1 square = 1 inch

Alphablocks

aby will love the letters and colors in these traditional, bright and cheery Alphablocks. They are machine-appliquéd squares, quilted and sewn together and with a foam rubber cube inside.

MATERIALS:
45″-wide cotton fabrics:
  ½ yard white
  ¼ **yard each red, yellow, blue, and green prints**
  Scraps of bright-colored solids (including gray, purple, light brown, beige, gold); prints; dotted and striped fabrics
Quilt batting, scraps or an 18″ × 30″ piece
½ **yard 18″-wide fusible webbing**
2 yards each black, red, and brown six-strand embroidery floss
Thread to match fabrics
Four 4″ cubes of foam

Enlarge the patterns for the block centers, following instructions in the how-to chapter. To make border pattern, draw a 4½-inch square with a 3⅛-inch square in the center. Cut out square, and then cut out inner square, leaving a frame border. Cut twenty-four 4½-inch squares each of white fabric for blocks and quilt batting. From each red, yellow, blue, and green print, cut six 4½-inch squares and six borders. Baste a border to each block along inner and outer edges. Zigzag-stitch along inner border. From enlarged designs, make the patterns for appliqué pieces, following instructions in the how-to chapter. Cut, appliqué, and embroider each letter onto center of white squares, following the individual letter instructions below. Use three strands of embroidery floss for hand embroidery. Baste border to each block along inner and outer edges. Zigzag-stitch along inner border.

Cut **A** from green striped fabric, apple from red, and leaf from green. Machine-embroider a green stem on apple. Use a yellow border.

Cut **B** from red dotted fabric, bear's face from light brown, and bow from yellow. Hand-embroider eyes and nose in black satin stitch and mouth in red backstitch. Use a blue border.

Cut **C** from blue print, cat from yellow print, and cat's bow from blue. Embroider eyes and nose in black satin stitch and mouth in red backstitch. Use a green border.

Cut **D** from green dotted fabric and duck from yellow. Machine-embroider wing outline in white and beak in orange. Hand-embroider eye in black satin-stitch. Use a red border.

Cut **E** from red print, egg and egg piece from yellow print, and bird from blue. Machine-embroider beak in orange. Hand-embroider eye in black satin stitch. Use a yellow border.

Cut **F** from green striped fabric, flower from blue print, leaves from green dotted fabric, and center from yellow. Machine-embroider stem in green. Use a yellow border.

Cut **G** from yellow print, grapes from purple, and leaves from dark green. Machine-embroider outline of individual grapes in purple and stem in green. Use a green border.

Cut **H** from yellow print and heart from red. Use a blue border.

Cut **I** from blue print, ice cream from red dotted fabric, and cone from light brown. Use a green border.

Cut **J** from red print, jester's face from beige, hat from red dotted fabric, hair from yellow, and collar and pompon from green dotted fabric. Hand-embroider eyes in brown satin stitch, mouth in red backstitch, and cheeks with tiny red running-stitches. Use a blue border.

Cut **K** from blue print and kite from red. Machine-embroider frame of kite in yellow, bows in green and red, and machine straight-stitch along string and tail in black. Use a yellow border.

Cut **L** from blue print, lamb's body from yellow-on-white print, face and feet from light brown. Machine-embroider ear with light brown. Hand-embroider eye and nose in brown satin stitch and

mouth in red straight stitch. Use a yellow border.

Cut **M** from green dotted fabric and mouse from gray. Machine-embroider tail in gray. Hand-embroider eyes and nose in black satin stitch and mouth in red backstitch. Use a red border.

Cut **N** from red print, bird from blue, nest from yellow, and five leaves from green. Machine-embroider branch in light brown. Hand-embroider eye in black satin stitch and beak in gold satin stitch. Use a red border.

Cut **O** from green dotted fabric and ocean from blue print. Use a yellow border.

Cut **P** from blue print, pear from yellow print, and leaf from green. Machine-embroider stem in green. Use a red border.

Cut **Q** from yellow, queen's face from beige, hair from light brown, collar from purple, and crown from gold. Hand-embroider eyes in brown satin stitch and mouth in red backstitch. Use a blue border.

Cut **R** from red and rabbit from light brown fabric, omitting tail from pattern. After appliquéing rabbit, using light brown thread machine-embroider line between ears and tail. Hand-embroider eyes and nose in brown and mouth in red. Use a green border.

Cut **S** from blue print and sun from yellow. Machine-embroider rays with yellow. Use a red border.

Cut **T** from yellow-on-white print, tulip from yellow, and leaves from green. Machine-embroider stem in green. Use a red border.

Cut **U** from green dotted fabric and umbrella from blue. Machine-embroider ribs with yellow, and handle and tip with light brown. Use a red border.

Cut **V** from yellow print, violet from purple, and leaf from green. Machine-embroider stem in green. Hand-embroider center in yellow satin stitch. Use a blue border.

Cut **W** from blue, wagon from red, and wheels from yellow. Machine-embroider handle of wagon in yellow. Use a green border.

Cut **X** from red dotted fabric, **Y** from yellow print, and **Z** from green dotted fabric. Use a blue border.

Baste a quilt-batting square to wrong side of each appliquéd square, stitching ¼ inch in from edge of square. Trim batting close to stitching. Matching print to border color, place a print square on each appliquéd square, right sides together. Pin layers together. Sew around edges of each square, leaving an opening for turning; stitch just inside basting line along side edges and taper ⅛ inch in from corners, as shown in Diagram 1. Trim fabric at corners. Turn each square right-side-out. Slipstitch edges of opening together. Machine-quilt along inner edge of border.

To hand-sew blocks together, use doubled thread. For sides, slipstitch four squares together so letters are upright. See Diagram 2. Slipstitch another square to bottom. Place foam block inside. Slipstitch another square to top of block. See Diagram 3.

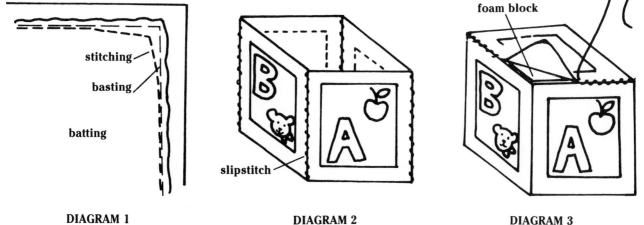

corner of block

stitching

basting

batting

slipstitch

foam block

DIAGRAM 1   **DIAGRAM 2**   **DIAGRAM 3**

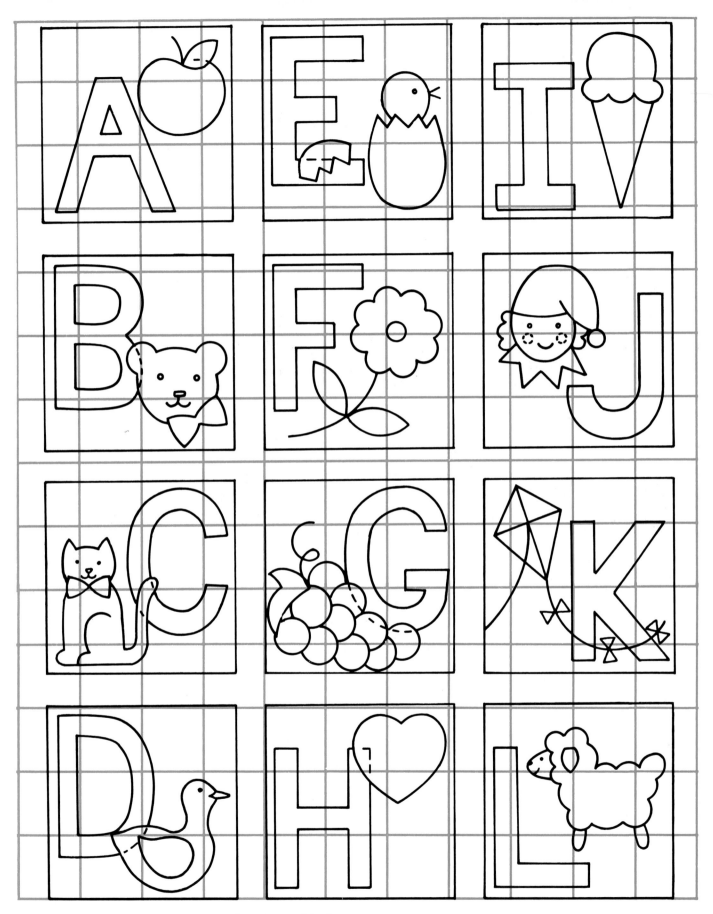

1 square = 1 inch

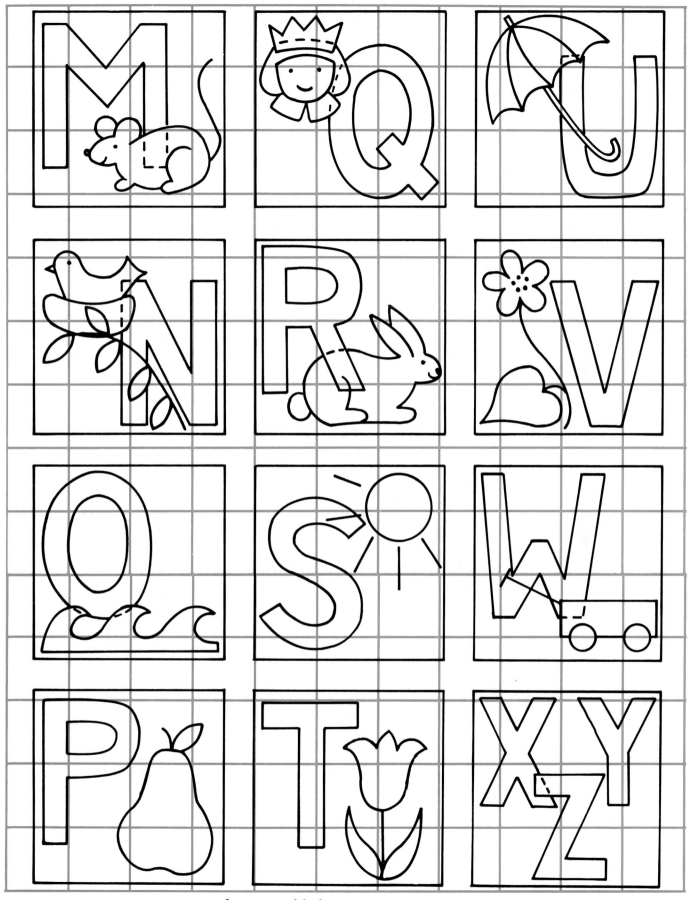

1 square = 1 inch

Mother Duck Pull Toy

Quack, Quack! A toddler can pull Mother Duck, and her two little ducklings can go along for the ride. Mother Duck is made of plain white cotton fabric. She's dressed in an eyelet collar and bow . . . and is wearing a felt hat! This charming toy is mounted on an easy-to-make wooden platform.

MATERIALS:
9″ × 5½″ × 1″ piece clear pine for base
2″ × 4″ × 1″ piece clear pine
Four 2½″-diameter wheels cut from clear pine
45″-wide cotton fabric:
   ¼ yard white
   ⅛ yard yellow-and-white print
8″ square each orange and yellow felt
14″ × 6″ piece quilt batting
½ pound polyester stuffing
4″ square fusible webbing
1 yard brown embroidery floss
¼ yard ½″-wide white eyelet ruffling
Yellow, white, and orange sewing thread
¼ yard each red and blue ¼″-wide satin ribbon
⅝ yard ⅜″-wide red-and-white gingham ribbon
½ yard ⅜″-wide blue-and-white gingham ribbon
8″ length ⁵⁄₁₆″-diameter wooden dowel
2 round wooden toothpicks
1″-diameter wooden bead
¾ yard red cotton cord or narrow ribbon
Two 1½″-long, ⅛″-diameter screws
Yellow and blue latex acrylic paint
Wood glue

TOOLS:
Drill; ³⁄₃₂″, ⅛″, ¼″, ⁵⁄₁₆″, and ⅜″ drill bits
Screwdriver
Paintbrush
Sandpaper

From white cotton, for Mother Duck, cut two body sides, one underside, and two wings. Reverse wing pattern (turn it over) and cut two more wings. Transfer dots to wrong side and placement markings for features and wings lightly to right side. Cut two wings from quilt batting. From yellow-and-white print, for ducklings, cut four bodies and eight wings (four left wings and four right wings—reverse pattern). Transfer dots to wrong side, seam lines to wrong side, and transfer placement for features and wings lightly to right side. From orange felt, cut four feet, two large upper bills, one large lower bill, two small lower bills, and two small upper bills. From yellow felt, cut two hat brims, two hat tops, and a ½″ × 2¼″ piece for crown.

Sew all seams right sides together, using ¼-inch seam allowances unless otherwise indicated, as follows:

Stitch body sides together along top edge between large dots. Matching dots, stitch underside to body sides, leaving an opening on one side between second and third small dots (counting from upper right to lower left). See Diagram 1. Clip seam allowance; turn right-side-out. Stuff upper portion of body. Drill two holes, ⅛-inch-diameter, 2½

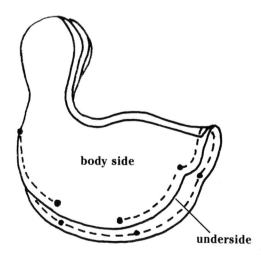

body side

underside

inches apart along center of small wooden block. Insert block along underside of duck's body and continue stuffing. See Diagram 2. Push bits of stuffing along side edges of block, but not below it. Slipstitch edges of opening together.

Baste batting to two wing pieces (be sure to make right and left wings). Stitch darts in all wings, and then slash along center, following instructions in how-to chapter. Right sides together, stitch padded wings to other wing pieces, leaving an opening between dots. Clip seam allowance. Turn right-side-out. Slipstitch edges of openings together. Quilt along broken lines. Pin wings to body sides along line; slipstitch securely in place. See Diagram 3.

Stitch large upper bills together along center top edge. Stitch upper and lower bill together, leaving end open. Turn right-side-out. Stuff bill; slipstitch to head along placement lines. With three strands of brown floss, embroider eyes, using satin stitch, and embroider lashes, using straight stitches.

Stitch feet together in pairs, leaving straight edge open. Clip and trim seam allowance. Turn right-side-out. Pad webbed ends of feet with a small amount of stuffing. Whipstitch straight edges together. Quilt along broken lines. Place ¼ inch of straight edge of feet under body so that feet slant to the front. Slipstitch feet to body along edge of underside.

Fuse two hat brims together and two top pieces together. Whipstitch one long edge of crown to top. Whipstitch ends together. Whipstitch center of brim to crown. Sew blue-and-white ribbon around crown. Tie a bow with remaining ribbon and sew to back of hat. Place a small amount of stuffing inside crown of hat. Sew hat to head of Mother Duck. Hem ends of eyelet. For collar, center a 20-inch piece of red-and-white gingham ribbon over top edge of eyelet and pin. Place collar around neck and tie a bow in front. Sew collar and bow in place.

For ducklings, stitch pairs of bodies and wings together along seam lines, leaving openings between dots. Clip seam allowance. Turn right-side-out. Stuff bodies firmly, and stuff wings so they remain slightly flat. Slipstitch opening closed. Slipstitch wings to body sizes. Sew upper and lower bills to head with whipstitches so bills are open. Embroider eyes with brown satin stitch and em-

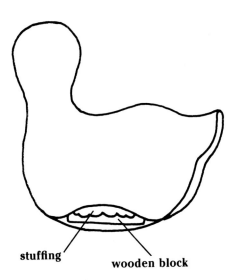

DIAGRAM 2

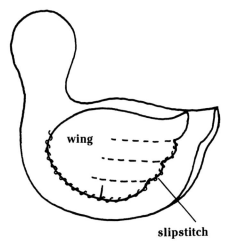

DIAGRAM 3

broider lashes with straight stitches. Tie red and blue ribbon around neck of each duckling and make a bow. Sew bows in place.

For wheels, drill a ⅜-inch-diameter hole in center of each wheel. Sand wheels. Cut four 1¼-inch lengths of dowel for the axles. Wrap masking tape around end before sawing to avoid splintering. Drill a 3/32-inch hole through each axle ⅛-inch from end. Cut four ⅝-inch lengths from widest section of toothpicks. Place a small amount of glue in hole and insert toothpick pieces. Allow to dry thoroughly.

For platform, drill two ⅛-inch-diameter holes in base along center line. One hole should be 3¾ inches from front and second hole should be 2½ inches behind first hole. Drill a ¼-inch-diameter hole at center, ½ inch from front edge. On sides, drill 5/16-inch-diameter holes 1½ inches from front and back. Make holes ⅜ inch deep. See Diagram 4.

Paint wooden bead, wheels and axles yellow. Paint base blue. You will need to apply three or four coats, allowing paint to dry between them. Insert axles through holes in wheels and glue ends in place in holes of base. Allow glue to dry.

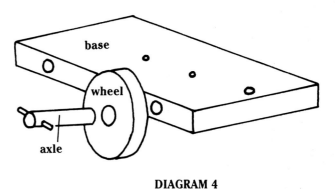

DIAGRAM 4

Using an awl or the point of scissors, carefully pierce fabric of underside at holes in block. Working from the bottom of base, insert a screw into each ⅛-inch hole until it shows on top of base. Hold duck firmly on base, aligning holes with screws. Screw duck to base.

Insert one end of cord through base and knot several times below platform. Insert other end through bead and tie or sew cord in place.

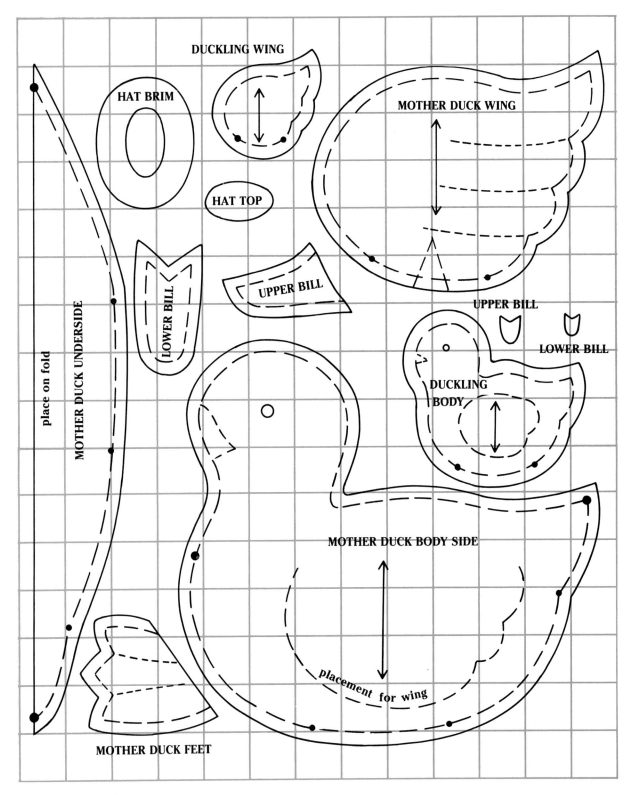

DUCKLING WING

HAT BRIM

MOTHER DUCK WING

HAT TOP

place on fold

MOTHER DUCK UNDERSIDE

LOWER BILL

UPPER BILL

UPPER BILL

LOWER BILL

DUCKLING BODY

MOTHER DUCK BODY SIDE

placement for wing

MOTHER DUCK FEET

1 square = 1 inch

Bouncing Babies

This string of smiling little dolls and perky hearts can be tied across a crib or bassinet. The set of bouncing babies is a perfect first toy . . . and gives Baby something bright and beautiful to focus on. The bouncing babies can also be used to decorate a wall.

MATERIALS:

6″ × 20″ pieces each of lavender print and blue print fabric
6″ × 4″ piece pink print
3″ square flesh-colored fabric
¼ pound polyester stuffing
3″ square fusible webbing (optional)
Six-strand embroidery floss: 2 yards each yellow and light brown; 1 yard pink; ½ yard bright pink and blue
Sewing thread to match fabrics
⅜ yard ¼″-wide pink ribbon
⅜ yard ¼″-wide pale green ribbon
2 yards ⅜″-wide white ribbon

Trace patterns for baby and heart, adding ¼-inch seam allowance to edges all around. Trace circle and features of baby's face. Cut four faces from flesh-colored fabric. Trace or draw features on faces. With fabric folded in half, wrong-side-out, cut two babies each from blue print and lavender print. Transfer seam line to wrong side of one fabric piece for each baby. In same manner, cut three hearts from pink fabric.

Fuse or baste face to center of right side of head on piece with seam line. Zigzag-stitch around face with matching thread. Right sides together, pin hearts together and two sides of babies together in pairs. Stitch around each shape, leaving an opening for turning between dots. Clip seam allowance along curves. Turn right-side-out. Stuff babies and hearts. Slipstitch edges of openings together.

To embroider faces, insert needle up through head and pull thread so knot is embedded inside the doll. When embroidery is complete, insert needle into head and bring it out in area of small square below head, and knot. Embroider eyes on

lavender babies, using three strands of blue floss and satin stitch. Embroider eyes on blue babies, using three strands of light brown and satin stitch. Using two strands of bright pink, embroider mouths with tiny backstitches. Embroider rosy heart-cheeks with satin stitch, using three strands of pink floss.

Using six strands of floss, work French knots around edge of face at dots for hair. Use light brown hair on lavender babies and yellow hair on blue babies. Cut pink and green ribbons in half, and tie four small bows. Sew bows to small square, covering knots from embroidery. Place hearts be-tween babies' arms, alternating colors of babies' suits. Using doubled thread, slipstitch hearts and arms together securely. Cut white ribbon in half. Fold each piece in half and sew center securely to outer arms of baby at each end. Use white ribbon ties to tie babies across crib, and make a bow.

This is a wonderful toy for a small baby to look up at and reach out for. Once Baby is old enough to crawl around and pull herself or himself up at the side of the crib, we recommend that you re-move this toy and use it to decorate the nursery wall.

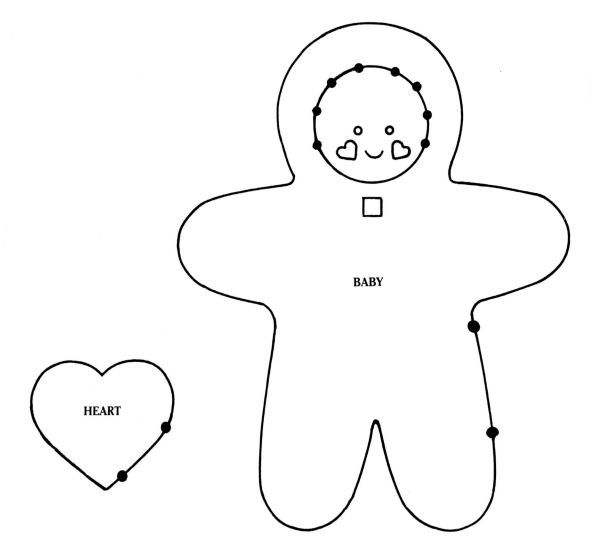

BABY

HEART

Mama Kanga and Joey

Mama Kanga has movable arms and a long tail. She's about 15 inches tall. Joey (baby kangaroos are called joeys) travels along in her pouch. This lovable toy will continue to delight your favorite child throughout the nursery years. It would make a wonderful birthday present . . . or make it for a special baby shower.

MATERIALS:
½ yard beige pinwale corduroy
13″ square beige-and-white print
11″ triangle red cotton fabric
3″ × 8″ piece yellow cotton fabric
1 pound polyester stuffing
Six-strand embroidery floss: 2 yards brown and
    1 yard red
Beige, red, and yellow sewing thread
1 yard carpet thread or buttonhole twist
Two ¾″-diameter buttons with shank

Enlarge patterns, following instructions in the how-to chapter. From beige corduroy, cut the following pieces for both Mama Kanga and Joey: two body sides, four legs, four arms, two tails, and two ears. From beige-and-white print, cut one body front and two ears each for Mama Kanga and Joey. For Mama Kanga, cut one pouch from each fabric.

Sew all seams right sides together, using ¼-inch seam allowance unless otherwise indicated, as follows:

MAMA KANGA

For Mama Kanga, stitch pouch pieces together along straight top edge. Turn right-side-out. Baste pieces together along seam line. Using corduroy side as right side, stitch darts in pouch. Baste pouch to lower part of body front. See Diagram 1. To reinforce neck curve on body side, stitch along seam line for ½ inch above and 1½ inches below dot. See Diagram 2. Clip seam allowance to stitching at ¼-inch intervals below dot. Sew body sides together along head and back, leaving an opening

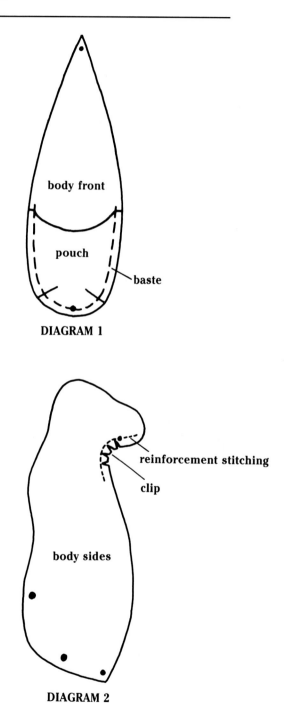

DIAGRAM 1

DIAGRAM 2

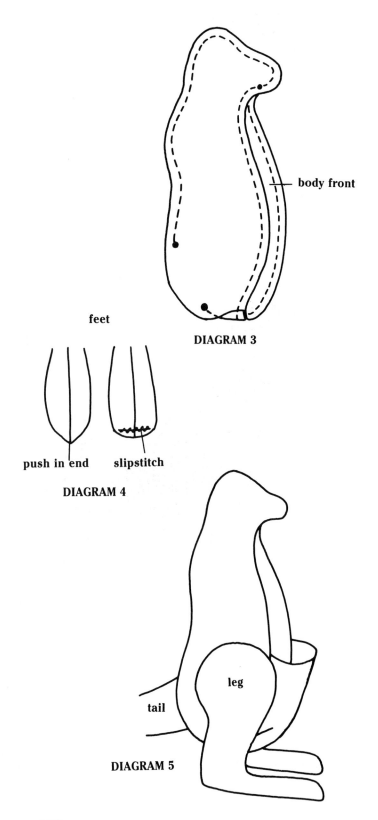

body front

DIAGRAM 3

feet

push in end   slipstitch

DIAGRAM 4

tail   leg

DIAGRAM 5

between large dots on back and small dots on front. Matching dots, stitch body front with pouch to body sides. See Diagram 3. Clip seam allowance along curves; turn right-side-out. Turn seam allowance under along opening on back; baste along edges. Stuff body firmly. Stitch tails together, leaving straight end open. Clip seam allowance along curves. Turn right-side-out. Stuff tail. Baste sides of open end together along seam line. Pin tail in top of body opening, matching dots. Slipstitch edges of opening to seam line of tail, then stitch remaining opening below tail together.

Stitch legs together in pairs, leaving an opening between dots. Clip seam allowance along curves and trim at corners. Turn right-side-out. Stuff legs so upper section is stuffed lightly and remains flat, and lower leg and foot are stuffed firmly. Slipstitch edges of opening together. Push in lower front end of foot to make a small miter. See Diagram 4. Slipstitch edges of miter together. Pin legs on body, matching placement lines; slipstitch legs securely in place. See Diagram 5.

Stitch pairs of arm pieces together, leaving an opening between dots. Clip seam allowance and turn right-side-out. Insert a button in each arm so shank is below **X.** Insert a pin through fabric and shank. Stuff arms. Slipstitch edges of opening together. Use heavy thread doubled in a long needle to attach arms to body. Insert needle through button shank in one arm. Push needle through body between **X's.** See Diagram 6. Insert needle through

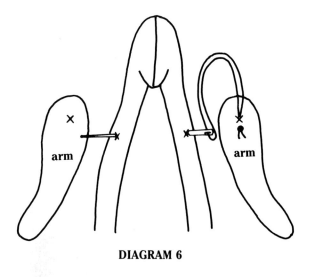

arm   arm

DIAGRAM 6

DIAGRAM 7

Joey

slipstitch

DIAGRAM 8

KERCHIEFS

11" 15½" 7½" 2½"

11"

DIAGRAM 9

button shank in second arm and then back through body at **X's** (but not necessarily at the exact same spot as before). Pull thread very tightly so body is a little indented around **X's.** Stitch through fabric of first arm close to **X** and knot thread securely. See Diagram 7. Bring needle out through arm and trim off end of thread so it doesn't show.

Stitch each print ear to a corduroy ear, leaving straight edge open. Clip and trim seam allowance along stitching. Turn right-side-out. Turn under seam allowance along open edge. Slipstitch sides together. Fold ear in half and place it along placement lines—ears should slant slightly forward. Slipstitch lower edge and about ⅛ inch of inner side edge to head.

Embroider eyes and nose with satin stitch, using three strands of brown floss. Make mouth, following lines on pattern and instructions for mouth of Terry Teddy on page 70.

JOEY

Joey is made almost in the same way as his mother, except that he does not have a pouch or a miter in the front of his feet, and his arms are sewn on (and do not move). Since he is quite a bit smaller, the pieces are harder to stitch and turn. You may want to trace the seamline onto one side of each arm, leg, ear, and tail. Stitch the seams, using very short stitch lengths, and trim the seam allowances to ⅛ inch before turning. Use a medium-size crochet hook (size E to H) or a similar thin, blunt object to help turn the pieces. On Joey's tail, leave the bottom edge open between the short end and the dot for easier turning. Then slipstitch the edges together. Slipstitch the arms and legs to the body as shown in Diagram 8.

To make Mama Kanga and Joey each a kerchief, cut a triangle of red fabric for Mama Kanga and a triangle of yellow for Joey, following the measurements given in Diagram 9. Turn under ¼ inch all around and stitch around the edges with matching thread. Tie kerchiefs around necks.

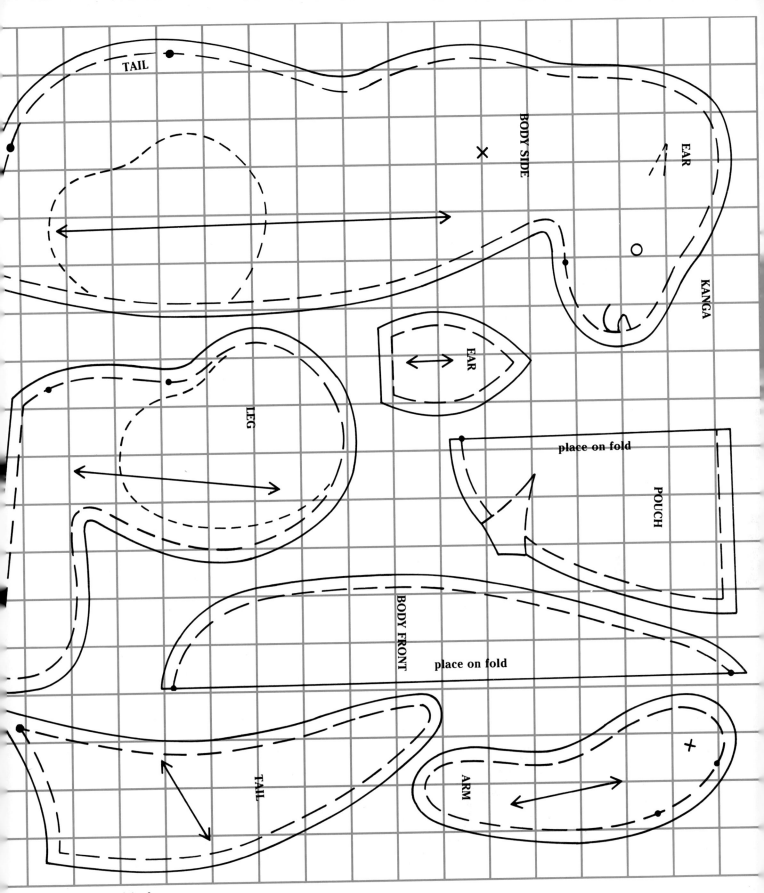

TAIL

BODY SIDE

×

EAR

KANGA

EAR

LEG

place on fold

POUCH

BODY FRONT

place on fold

TAIL

ARM

+

1 square = 1 inch

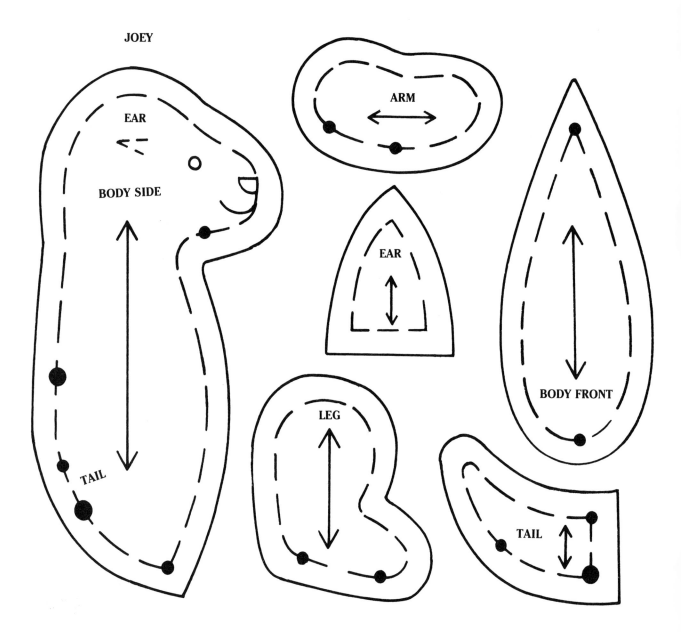

JOEY

ARM

BODY SIDE

EAR

BODY FRONT

LEG

TAIL

EAR

TAIL

1 square = 1 inch

BABY'S

CLOTHES

Bonnets for Boys and Girls

hese cool and crisp bonnets are perky and practical for the beach or the backyard. They're easy to make, and you can use different fabrics, ribbons, and trims for imaginative variations. Be sure to take a snapshot of your baby wearing a bonnet—it will make a great "baby picture" for Baby's future high-school yearbook.

EYELET CAP

MATERIALS:
½ yard white eyelet with embroidered border design
¼ yard pastel cotton fabric
White and pastel sewing thread
1 yard ⅝″-wide white satin ribbon
1 yard ⅜″-wide pastel ribbon
¼ yard ¼″-wide light green ribbon

Enlarge patterns for cap, following instructions in the how-to chapter. From eyelet, cut crown with long straight edge of pattern along scalloped edge of fabric. Cut one back from eyelet. Cut one crown and two backs from pastel fabric.

Right sides together, stitch eyelet to pastel along ends of crown. Trim seam allowance; turn right-side-out. Baste layers together along scalloped edge. Trim pastel fabric even with scallops. Zigzag-stitch along scalloped edge. Gather long edge of bonnet between notches. Baste one pastel back to wrong side of eyelet back. Right sides together, matching notches and dot, pin and then stitch crown to back. Grade seam allowance, following instructions in the how-to chapter. Press long curved edge on remaining back under along seam line for lining. Right sides together, stitch back to back of bonnet along lower edge. Grade seam allowance as before. Fold lining to inside of bonnet and slipstitch edge along seam. Cut four 1½-inch pieces of ¼-inch green ribbon; fold in half to make loops. Place two loops on each side of bonnet with ends below line in front corner. Cut

two 14-inch pieces of ⅝-inch ribbon. Turn under ½ inch on one end of each piece; make a pleat in center of fold. Sew fold to line over ends of loops. Cut two 18-inch pieces of pink ribbon and make ribbon roses, following instructions in the how-to chapter. Sew roses to fold of white ribbon. Trim ends of ribbon diagonally.

BOY'S CLASSIC WHITE BONNET

MATERIALS:
¼ yard white piqué or seersucker
¼ yard white cotton fabric for lining
11″ × 3″ piece stiff interfacing
Blue and white sewing thread
1 yard ⅜″-wide blue and white striped ribbon
1⅛ yards ⅛″-wide blue satin ribbon

Enlarge pattern for classic bonnet back and large boy's brim, following instructions in the how-to chapter. From outer fabric, cut 5¾″ × 15″ piece for crown, one back, and two brims. Cut crown and back from lining. Cut brim from interfacing.

Leave ⅜-inch seam allowance on all seams. On outer fabric and lining pieces, make one row of gathering stitches along seam line of long edge of crown. Right sides together, ease edge to fit curved edge of back; stitch seam. Grade and clip seam allowance, following instructions in the how-to chapter. Topstitch ⅛ inch from seam on back.

Baste interfacing to wrong side of one brim. Right sides together, stitch brims together along curved edge. Grade and clip seam allowance as above. Turn right-side-out. Baste straight edges together. Hand-baste ⅛-inch-wide ribbon ¼ inch in from curved edge of brim, easing it to fit smoothly. Stitch along edges of ribbon with blue thread. Right sides together, matching centers, stitch brim to bonnet along front edge. Right sides together, stitch lining to bonnet along edges, leaving a 2-inch opening for turning on lower edge of back. Grade seam allowance; clip corners. Turn right-side-out. Slipstitch edges of opening together. Hand-baste

⅛-inch ribbon to crown and back, ¼ inch in from outer edges. Stitch along edges of ribbon, using blue thread. Cut striped ribbon in half. Turn ½ inch on one end of each piece to right side. Place a ribbon under each front corner diagonally. Sew ends in place on underside.

GIRL'S CLASSIC EYELET BONNET

MATERIALS:

¼ yard white eyelet fabric
¼ yard white fabric for brim and lining
½ yard ⅜"-wide lace ruffling
⅝ yard 2"-wide eyelet edging
½ yard ⅝"-wide embroidered ribbon
8" × 13" piece very stiff interfacing or crinoline
1 yard ⅝"-wide white satin ribbon
White sewing thread

Enlarge pattern for classic bonnet back and girl's brim, following instructions in the how-to chapter. From eyelet fabric, cut 5¾" × 15¼" crown and one back. From white cotton fabric, cut two brims with center on fold, one crown lining, and one back lining. Cut brim from stiff interfacing.

Leave ⅜-inch seam allowance on all seams. Right sides together, stitch lace ruffling along curved edge of back. On both eyelet and lining pieces, make one row of gathering stitches along seam line of one long edge of crown. Right sides together, ease edges to fit curved edge of backs; stitch seam. Grade and clip seam allowance, following instructions in the how-to chapter. Right sides together, stitch eyelet to lining along edges, leaving a 2-inch opening for turning on lower edge of back. Grade seam allowance as before; trim corners. Turn right-side-out. Slipstitch edges of opening together.

Baste interfacing to one brim piece. Stitch brims together along outer curve. Grade and clip seam allowance. Turn right-side-out. Baste edges together along seam line of inner curve. Trim seam allowance to ¼ inch. Matching centers, stitch seam line of brim to bonnet ⅛ inch from edge of eyelet fabric edge. See Diagram 1. Gather raw edge of eyelet edging to about 14¼ inches to fit over brim. Stitch edging to seam line of brim. Trim seam al-

lowance of edging. Turning under ½ inch at ends, stitch a length of embroidered ribbon to front edge of bonnet. Cut white ribbon in half. Turn under ¾ inch on one end of each piece. Place end diagonally over corner; stitch to bonnet ⅝ inch from fold. Trim ends of ribbon diagonally.

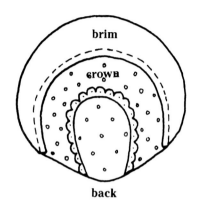

DIAGRAM 1

RUFFLED BONNET

MATERIALS:

⅜ yard gingham or print fabric
7" × 18" piece white cotton fabric for lining
1 yard 2½"-wide eyelet edging
½ yard eyelet beading
White thread
½ yard ¼"-wide ribbon to match fabric
One ⁵⁄₁₆"-diameter white button
2" piece narrow elastic cording

Enlarge pattern for ruffled bonnet, following instructions in the how-to chapter. Cut bonnet from fabric and lining. Cut two 1¼" × 16" bias strips from fabric, following instructions in the how-to chapter.

Leave ⅜-inch seam allowances on all seams. To make pleats on bonnet and lining, fold lines together in direction of arrows; baste along seam lines. Cut a 31-inch length of eyelet edging and taper raw edge at ends. See Diagram 1. Gather raw edge of eyelet edging to long unpleated edge of bonnet with right sides together, beginning and ending ⅜ inch from sides. Stitch seam. Fold 1¼-inch elastic cord in half to make a loop. Baste loop

RUFFLED BONNET

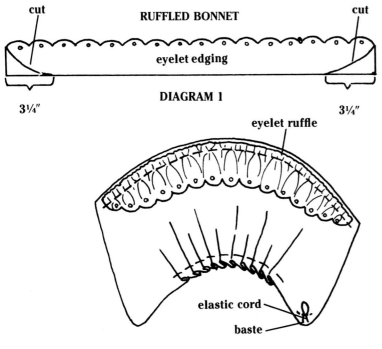

cut   cut

eyelet edging

DIAGRAM 1

3¼″   3¼″

eyelet ruffle

elastic cord

baste

DIAGRAM 2

to back corner of one side. See Diagram 2. Press under long front edge of lining. Right sides together, stitch lining to bonnet along sides and pleated edge. Grade seam allowance, following instructions in the how-to chapter. Turn right-side-out. Baste lining to bonnet over seam of edging. Topstitch around entire bonnet ⅛ inch from edge. Insert ribbon through eyelet beading. Stitch beading along front edge of bonnet, turning under ½ inch on ends. Right sides together, fold each bias strip in half lengthwise; stitch ¼ inch from long edge. Turn right-side-out. Tuck under ¼ inch on ends of tube and slipstitch edges together. Make a ¾-inch-long loop at one end and stitch diagonally to corner of beading. Sew button to back corner opposite elastic loop.

BOY'S QUILTED BONNET

MATERIALS:
⅜ yard light blue cotton fabric with white dots
10″ × 18″ piece quilt batting
¾ yard ½″-wide lace edging
Light blue and white sewing thread
1 yard ⅜″-wide white satin ribbon

For a summer bonnet:
Omit quilt batting
Scrap of stiff interfacing
Add: Two ⁵⁄₁₆″-diameter buttons
3″ piece of narrow elastic cord

Enlarge pattern for **T**-shaped bonnet and boy's brim. Cut two bonnet pieces and two brims from light blue fabric. Cut one bonnet and one brim from quilt batting.

Baste quilt batting to one bonnet and one brim along seam line, ⅜ inch in from edge. Right sides together, stitch brims together along curved edge and side ends. Trim batting close to stitching. Trim and clip seam allowance. Turn right-side-out. Baste straight edges together. Topstitch ¼ inch from curved edge. Next, stitch sides to back on both bonnet pieces. See Diagram 1.

BOY'S QUILTED BONNET BRIM

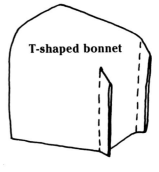

T-shaped bonnet

DIAGRAM 1

Stitch brim to center of long edge of bonnet piece with quilt batting. Right sides together, stitch bonnet pieces together along edges, leaving an opening between dots for turning. Trim batting close to stitching. Trim seam allowances. Turn right-side-out. Slipstitch edges of opening together. Baste, then stitch lace around bonnet ⅞ inch from front, side, and lower back edge, mitering corners. Cut two 14-inch pieces of ribbon. Turn under ⅝ inch at one end of each piece. Lap folded end of ribbon diagonally over corner of bonnet; stitch ½ inch from fold of ribbon.

To make a boy's summer bonnet from this pattern, omit quilt batting. Cut one brim from stiff interfacing and baste or fuse it to one brim piece. Stitch brims together same as above. Baste brim to

one bonnet piece. Fold a 1¼-inch piece of narrow elastic cord in half and baste it to each back corner of sides. See Diagram 2 of Ruffled Bonnet on page 114. Right sides in, stitch bonnet pieces together around T-shape, leaving an opening at back for turning. Trim seam allowance and clip to corners between sides and back. Turn right-side-out. Slipstitch edges of opening together. Apply lace to front, sides, and lower edge of back, ⅞ inch from edge, mitering corners and turning under ends of lace at edges. Sew ⁵⁄₁₆-inch-diameter buttons to lower sides of back. Sew ribbon on same as quilted bonnet.

GIRL'S SUMMER BONNET

MATERIALS:
⅜ **yard floral print cotton fabric**
1 yard ½″-wide eyelet ruffling
Pink thread
1¼ yards ¼″-wide pink ribbon
¾ yard ⅜″-wide pink ribbon

For a quilted bonnet, add a 10″ × 18″ piece quilt batting.

Enlarge pattern for T-shaped bonnet. Cut two bonnet pieces from floral print fabric. (Read on for quilted bonnet.) Right sides together, stitch eyelet ruffling to one bonnet piece along sides and long front edge, ⅜ inch in from edge, making tiny pleats at corners for extra fullness. See Diagram 1. Narrowly hem ends of eyelet ⅜ inch from ends of sides. Stitch 3½-inch length of eyelet ruffling to lower edge of back and finish sides in same man-

ner. Use ⅜-inch seams. Stitch bonnet pieces together along edges, leaving an opening for turning at lower back. Trim seam allowance. Clip to corners between sides and back. Turn right-side-out. Slipstitch edges of opening together. Topstitch ⅛ inch from edges without eyelet ruffling. Beginning 4½ inches from end of ¼-inch-wide ribbon, baste, then stitch ribbon to sides and front along edge of eyelet ruffling, mitering corners. Trim ribbon 4½ inches from end of stitching. Leaving 4½-inch ends, stitch ¼-inch-wide ribbon to lower edge of back in same manner. Tie a bow on each side, using one ribbon end from front and one from back. Cut ⅜-inch-wide ribbon in half across width. Fold ½ inch at one end of each piece to right side. Place ribbon under each front corner diagonally. Sew ends in place on underside.

To make a quilted bonnet, cut one T-shaped bonnet piece from quilt batting as well as two from fabric. Baste batting to one fabric piece. Right sides together, stitch sides to back. See Diagram 1 for Boy's Quilted Bonnet on page 114. Baste eyelet ruffling around entire bonnet piece with batting, making tiny pleats at front corners same as above. Stitch ends of eyelet together; zigzag-finish ends. Right sides together, stitch bonnet pieces together, leaving an opening for turning in center of back edge. Trim batting close to stitching; trim seam allowance. Turn right-side-out. Baste, then stitch ribbon around edges, mitering at corners. Make ⅜-inch-wide ribbon ties same as above. From remaining ¼-inch-wide ribbon, make two tiny bows and sew to corners of bonnet, if you wish.

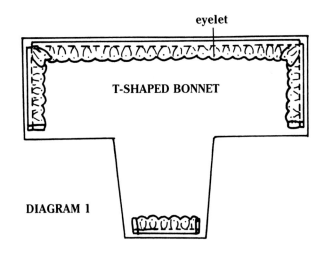

T-SHAPED BONNET

eyelet

DIAGRAM 1

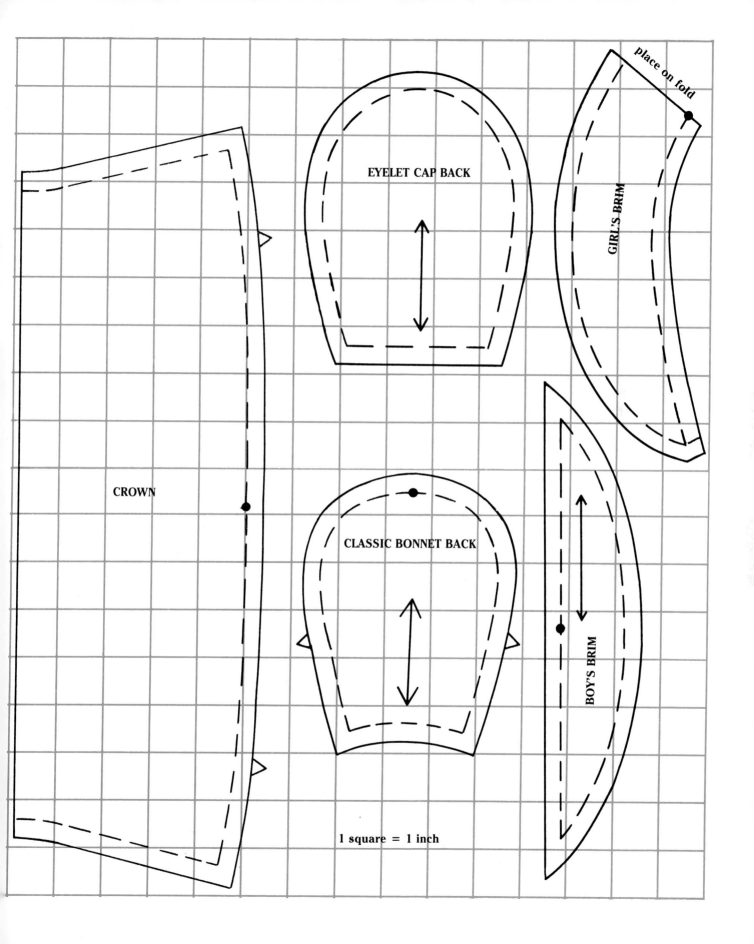

EYELET CAP BACK

place on fold

GIRL'S BRIM

CROWN

CLASSIC BONNET BACK

BOY'S BRIM

1 square = 1 inch

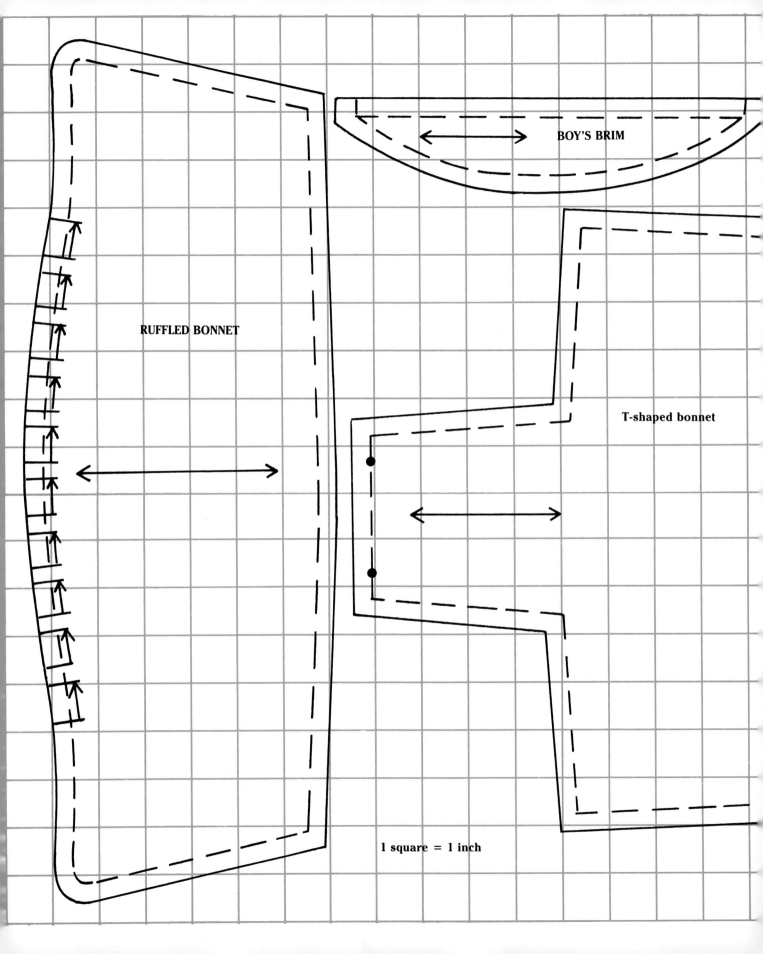

BOY'S BRIM

RUFFLED BONNET

T-shaped bonnet

1 square = 1 inch

Smocked Rompers

Rompers are fun for boys and girls to wear on dress-up occasions. For a little boy's classic, make romper in white, with a Peter Pan collar and a tie belt. For a little girl, make romper in a dainty print, with a ruffled collar and a wide sash. Both versions are decorated with almost the same simple stitches.

SIZES:
Newborn (3 months) [Small (6 months)—Medium (12 months)]

MATERIALS:
Solid or floral print cotton fabrics, such as lawn, broadcloth or percale, 2 yards 36″-wide fabric, 1¾ yards 45″-wide fabric

⅜ yard ½″-wide single-fold bias tape to match fabric

Matching sewing thread

Contrasting sewing thread to baste smocking pleats

Two ⁵⁄₁₆″-diameter buttons

3 large snaps

¾ yard ¼″-wide elastic

Hot-iron transfer with dots ⅜″ apart in rows ⅜″ apart, *or* 1 large sheet eight-to-the-inch graph paper

For boy's white romper:

⅛ yard 18″-wide lightweight interfacing

Six-strand embroidery floss, 12 yards blue, 1 yard peach

¾ yard ¼″-wide lace edging

For girl's floral print romper:

Six-strand embroidery floss, 6 yards each mint green and peach, 1 yard blue, and ½ yard white

¾ yard ⅜″-wide lace edging

You may wish to use ¼ yard matching solid color lightweight cotton lining fabric, because a print fabric may tend to show through yoke.

Enlarge patterns for the size romper you wish to make, following instructions in the how-to chapter. From fabric, cut two fronts; two backs; two yoke fronts; two yoke backs; two sleeves.

For boy's white romper, cut four collar pieces; two ties, 3½″ × 11½″ [12″—12½″]; and two yoke backs and one yoke front for lining. Cut two collars from interfacing.

For girl's print romper, cut a 2″ × 26″ [27″—28″] strip for ruffled collar and two ties, 3½″ × 22″ [23″—24″]. For lining, cut two yoke backs and one yoke front.

Stitch all seams right sides together, using ⅝-inch seam allowance unless otherwise indicated, as follows:

Stitch fronts together along center seam. Trim seam allowance to ¼ inch; zigzag-finish seam allowance edges on each side. Following instructions for smocking in the how-to chapter, transfer or mark ten horizontal rows of smocking dots to fit across top edge of front between armhole seam lines. Be sure center dot of each row falls on center seam. Position the rows on front so that the top auxiliary row is ⅜ inch from the edge of the fabric and the second row is ⅛ inch below seam line. Following either Diagram 1 or 2 in the instructions for smocking, transfer or mark dots. Transfer or mark four horizontal rows of smocking dots to fit across top edges of backs between center back and armhole seam line, spaced same as on front. Gather fabric so top edges are 1 inch narrower than lower edge of yokes; knot threads securely.

Use the smocking diagram on page 126 for the front to work stitches, following instructions in the how-to chapter. Cut floss in 18-inch lengths and use three strands for stitching. Use light blue floss for boy's white romper for all rows of embroidery shown on chart, and peach for heart. For girl's print romper, use colors indicated at right of diagram. Work cable stitch across row 1. For rows 2 and 3, begin in center and work trellis stitch with three

wave stitches to each side. Work chart in reverse
for right-hand side. Turn work upside down and
stitch left to right to make stitching the left half
easier. (If you are left-handed and stitch right to
left, turn work upside down for right-hand half.)
Between rows 3 and 4 and rows 4 and 5, work
partial rows of trellis stitch, leaving area of large
diamond open. Work trellis stitch between rows 5
and 6. Work one row cable stitch across row 7.
Work wave stitch between cables and row 8.

For boy's romper, in center of large diamond,
work top row of heart with wave stitch and bottom
row of heart with trellis stitch. For girl's romper,
stitch flower in center on large diamond, following
diagram. Work one French knot for center with
white. Using lazy-daisy stitch, embroider petals
with light blue and leaves with mint.

For back of boy's romper, use light blue floss.
For back of girl's romper, use mint green floss. Following smocking diagram for back, stitch one row
of cable stitch across row 1. Work one row of wave
stitch between cables and row 2.

Narrowly hem lower edges of sleeves. Transfer
or draw two rows of dots to wrong side, ½ inch
above lower edge between underarm seam lines.
Gather dots to 4½″ [5″—5½″]. Make a row of cable
stitch along each row.

When all smocking is completed, remove gathering threads. Stitch backs together below dot on
center back seam. Trim seam allowance to ¼ inch;
zigzag-stitch edges together. Clip almost to stitching at dot. From a scrap of fabric, cut a placket
1½″ × 9½″. Open out upper edge of center back
seam. Pin and then stitch edge of placket to edges
of back, ¼ inch from edge. See Diagram 1. Turn
¼ inch to wrong side along other edge of placket.
Fold placket in half lengthwise; slipstitch edge in
place over seam. See Diagram 2. Topstitch along
inner edge of placket, if you wish. Press placket
away from the back on left back and to the wrong
side of the right back. Baste right back along upper
edge. See Diagram 3.

Pin and then stitch front yoke to front, and back
yokes to back, matching centers. See Diagram 4.
Grade seam allowance, following instructions in
the how-to chapter; press toward yoke. Stitch front
yoke to back yokes at shoulders.

For boy's collar, fuse or baste interfacing to
wrong side of two collar pieces. Stitch each of

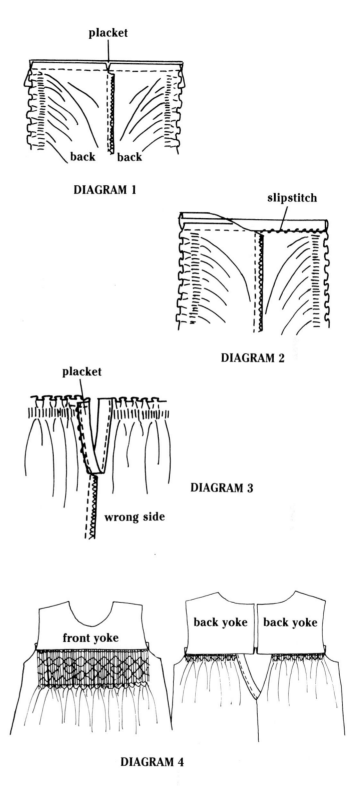

DIAGRAM 1

DIAGRAM 2

DIAGRAM 3

DIAGRAM 4

121

these two pieces to one remaining collar piece along ends and outer curve. Grade and clip seam allowance. Turn right-side-out. Baste inner curved edges together along seam lines. Sew ¼-inch-wide lace edging under lower edge of collars. Be sure to make a right and left collar. Make a tiny row of running stitches ⅛ inch from finished edges, using three strands of blue floss. Baste collars to neck edge of yokes between center front and center backs.

For girl's ruffled collar, narrowly hem one long edge and ends of collar strip. Stitch lace over long hemmed edge, using three strands of peach floss and running stitches. Gather collar evenly to neck edge between center backs; baste it in place along seam line.

For facing, stitch yoke front to yoke backs at shoulders. Press under lower edges of yoke along seam line; trim seam allowance to ¼ inch. Pin and then stitch facing to collar and yoke along neck and back edges. Grade and clip seam allowance. Turn facing to inside; slipstitch lower edges in place along seam line. Topstitch just below neck edge to hold facing to yokes if necessary.

Baste sleeve edges together. Gather top edge of sleeves between notches. Matching notches and dot to shoulder seam, gather sleeve evenly to sleeve edge of front and back; stitch seam. Trim seam allowance to ¼ inch; zigzag edges together.

For boy's romper, fold ties in half lengthwise; stitch ¼ inch from end and long edges. Turn right-side-out. Baste unfinished ends to side edge of backs just below armhole seam.

For girl's romper, narrowly hem long edges and one end of ties. Fold hemmed end diagonally to long edge for pointed tie end; slipstitch edges together. Be sure to make a right and left tie. Make a ½-inch pleat in center of unfinished end. Baste pleated end to side edge of backs just below armhole seam.

Stitch front to back along side and under arm seams. Trim seam allowance to ¼ inch; zigzag edges together. Turn under ¼ inch, then ⅜ inch along lower edge of legs. Stitch along top edge to make a casing. Cut a 12″ [12½″—13″] length of elastic. Insert elastic in casing; stitch ends in place ¼ inch from ends.

Press open one fold of bias tape. With ends of tape extending ½ inch beyond edge, stitch crease of bias tape to right side of front and back inside leg seam, ¼ inch from edge. See Diagram 5. Turning in ends, fold bias tape to wrong side; slipstitch ends and edge in place. See Diagram 6. Sew snaps between front and back at leg edges and center of inside leg seam. Make two buttonholes on right back at positions indicated, ½ inch from neck and lower edge. Sew buttons to left back.

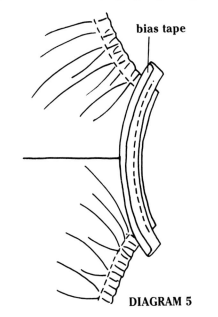

bias tape

DIAGRAM 5

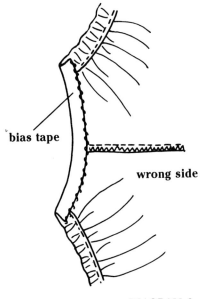

bias tape

wrong side

DIAGRAM 6

Classic Smocked Dress

his classic raglan-sleeved dress is my version of a style that is always popular. It is decorated with a beautifully simple design of hearts and diamonds, with French-knot flowers. Tradition and comfort go hand-in-hand in a sewing project easy enough for a beginner.

SIZES:
Newborn (3 months) [Small (6 months)—Medium (12 months)]

MATERIALS:
Peach fabric, such as lawn or broadcloth, 1¼ yards 36″-wide fabric *or* 1 yard 45″-wide fabric
Six-strand embroidery floss, 8 yards peach, 6 yards off-white, 4 yards light blue, and 2 yards mint green
Peach sewing thread
Contrasting-color sewing thread to baste smocking pleats
3 medium-size snaps
Hot-iron transfer with dots ⅜″ apart in rows ⅜″ apart *or* 1 large sheet eight-to-the-inch graph paper

Enlarge the patterns for the size dress you wish to make, following instructions in the how-to chapter. From fabric, cut one front, two backs, two sleeves, one neck binding, and one 1½″ × 10″ placket.

Stitch all seams right sides together, using ⅝-inch seam allowance unless otherwise indicated, as follows:

Narrowly hem lower edge of sleeves. Following Instructions for Smocking in the how-to chapter, transfer or draw two rows of dots on wrong side ½ inch above lower edge between underarm seam lines. Make rows of running stitches across dots, but do not gather.

Make a row of basting stitches along center front for 4 inches at top edge of dress. Matching notches, stitch the sleeves to the front and backs along armhole seams. Trim seam allowance to ¼ inch; zigzag-stitch edges of seams together. Transfer or mark nine rows of smocking dots to the wrong side of neck edge, using the method for curved edges, following instructions in the how-to chapter. Center line of front should fall halfway between vertical rows of dots. Position the rows horizontally so that top auxiliary row is ⅜ inch from the edge of the fabric and the second row is ⅛ inch below seam line. Gather the dots so the first row of gathers measures 10½″ [10¾″—11″] around the neck edge and the bottom row measures about 23 inches; knot ends securely. Gather lower edge of sleeves to 6″ [6½″—7″] and knot ends.

Following the smocking diagram for neck edge, work smocking stitches, following instructions in the how-to chapter. Cut floss into 18-inch lengths and use three strands for stitching. With peach, work cable stitch across row 1. Between rows 1 and 2, work cable-wave combination, beginning at center front and working to each side. Turn work upside down and stitch left to right to make stitching the left half easier. (If you are left-handed and stitch right to left, then turn work for right-hand half.) With peach, work cable-wave combination between rows 2 and 3. To make upper half of diamond shape, with peach, work cable-trellis combination from row 3 to just below row 4. Repeat the same stitches with off-white one-half row below peach row. To make lower half of diamonds, work same cable-trellis combination in opposite direction with off-white. Repeat the same stitches with peach one-half row below off-white. With off-white, work a French knot in the center of diamonds along row 5. With blue, work five French-knot petals around center. Work a green lazy-daisy leaf on each side of flower. With peach, work a row of cable stitches along each row of gathering stitches on sleeves. When smocking is completed, remove all gathering threads.

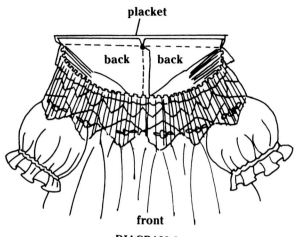

placket

back   back

front

DIAGRAM 1

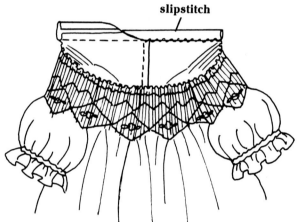

slipstitch

DIAGRAM 2

placket   baste

back   back

DIAGRAM 3

Stitch backs together below dot on center back with a French seam, following the instructions in the how-to chapter. Clip seam allowance to dot at top of seam. Trim seam allowance above dot to ¼ inch. Trim neck edge seam allowance to ¼ inch. Open out upper edge of seam and pin, then stitch edge of placket to back, ¼ inch from edge. See Diagram 1. Turn ¼ inch to wrong side along other edge of placket. Fold placket in half lengthwise; slipstitch edge in place over seam. See Diagram 2. Topstitch along inner edge of placket if you wish. Press right placket away from back. Press left edge of placket to inside; baste edge in place along upper edge. See Diagram 3.

Pin neck binding to dress, matching center fronts and backs and dots to seams. Ends of binding extend ⅝ inch past edge of dress. See Diagram 4. Stitch seam ¼ inch from edge. Grade seam allowance, following instructions in the how-to chapter. Fold ¼ inch to wrong side along other edge of binding, turning under ends. Fold binding in half lengthwise; slipstitch edge in place over seam. See Diagram 5.

Stitch fronts to back along sides and under arm with French seams. Turn under 1½ inches twice on lower edge of dress; slipstitch hem in place. Sew three sets of snaps evenly spaced apart along placket opening with first at top and last about 1 inch from bottom.

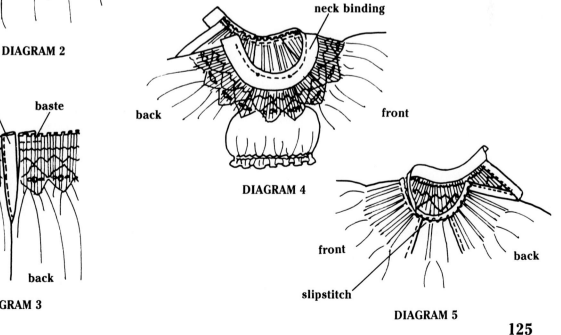

neck binding

back   front

DIAGRAM 4

front   back

slipstitch

DIAGRAM 5

125

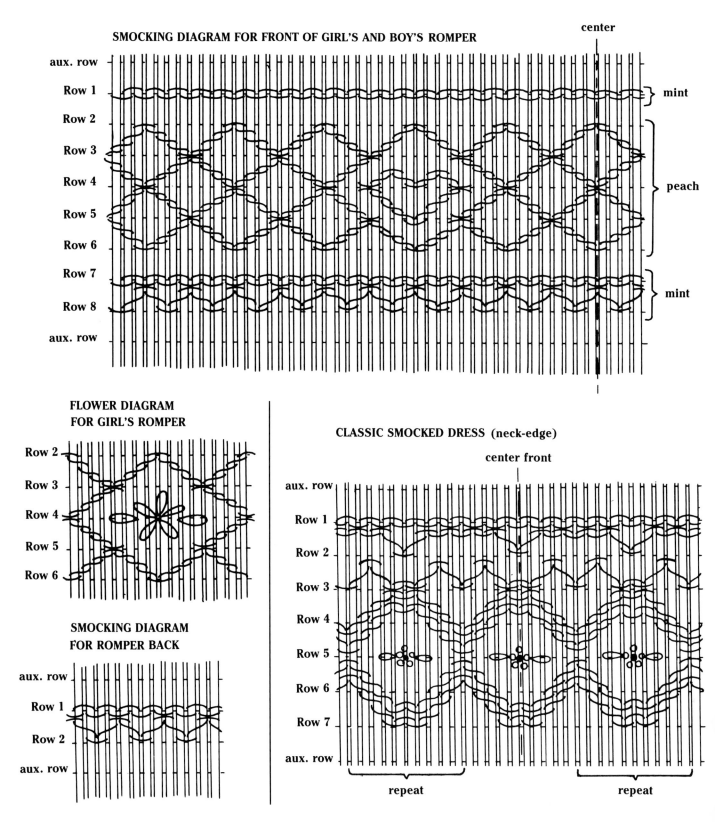

SMOCKING DIAGRAM FOR FRONT OF GIRL'S AND BOY'S ROMPER

center

aux. row
Row 1 — mint
Row 2
Row 3
Row 4 — peach
Row 5
Row 6
Row 7 — mint
Row 8
aux. row

FLOWER DIAGRAM
FOR GIRL'S ROMPER

Row 2
Row 3
Row 4
Row 5
Row 6

CLASSIC SMOCKED DRESS (neck-edge)

center front

aux. row
Row 1
Row 2
Row 3
Row 4
Row 5
Row 6
Row 7
aux. row

repeat   repeat

SMOCKING DIAGRAM
FOR ROMPER BACK

aux. row
Row 1
Row 2
aux. row

126

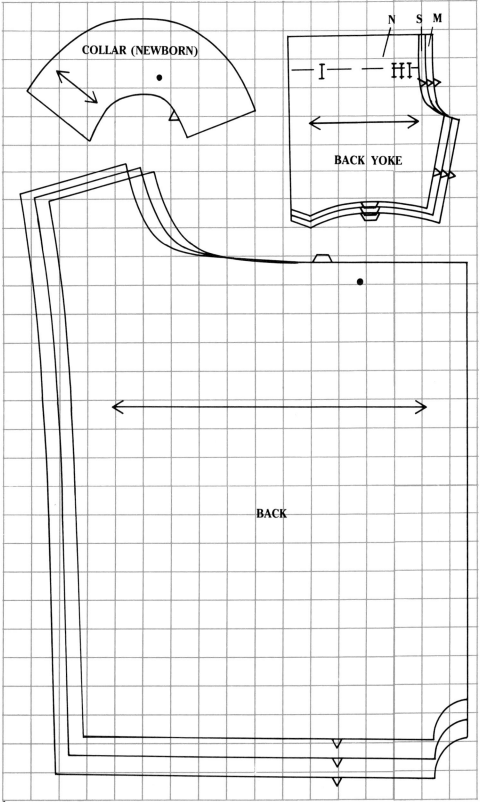

COLLAR (NEWBORN)

N S M

BACK YOKE

BACK

1 square = 1 inch

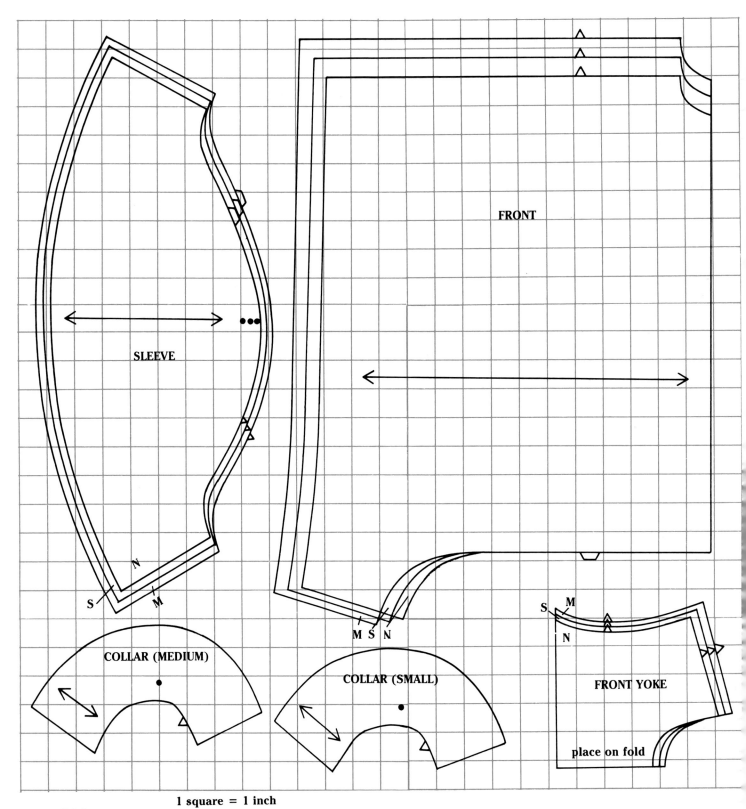

SLEEVE

FRONT

COLLAR (MEDIUM)

COLLAR (SMALL)

FRONT YOKE

place on fold

1 square = 1 inch

128

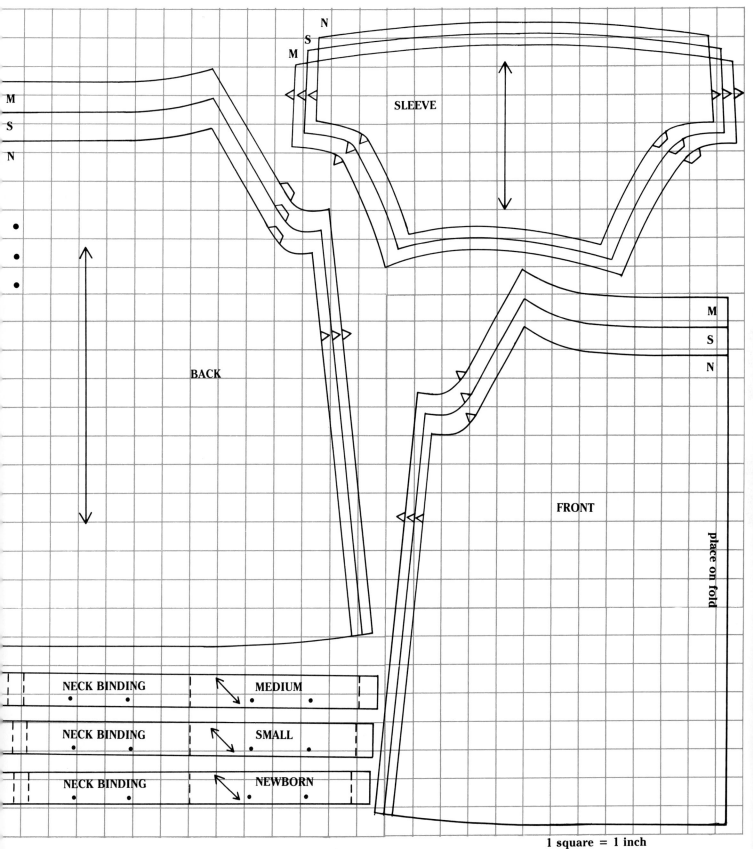

SLEEVE

M
S
N

M
S
N

BACK

FRONT

M
S
N

place on fold

NECK BINDING · · | MEDIUM · ·

NECK BINDING · · | SMALL ·

NECK BINDING · · | NEWBORN · ·

1 square = 1 inch

Best-Foot-Forward Shoes

A n upbeat alternate to baby booties, these cloth shoes keep Baby's tootsies warm in style. For dress-up occasions, there are satin tie shoes trimmed in baby-blue . . . and satin slippers with lace and ribbon roses. The sneakers and calico Mary Janes are for everyday fun. And the Bunny Boots are just right for bedtime story time. These shoes are fun for you to make and fun for Baby to wear.

TIE SHOES

MATERIALS:
For sneakers:
4½" × 22" piece red canvas
4½" × 22" piece white flannel
2 yards white double-fold bias tape
White thread
¼ yard ⅜"-wide red, white, and blue striped ribbon
12 red eyelets
1 pair of small shoe laces

For satin dress shoes:
4½" × 22" piece white satin
4½" × 22" piece white flannel
2 yards light blue double-fold bias tape
Light blue thread
1 yard ⅛"-wide white satin ribbon
12 white eyelets

Trace patterns for tie shoe sides, tongue, and sole. Cut two of each piece from each outer fabric and flannel.

Wrong sides together, baste flannel to fabric ⅛ inch from edges. For sneaker, baste ribbon to shoe sides between broken placement lines. Bind upper edges of sides and tongue. See Diagram 1. Insert eyelets in sides at open dots. Lap sides over tongues along broken lines. Stitch along each edge of bias tape for ¾ inch above lower edge. See Diagram 2. Make a row of gathering stitches around front of shoe. Gather slightly to round toe of shoe without puckering fabric. See Diagram 3. Bind lower edge of sides and front, beginning on left side of right shoe and right side of left shoe. Pull up basting thread on sole to round front and back curve slightly without puckering fabric. See Diagram 4. Compare shoe top and sole to make sure

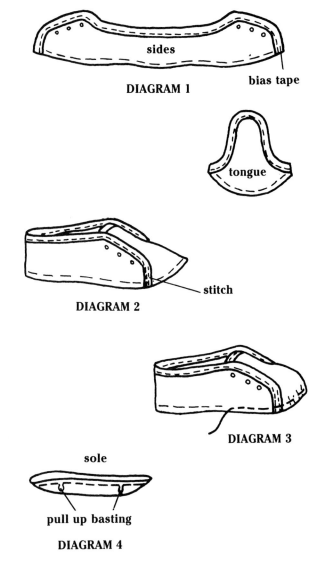

DIAGRAM 1

sides

bias tape

tongue

DIAGRAM 2

stitch

DIAGRAM 3

sole

pull up basting

DIAGRAM 4

edges are approximately the same length. Bind edges, beginning on the left side of right shoe and the right side of left shoe. Turn under ¼ inch on end of binding and stitch over beginning edge. Matching center front and back, pin and then slipstitch edges of shoe to sole. Insert shoe laces into eyelets of sneakers. Cut ⅛-inch ribbon in half and insert in eyelets of dress shoes.

SATIN SLIPPERS

MATERIALS:
6″ × 18″ piece white satin
6″ × 18″ piece white flannel
1¼ yards white double-fold bias tape
11″ piece 1″-wide lace edging
White sewing thread
1¼ yards ⅜″-wide white satin ribbon
1 yard ⅜″-wide pink ribbon
4″ piece ¼″-wide green ribbon

Trace patterns for slipper and sole. Cut two of each piece from satin and from flannel.

Right sides together, stitch satin slipper to flannel along inner curve, ¼ inch from edge. Trim and clip seam allowance. Turn right-side-out. Open out backs along straight back edge. Matching seams, stitch back edges together and then turn right-side-out again. See Diagram 1. Baste lower edges of satin and flannel slippers together ⅛ inch from edge. Pull up basting stitches to round front of shoe without puckering fabric. See Diagram 2. Wrong sides together, baste flannel sole to satin sole, ⅛ inch from edge. Pull up basting stitches without puckering fabric to round front and back curves of sole. See Diagram 4 of tie shoes. Compare sole and slipper to make sure edges are approximately the same length. Bind lower edge of shoe and edge of sole, following instructions in the how-to chapter. Begin binding on right side of pieces for left shoe and left side of pieces for right shoe. Turn under ¼ inch on end of binding and stitch over beginning edge. Matching center front and back, slipstitch slippers to soles.

Cut lace in half. Right sides together, sew ends of pieces together close to edge; zigzag or overcast raw edges of lace seam. By hand, make a row of gathering stitches along straight edge of lace. Pull thread to form a ruffled circle. Sew lace to front of

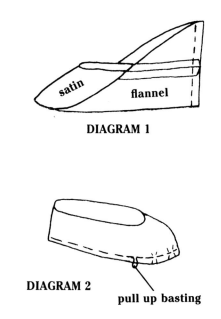

DIAGRAM 1

DIAGRAM 2

pull up basting

slipper. Cut pink ribbon in half. Make each piece into a ribbon rose, following instructions in the how-to chapter. Trim ends of two 2-inch pieces of green ribbon diagonally. Make a pleat in center so it is slightly **V**-shaped. Right side down, sew green ribbon to wrong side of rose. Sew rose to center of ruffled circle. Cut white ribbon in half. Lap center ⅛ inch over back of shoe. Stitch 1 inch at center of ribbon to back of shoe. Trim ends of ribbon diagonally.

CALICO MARY JANES

MATERIALS:
6″ × 22″ piece floral print cotton fabric
6″ × 20″ piece white flannel
1⅞ yards matching double-fold bias tape
Thread to match fabric and bias tape
Two ⅜″-diameter buttons

Following broken line of slipper for top edge, trace patterns for slipper, sole and strap. Cut two of each piece from floral print. Cut slipper and sole from flannel.

Right sides together, stitch straight back edge of each slipper together. Trim seam allowance of flannel pieces to ⅛ inch from stitching. Right sides out, baste flannel pieces to fabric pieces ⅛ inch from edges. Pull up basting thread on front of slipper piece and front and back of sole to round edges without puckering fabric. See Diagram 2 for satin slippers and Diagram 4 for tie shoes. Compare sole and slipper to make sure edges are approximately the same length. Bind upper and lower edge of slipper and edge of sole, following instructions in the how-to chapter, and beginning and ending binding at back seam of slipper. On sole, begin and end binding on left side for right shoe and right side for left shoe. Turn under ¼ inch on end of binding and stitch over beginning edge. Matching center fronts and backs, slipstitch sole to slipper.

Fold straps in half, right sides together; stitch along edges, leaving an opening between dots. Trim and clip seam allowance. Turn right-side-out. Topstitch ⅛ inch from edge of straps. Make a ⅜-inch buttonhole along line on strap. Sew strap end without buttonhole to inside edge of each shoe along placement lines. Sew button to opposite side of shoe at dot.

BUNNY BOOTS

MATERIALS:
¼ yard white flannel
4″ × 10″ piece pink flannel
3″ square lightweight cardboard
½ yard each light blue, pink, and tan six-strand embroidery floss
White sewing thread
12 yards white sport-weight yarn
⅜ yard ⅛″-wide elastic
Small embroidery hoop

Enlarge pattern for boots. Trace two fronts to right side of white flannel, drawing cutting line and features. Leave enough extra fabric around front edge so that fronts can be inserted in an embroidery hoop. Using three strands of floss, embroider eyes in light blue satin stitch, nose in pink satin stitch, and mouth in pink backstitch. Using two strands of tan, embroider whiskers with straight stitch. When embroidery is complete, cut out fronts. Cut two backs, two soles, and four ears from white flannel. Cut four ears from pink flannel.

Stitch all seams right sides together, using ⅜ inch seams. To finish seams of boots, trim seam allowance to ¼ inch; zigzag-stitch along edge of seam allowance.

Narrowly hem top edge of front and back. Cut elastic in half; stretch and stitch it along broken line of front and back. Stitch remaining side seams. Matching dots to side seams, stitch sole to lower edge of front and back.

Stitch each pink ear to a white ear ¼ inch from edge, leaving straight end open. Trim and clip seam allowance. Turn right-side-out. Turn seam allowance under along lower edge; slipstitch. Fold each ear in half lengthwise; sew lower edge together. Stitch ears to boots along lines on front.

From cardboard, draw and cut four 1½-inch diameter rings with ½-inch-diameter circle in center. Cut yarn in half. From each half, set aside an 8-inch piece for tying center. Following instructions in the how-to chapter, make two pompons. Sew pompon tail to back of boots.

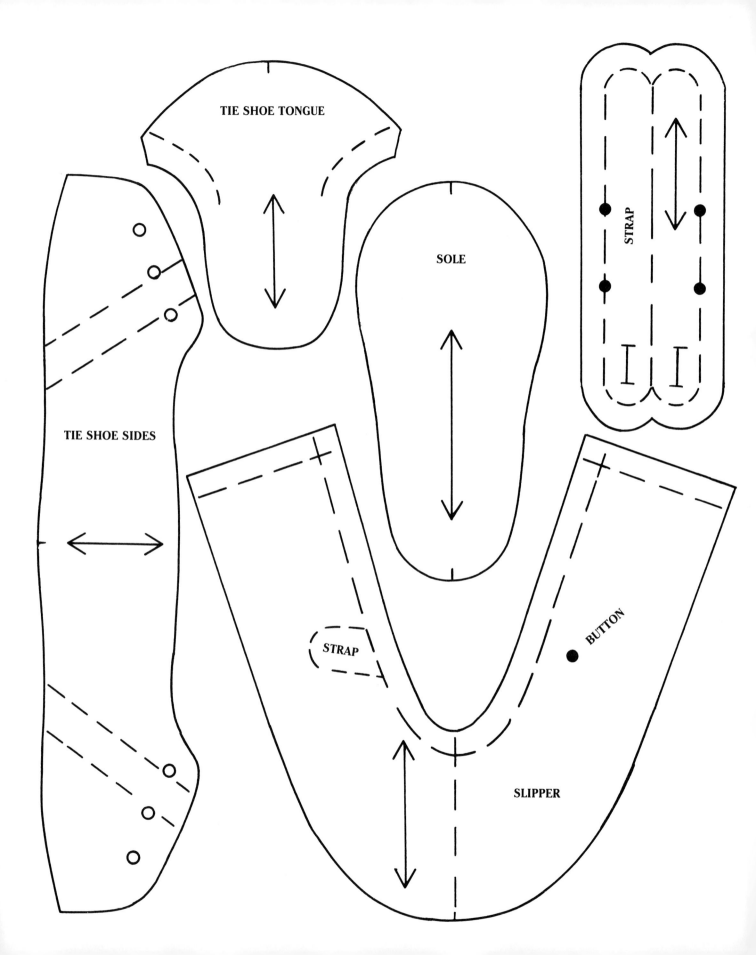

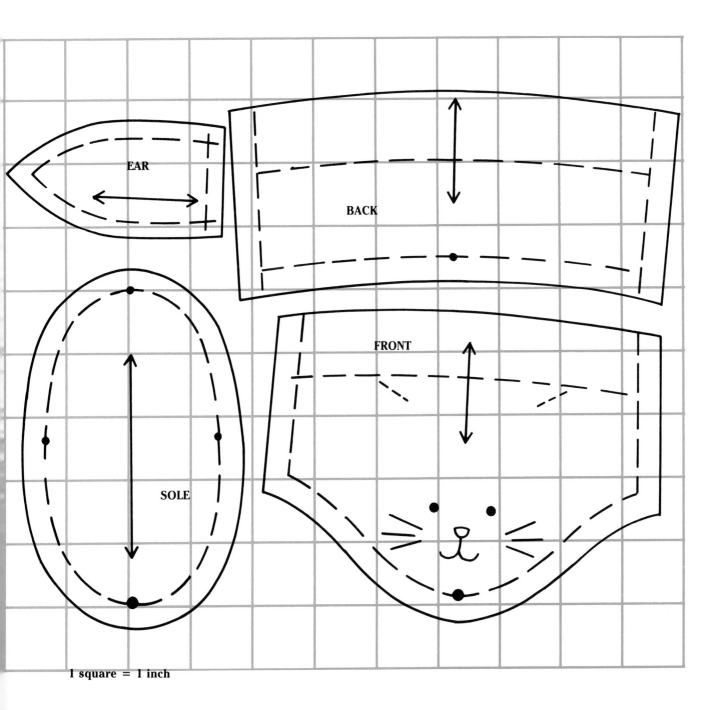

EAR

BACK

FRONT

SOLE

1 square = 1 inch

Home-from-the-Hospital Knitted Sweater Set

Bring your baby home from the hospital in this classic white sweater set . . . or make it as a gift for a newborn. Before the baby is born, make it in unisex colors of lavender or yellow. Or complete the knitting and then weave in ribbons later—pink ribbons if it's a girl or blue ribbons if it's a boy.

Some knitting experience is recommended.

SIZES:

3 months [6 months—12 months]
Chest measurement of finished sweater: 18″ [20″—22″]

MATERIALS:

Brunswick Fore 'N' Aft (acrylic sport-weight) yarn, 3 [3—4] (50 gr–1¾ oz) skeins white
Circular knitting needles, sizes 3 (3.25 mm) and 5 (3.75 mm) or sizes that give you the correct gauge
Set of four double-pointed (dp) needles, size 5 (3.75 mm)
6 yards ¼″-wide pastel satin ribbon
¾ yards ¼″-wide white satin ribbon
¾ yards ⅝″-wide white satin ribbon
Six ⅜″-wide white heart-shaped buttons
Pastel thread to match ribbon
Tapestry needle
2 each 2″-long and 4″-long stitch holders

GAUGE: In stockinette st, 5 sts = 1″

Note: See page 214 for Knitting Abbreviations and Terms.

Pattern Stitch: *Row 1* (right side): Knit. *Row 2:* Purl. *Row 3:* Knit. *Row 4:* Purl. *Rows 5–8:* Knit. *Row 9* (eyelet row): K 1, * yo, k 2 tog; repeat from * across. *Rows 10–12:* Knit. *Rows 13–18:* Repeat rows 1 and 2 three times. Repeats Rows 5–18 for pattern.

SWEATER

Body: On smaller circular needle, cast on 95 [105—115] sts. Do not join, but work back and forth as on straight needles. Work in ribbing as follows:

Row 1 (right side): K 1, * p 1, k 1; repeat from * across.
Row 2: P 1, * k 1, p 1; repeat from * across. Repeat these 2 rows once more.
Row 5 (buttonhole row): K 1, p 1, k 1, yo, k 2 tog (buttonhole made), * p 1, k 1; repeat from * across. Repeat row 2 once, then rows 1 and 2 once.

Change to larger circular needle. Now start pattern as follows:

Row 1 (right side): (K 1, p 1) 3 times for front buttonhole band, place a marker on needle, k to within last 6 sts, place a marker on needle, (p 1, k 1) 3 times for front button band.
Row 2: (P 1, k 1) 3 times, slip marker, p to marker, slip marker, (k 1, p 1) 3 times. Keeping 6 sts at beg and end of row in ribbing as established, work pattern st between markers (*note:* next row is Row 3 of pattern) and, spaced every 1¼″ [1½″—1¾″] above last buttonhole, make another buttonhole on right-side row, same as before. Work even until piece measures 5″ [6″—7″], ending on the wrong side.

To divide work for armholes: Next row: Work first 24 [26—28] sts and place on a holder for right front, bind off next 5 [6—7] sts for armhole, work until there are 37 [41—45] sts on right point (back sts), place remaining 29 [32—35] sts on another holder.

Back: Working on back sts only, continue in pattern as established and dec 1 st at beg and end of

136

every other row twice (33 [37—41] sts). Work even until armholes measure 3½″ [3¾″—4″]. For shoulders, bind off 4 [4—5] sts at beg of next 2 rows, then 4 [5—5] sts at beg of next 2 rows. Place remaining 17 [19—21] sts on a holder to be worked later for back of neck.

Left front: Place remaining 29 [32—35] unworked sts from holder onto larger circular needle. With right side of work facing you, attach yarn to first st. Bind off first 5 [6—7] sts for armhole, work remaining 24 [26—28] sts for left front. Continue front band and pattern as established, and, at arm edge, dec 1 st every other row twice. Work even on 22 [24—26] sts until armhole measures 1½″ [1¾″—2″], ending at front edge.

Next row: Work first 9 [10—11] sts and place on a holder for neckband; complete row. Continue in pattern, and at neck edge bind off 2 sts twice, then dec 1 st on next row once. Work until armhole measures same as for back. For shoulders, at arm edge, bind off 4 [4—5] sts once, then 4 [5—5] sts once.

Right front: Place right front sts from holder onto larger circular needle. With wrong side of work facing you, attach yarn to first st. Continue front band and pattern as established, and at arm edge dec 1 st every other row twice. Complete to correspond to left front, continuing to make buttonholes as before (a sixth buttonhole will be on neckband).

Sleeves: On smaller circular needle, cast on 31 [33—35] sts. Work in ribbing same as for body until 10 [8—12] rows are completed. Change to larger circular needle and work in pattern st, increasing 1 st at beg and end of every inch 2 [3—4] times, working added sts in pattern. Work even on 35 [39—43] sts until sleeve measures about 5¼″ [6″—7¼″] from beg. End with a same pattern row as body at underarm, so that pattern rows on yoke and sleeve cap line up.

Sleeve cap: Bind off 3 [3—4] sts at beg of next 2 rows. Dec 1 st at beg and end of every other row 4 [5—6] times. Bind off 2 sts at beg of next 6 rows. Bind off remaining 9 [11—11] sts.

Finishing: Block sweater and sleeve pieces fol-
lowing instructions on page 20. Leaving ½-inch ends, weave pastel ribbon through each eyelet row of knitted pieces. Turn under ¼ inch twice on each ribbon end and sew in place on wrong side. Sew shoulder and sleeve seams; sew sleeves in place.

Sew shoulder seams. *Neckband:* Slip sts of left front, back, and right front onto smaller circular needle. With right side of work facing you, attach yarn and rib first 6 sts of right front as established, k remaining 3 [4—5] sts, pick up and k 12 sts around shaped right front neck edge, k 17 [19—21] sts of back, pick up and k 12 sts around shaped left front neck edge, k 3 [4—5] sts of left front, rib last 6 sts as established (59 [63—67] sts). Now work in k 1, p 1 ribbing for 6 rows, working last buttonhole on right front. Bind off in ribbing.

Sew sleeve seams. Sew sleeve caps to armholes, matching pattern rows. Sew on buttons opposite buttonholes.

BONNET

On smaller circular needle, cast on 65 [67—71] sts for front edge. Work in k 1, p 1 ribbing, same as for sweater body, for 14 rows. *Next row:* Bind off 4 sts, k to end. *Next row:* Bind off 4 sts, p to end (57 [59—63] sts). Starting with row 3, work in pattern st until bonnet measures 5¾″ from beg, ending on the wrong side. *Next row:* Bind off 21 sts, k to end. *Next row:* Bind off 21 sts, p to end. Work even in stockinette st (k 1 row, p 1 row) on 15 [17—21] sts for 4″ for back of bonnet. Slip sts onto holder. Sew side edges of back to adjacent bound-off edges of bonnet sides. *Neck-edge ribbing:* With smaller circular needle, pick up and k 53 [55—59] sts around neck edge of bonnet, including sts from holder. Work in k 1, p 1 ribbing for 4 rows. Bind off in ribbing. Sew edges of neck ribbing to bound-off sts of front ribbing. Block bonnet following instructions on page 20. Weave pastel ribbon through eyelet rows and sew ribbon ends in place as for sweater. Fold half of front ribbing back to form cuff. Cut ⅝-inch-wide ribbon in half for ties. Securely sew a ribbon end to each front corner of bonnet inside folded cuff. Tack cuff in place over ribbon ends.

BOOTIES

Starting at top of leg, on larger circular needle, cast on 25 [25—29] sts. Work in stockinette st (k 1 row, p 1 row) for 8 rows. Knit 4 rows. *Next row* (eyelet row): K 1, * yo, k 2 tog; repeat from * across. K 3 rows. Work in stockinette st for 1" [1¼"—1½"], ending with a p row. Work eyelet row as before. P 1 row, k 1 row, p 1 row.

To divide for foot: K 9 [9—10] sts and place on a holder for right side, k 7 [7—9] for instep, place remaining 9 [9—10] sts on a holder for left side. Work in stockinette st on instep sts for 2" [2¼"—2½"], ending with a p row. Slip instep sts to dp needle. Slip right-side sts to another dp needle. K right-side sts, then pick up and k 8 [9—10] sts along right side of instep, k instep sts, pick up and k 8 [9—10] sts along left side of instep, k left-side sts from holder. Divide 41 [43—49] sts onto three dp needles and mark beg of rnds at center back. Work around as follows: (P 1 row, k 1 row) 5 times, decreasing 4 [4—6] sts evenly spaced around last row. K 3 more rows, decreasing 1 st at center of last row. K 1 row. Bind off all sts.

Finishing: Sew bound-off sts tog to form center sole seam; sew back seam. Turn under ¼ inch at top edge of leg for hem and sew in place. Weave pastel ribbon through upper eyelet row, sewing ribbon ends in place as for sweater. Cut ¼-inch-wide white ribbon in half. Beginning at front, weave ribbon through lower eyelet row of each bootie. Tie in bow.

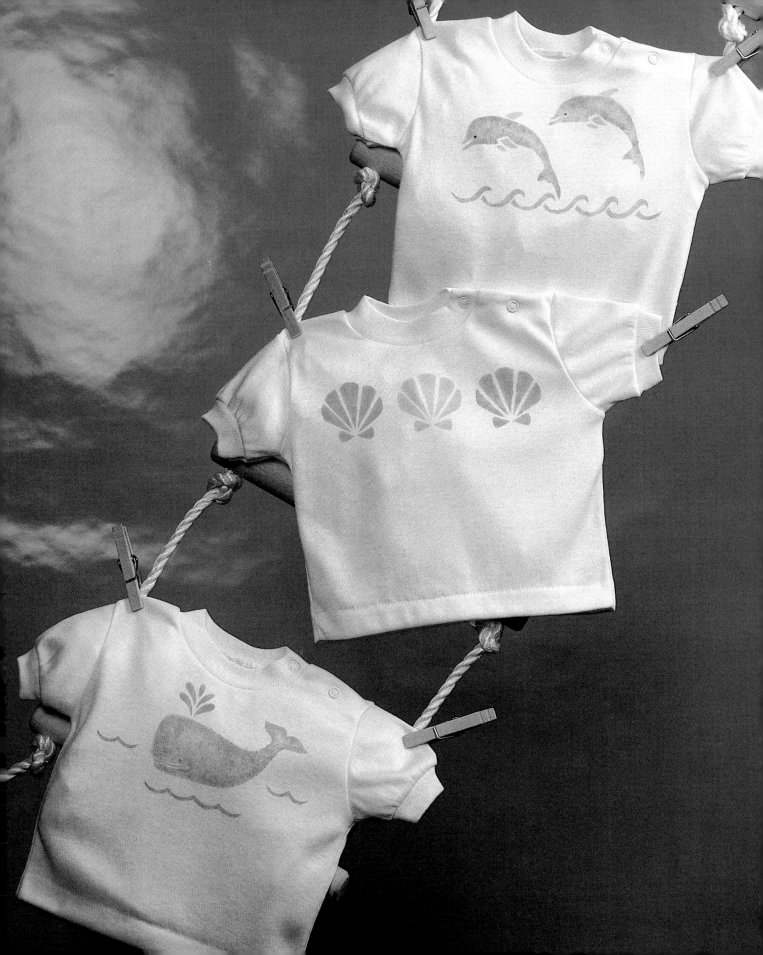

Stenciled T-shirts

Stenciling a few purchased, baby-sized T-shirts is a quick and easy way to extend Baby's summertime wardrobe. Fun to make, and very packable for vacations or weekends at the beach.

MATERIALS:
One or more white cotton T-shirts
Textile paints
Stencil brush with bristles ¼″ in diameter
Small watercolor paint brush
X-Acto® knife
Translucent acrylic sheets for stencils
Small containers to mix paint in
Tracing paper
Pencil
A few plastic spoons or Popsicle sticks
Masking tape
8½″ × 11″ cardboard
Paper toweling
A container of water to clean brushes
Paper to cover work surface

To make stencils, trace motifs onto tracing paper, arranging and spacing the elements of the design as desired. The T-shirts I used are size 12 months. For smaller sizes you may wish to use only one dolphin, one or two shells, and eliminate the waves from the side of the whale to fit the motif on the shirt. Usually, one stencil is cut for each color. If the shapes in two different colors appear far apart in the design, they may be cut on the same stencil. You may even cut all three shells on one stencil: Just be neat and careful when applying the paint. Eyes are shown for placement only—do not cut them out.

Cut pieces of translucent acrylic sheet 1 inch larger than the design on all sides. Place the translucent sheet over the design and trace the entire design in the center. Place the stencil over cardboard and cut out the shapes with an X-Acto® knife. Cut smaller areas first, but disregard eyes.

Rotate the stencil and cut out each shape *without* lifting the knife.

Mix the textile paints to get the exact color or shade you want. For the colors used on these shirts, mix green, blue, and white for mint green; mix white with orange, with yellow, and with blue for pastel shades. Mix enough of each color to complete the project. For these designs, 1 or 2 teaspoons of paint is all that is needed.

If you have never stenciled before, you may wish to test the stencils and practice on scrap fabric first.

Cover working surface with paper. Insert cardboard inside shirt so paint will not bleed through onto back. Position the main stencil on shirt, centering the design vertically. Tape it in place. Begin at the top left if you are right-handed (or the top right if you are left-handed). Dip the tip of the stencil brush into the paint with the brush held upright. Rub the brush in a circular motion on a few paper towels to work the paint into the bristles and remove excess paint. Test the brush on the paper towels or on a scrap of fabric to check the density of the paint. Hold the stencil down against the fabric to keep it from shifting as you paint. This is especially important when working on knits, since they tend to stretch. Holding the brush upright, with the bristles flat on the surface of the stencil, brush over the edge of the shape. Do not brush toward the stencil edge, since some paint could be forced under the edge. Work around the shape, building up to the color density that you desire. On large shapes, more paint may be applied to the edges than the center to create a three-dimensional look. Once the design is complete, carefully lift the stencil off the fabric. When the paint is dry to the touch, tape down the next stencil, aligning it with the painted design, and continue. Afterward, add a dot of paint for the eyes on the dolphins and whales, using the small brush.

When finished, follow the paint manufacturer's instructions for setting the color.

Heirloom Christening Ensemble

This heirloom outfit will be treasured generation after generation. The ensemble is embroidered and embellished with satin ribbons and dainty cotton lace. The size can be adjusted by gathering the ribbons for sizes up to six months . . . An ambitious project, but well worth the time and effort.

SIZE:
Adjustable to fit newborn to 6 months.

MATERIALS:
4 yards white lawn, voile, batiste or other lightweight cotton or cotton blend fabric
6 skeins white six-strand embroidery floss
White cotton lace:
  6 yards 1"-wide edging with beading
  2½ yards ½"-wide edging
  3 yards ½"-wide beading
White sewing thread
White satin ribbon:
  6 yards ⅛"-wide
  3 yards ¼"-wide
  3 yards ⅝"-wide
Five ⁵⁄₁₆"-diameter buttons
Embroidery hoop

Enlarge the patterns, following instructions in the how-to chapter. From the full-size embroidery patterns, trace the floral vine motif onto the lower edge of the gown front and back patterns, 1 inch in from cutting line. Trace curved line of vine, leaves, and the center dot only of the flower. On the jacket, following the design indicated on the pattern, trace the vine 1¼ inches in from the cutting edge. On the bonnet, trace the design along the edges indicated on the pattern 1 inch in from the cutting line. Trace the heart motifs onto the pattern pieces as indicated. In addition, draw a pattern for heart strip, 2¾" × 44½". Beginning with a half-heart ½ inch from end, trace thirteen hearts onto strip, 1⅝" apart. Finish with another half-heart ½ inch from remaining end. See Diagram 1. Then draw a floral vine strip 2" × 44½". Trace floral vine motif along strip 1¼ inches from lower edge. Using a pencil, trace all patterns along with embroidery motifs onto fabric, very lightly. Reverse patterns and trace another gown back, gown sleeve, jacket front, and jacket sleeve. Leave enough fabric along edges to insert embroidery motifs in a hoop, but do not spread pieces out over entire fabric.

Use three strands of white floss for all embroidery. To embroider the floral vine, backstitch along the line; embroider the flowers with six French knots worked around the drawn center knot, and

HEART

VINE

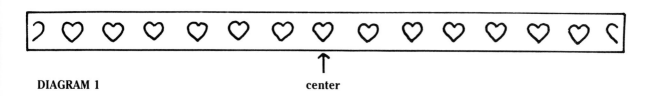

DIAGRAM 1

center

DIAGRAM 2

stitch

zigzag

DIAGRAM 3

trim

DIAGRAM 4

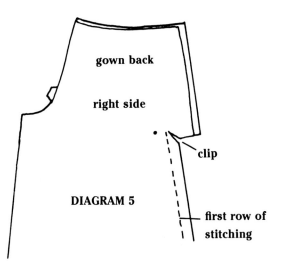

gown back

right side

clip

DIAGRAM 5

first row of stitching

embroider leaves with lazy-daisy stitch. For the heart, work ⅛-inch-long backstitches along the outline and the stem. Embroider flowers with French knots and leaves with lazy-daisy stitch. Bring needle up at center top of heart. On top of fabric, run floss back and forth through backstitches in a continuing **S**-shaped curve. See Diagram 2. When embroidery is completed, cut pieces from fabric and press lightly from the wrong side.

Omitting embroidery, cut two more jacket fronts; one jacket back; and two jacket sleeves for lining; front ruffle, 5″ × 45″; two back ruffles, 5″ × 23″; bonnet lining; slip back and front; and slip facings.

Use ⅝-inch seam allowance unless indicated.

GOWN

For gown, join backs to front along side seams with French seams, following instructions in the how-to chapter. Stitch along seam line of lower edge. Trim seam allowance to ⅛-inch. Finish edge with zigzag stitch. See Diagram 3. Stitch ¼-inch in from edge along top and bottom of heart strip and top of floral vine strip. Finish edge same as for gown. Baste lace beading to lower edge of gown, covering finished edge; stitch along edge of lace. Baste and stitch remaining edge of lace to top of heart strip. In same manner, join floral vine strip with lace beading to lower edge of heart strip.

Join back ruffles to front ruffle along ends with French seams. Narrowly hem one long edge of ruffle, following instructions in the how-to chapter. Place beading edge of 1-inch-wide lace on right side of hemmed edge of ruffle. Baste and stitch lace in place. Right sides together, gather top edge of ruffle evenly to lower edge of floral vine strip; stitch seam. Trim seam allowance to ¼ inch; zigzag-stitch along edge. Weave ⅛-inch-wide ribbon through beading of lace. Sew ends of ribbon to lace and invisibly tack ribbon and lace together every few inches.

Narrowly hem lower edge of sleeves. Baste and stitch hemmed edge over straight edge of ½-inch-wide lace edging. Make a small buttonhole at the lower center of sleeve, as indicated on pattern piece. For each sleeve casing, cut a 1″ × 10½″ bias strip and make it into single-fold bias tape, following instructions in the how-to chapter. Trim edges to generous ⅛ inch. See Diagram 4. Pin casing to sleeve, ½ inch from lower edge of fabric. Stitch along top and bottom of casing, beginning and ending 1½ inches from ends. Join front and back edges of sleeves with French seam, keeping casing ends free. Turn under ends of casing over seam and stitch in place. Right sides together, stitch sleeves to front and back. Trim seam allowance to ¼ inch; zigzag along edges.

Stitch buttonhole in center of front. For waistline casing, cut a 1½-inch-wide bias strip 30 inches long and press in same manner as sleeve casing. Trim edges to ¼ inch from fold. Pin casing to front and back at position indicated by broken lines. Stitch along top and bottom of casing, beginning and ending 1½ inches from center back seam. Join center back edges below dot with a French seam. When first row of stitching on French seam is complete, clip to top of stitching ¼ inch from dot. See Diagram 5. Complete French seam at center back. On right back, press under ¼ inch on side and lower edges of center back placket above dot. Fold side edge to wrong side along center back; stitch in place. See Diagram 6. On left back, press under ¼ inch on lower edge of center back placket. Fold edge to wrong side of center back; fold again along center back. Stitch along edge. See Diagram 7. Turn under ends of waistline casing at center back seam and stitch edges in place.

Narrowly hem ends of a 13-inch piece of ½-inch-wide lace edging. Stitch lace around gown neckline with top edge just inside seam line. Trim seam allowance to ⅜ inch. Cut a 1⅜″ × 14″ bias strip for neck binding. Make a ¼-inch buttonhole at center, ⅜ inch from long edge. See Diagram 8. Right sides together, with buttonhole at center front, stitch bias strip to neckline ⅜ inch from top edge. Trim seam allowance. Fold binding to wrong side ⅜ inch from seam, turning under ends and edge along stitching. Slipstitch casing in place.

Cut two 14 inch lengths of ¼-inch-wide ribbon. Insert ribbon into neckline casing at back and bring ends out through buttonhole. Stitch across casing at back to hold end of ribbon. On left side of back opening, make buttonholes indicated on pattern, plus one along lower edge of neckline casing. Cut two 16-inch pieces of ¼-inch-wide ribbon; insert into sleeve casings through center buttonhole. Cut a 65-inch length of ⅝-inch-wide ribbon. Insert into waistline casing of gown through buttonhole at center front.

JACKET

For the jacket, with right sides together, stitch sleeves to fronts and back along notched armhole edge. Trim seam allowance to ¼ inch. Stitch lining pieces together in the same manner. Make buttonholes on fronts of embroidered pieces near neckline where indicated on pattern. Right sides together, stitch lining to jacket, leaving an opening for turning in center of lower back edge. Trim and grade seam allowance. Turn right side out. Stitch ⅜ inch from neck edge to form a casing. Narrowly hem ends of two 8½-inch lengths of 1-inch-wide

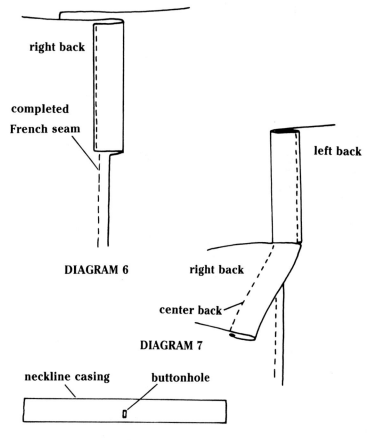

DIAGRAM 6

DIAGRAM 7

DIAGRAM 8

lace edging. Baste, then stitch beading portion over end of sleeve. Insert ⅛-inch-wide ribbon through beading and tack ends in place. Right sides together, stitch fronts to back along sleeve and side seams, ¼ inch from edge. Baste, then stitch lace around front and lower edge of jacket, mitering lace at corners, following instructions in the how-to chapter. Narrowly hem ends of lace at neck edge. Insert ⅛-inch-wide ribbon in beading. Tack ribbon in place at ends and at corners. Cut a 30-inch length of ¼-inch-wide ribbon; insert through neck casing.

BONNET

Use ⅜-inch seam allowance for bonnet. Press under seam allowance on two short ends of bonnet and lining. Right sides together, stitch bonnet to lining along remaining edges. Grade and trim seam allowance, following instructions in the how-to chapter. Turn right-side-out. Baste, then stitch 1-inch-wide lace edging around embroidered edges, mitering lace at corners. Narrowly hem ends at back. Insert ⅛-inch-wide ribbon through beading; tack ends and mitered corners in place. Baste, then stitch ½-inch-wide lace beading along remaining straight edge at back opening of bonnet, turning under ends. Slipstitch short edges and lace together at back. Insert a 14-inch length of ⅛-inch-wide ribbon through beading. Gather ribbon and tie a bow. Cut two 16-inch lengths of ⅝-inch-wide ribbon. Turn under 1 inch on end and sew to corner of bonnet, making a tuck in ribbon. Trim ends of ribbons diagonally.

SLIP

For slip, stitch front to back at sides with French seams. Right sides together, stitch front facing to back facing at sides. Turn under ¼ inch on lower edge of facing; stitch edge in place. Pin, then stitch facing to upper edge of slip, right sides together, matching seams and notches. Grade and clip seam allowance, following instructions in the how-to chapter. Turn facing to inside. Tack facing to seams at sides. Narrowly hem lower edge, or finish with zigzag stitch. See Diagram 3. Pin, then stitch ½-inch-wide lace edging over lower edge. Seam ends of lace; finish with zigzag stitch. Make buttonholes on front at positions indicated. Sew buttons to dot on back.

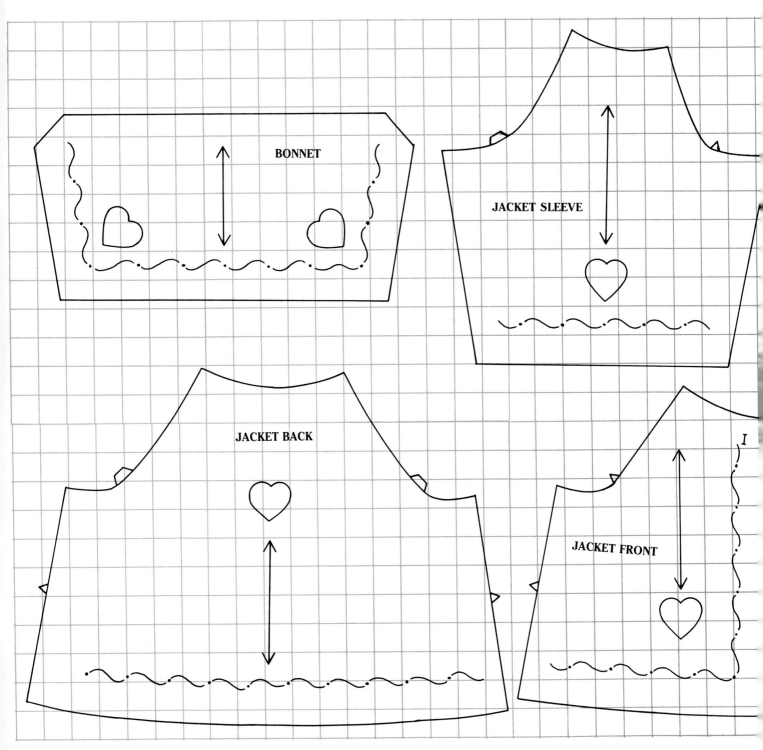

BONNET

JACKET SLEEVE

JACKET BACK

JACKET FRONT

I

1 square = 1 inch

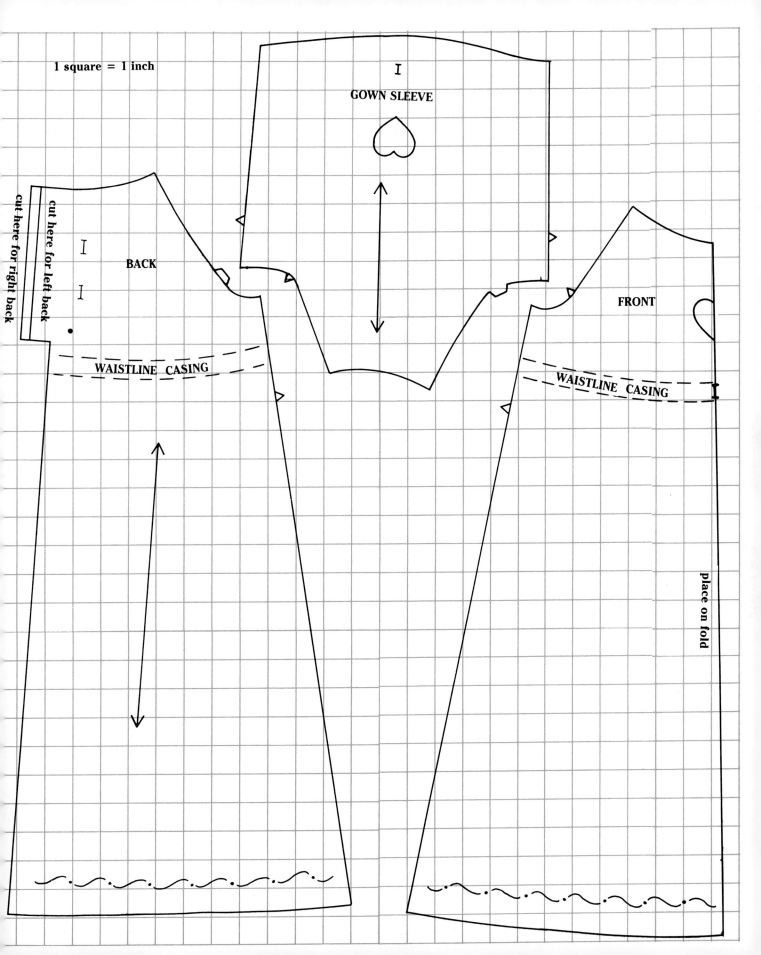

1 square = 1 inch

GOWN SLEEVE

cut here for right back

cut here for left back

BACK

WAISTLINE CASING

FRONT

WAISTLINE CASING

place on fold

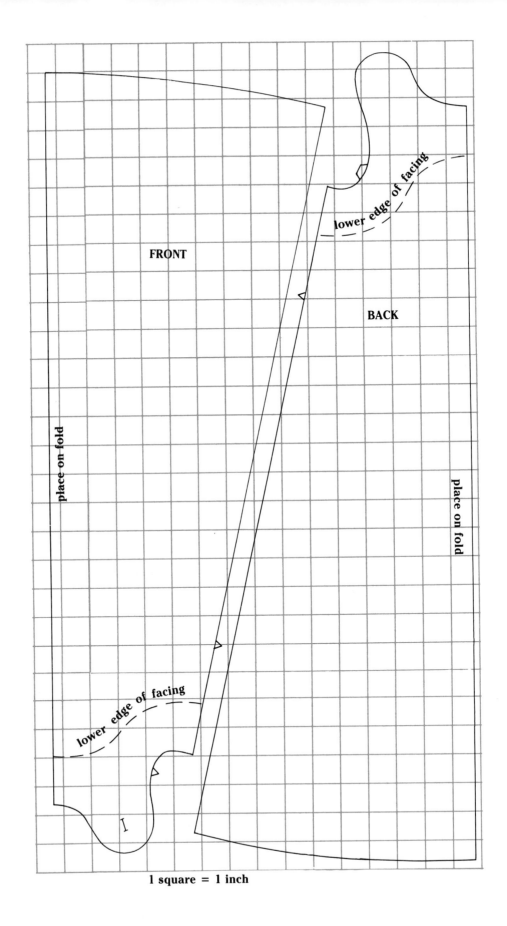

FRONT

BACK

lower edge of facing

lower edge of facing

place on fold

place on fold

1 square = 1 inch

Sunbonnet Sue Pinafore Ensemble

This cool eyelet pinafore is ideal for warm summer days. It's trimmed with eyelet ruffles . . . and the "basket" pocket holds a tiny, adorable doll. The doll's sunbonnet matches the girl's, so both of them can be protected from too much sun.

SIZES:

Small (12 months), medium (18 months), large (24 months)

MATERIALS:

45"-wide white eyelet fabric, 1⅛ yards for small, 1¼ yards for medium and large

½ yard print fabric for sunbonnet and trim

6" × 8" piece yellow-and-white gingham

4½" × 12" piece dot or print to coordinate with print fabric

4" square solid color to match cotton print

4" square muslin

¼ yard lightweight cotton lining fabric

About 1 handful polyester stuffing

¼ yard 18"-wide medium-weight interfacing or fusible webbing

6" × 18" piece stiff interfacing or crinoline

½ yard each brown and red six-strand embroidery floss

2¼ yards white single-fold bias tape

3 yards 3"-wide white eyelet edging

10" piece ¼"-wide lace

Sewing thread to match fabrics

6"-length ¼"-wide red ribbon

16" piece 1"-wide white grosgrain ribbon

1½ yards ¼"-wide elastic

3¼ yards ⅛"-diameter cotton cording

Six ⁵⁄₁₆"-diameter white buttons

Enlarge pattern for the size pinafore and sunbonnet you wish to make. ⅝-inch seam allowances are included on pattern. With fabric folded in half, cut one front, two backs, one yoke front, two yoke backs, and two bloomer pieces. Cut two sleeve ruffles from eyelet edging, placing straight edge of pattern along scalloped, embroidered edge of eyelet. Cut one front yoke and two back yokes from lining. Lightly trace outline of basket and handle in position on left side of pinafore front. Make a pattern for basket bottom, *adding* ¼-inch seam allowance. Cut two baskets from gingham and one from medium-weight interfacing. From remaining gingham, cut an 8½" × 1"-wide bias strip for basket handle. From print, cut bonnet back, two brims, two 1½" × 15" ties and 1¼-inch-wide bias strips to make a 3¼-yard length. Cut bonnet brim from stiff interfacing. For doll, trace most patterns from book. Cut two brims and a 3-inch-diameter circle for bonnet back from print, two dress pieces, and four sleeves from coordinating print, four shoes from solid fabric, and two hands and a 2¾-inch-diameter circle from muslin.

PINAFORE

Baste or fuse interfacing to one basket bottom. Right sides together, stitch basket bottom pieces, leaving an opening along straight edge for turning. Trim and clip seam allowance along curves. Turn right-side-out. Turn under edges of opening. Topstitch along lines of rim of basket. Pin basket bottom to front. Make single-fold seam binding from gingham bias strip, following instructions in the how-to chapter. Press and stretch bias strip into a curve along lines of basket handle on front, tucking ends under basket bottom. Stitch along edge of each edge of handle and along side and lower edge of basket bottom.

Cut two 1¼-inch-wide strips of medium-weight interfacing the length of pinafore center back edge. Baste or fuse interfacing to wrong side of center, ¼ inch from edge. Fold ¼ inch to wrong side of back edge over interfacing; stitch along edge. See Diagram 1. Fold center back under along inner edge of interfacing; baste along top and lower edges.

Following instructions in the how-to chapter, make piping from cording and bias strips of print fabric. Stitch all seams of pinafore, bloomers, and bonnet with right sides together, using ⅝-inch seams, as follows (use zipper foot to stitch all seams with piping):

Baste piping to lower edge of yoke front and backs. Gather top edge of front to fit front yoke between notches; stitch seam. Gather top edge of backs to fit back yokes between notch and dot; stitch seam. Grade seam allowances, following instructions in the how-to chapter; press toward yoke. Stitch fronts to back at shoulder seams. Stitch piping along neck edge and armhole edge of yoke. See Diagram 2. Gather ruffle to fit armhole edge of yokes, matching dot to shoulder seam. Stitch in place.

For yoke lining, stitch backs to front at shoulder seams. Press under ⅝ inch along armhole and lower edges. Stitch lining to yoke along center back and neck edge. Trim and clip seam allowance.

Stitch pinafore front to backs along side seams. Zigzag-finish seam allowances. Press open one edge of bias tape. Right sides together, pin bias tape to armhole edge of front and back, placing crease along seam line and easing tape around curve. See Diagram 3. Stitch along seam line. Trim seam allowance to ¼ inch; clip along curves. Turn bias tape to wrong side. Slipstitch lower edge of front and backs. Slipstitch lining to yoke along lower and armhole edges.

Stitch piping to lower edge of pinafore. Narrowly hem ends of a 2-yard length of eyelet edging. Gather top edge of eyelet edging evenly to fit lower edge of pinafore; stitch in place. Press open one fold on bias tape. Pin, then stitch, crease along seam line of lower edge over eyelet ruffle and piping. See Diagram 4. Trim tape ½ inch from end of seam. Grade seam allowance of eyelet fabric, piping, and eyelet ruffle. Turn in ends even with center

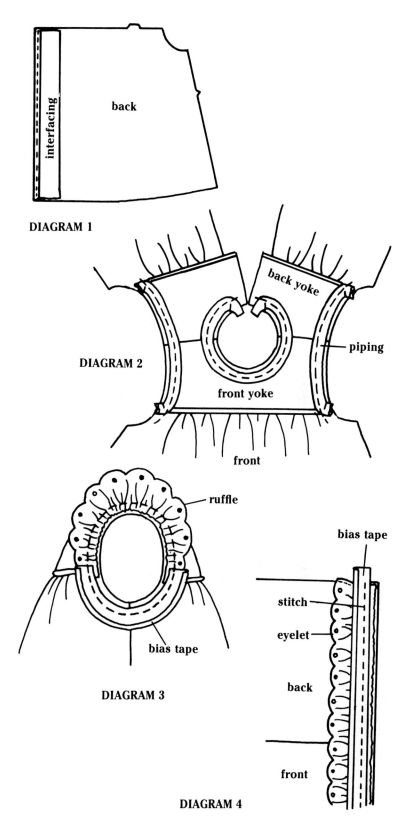

DIAGRAM 1

DIAGRAM 2

DIAGRAM 3

DIAGRAM 4

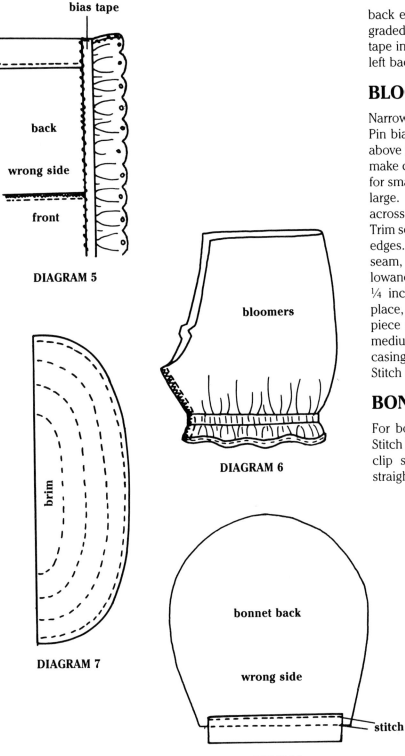

bias tape

back

wrong side

front

DIAGRAM 5

brim

DIAGRAM 7

bloomers

DIAGRAM 6

bonnet back

wrong side

stitch

DIAGRAM 8

back edge, and fold bias tape to wrong side over graded seam allowance. Slipstitch top edge of bias tape in place. See Diagram 5. Make buttonholes in left back. Sew buttons to right back along center.

BLOOMERS

Narrowly hem long lower edge of bloomer pieces. Pin bias tape to wrong side of each piece ¾ inch above finished edge. Stitch along edges of tape to make casing. Cut two pieces of elastic, 10¼ inches for small, 11 inches for medium, or 11¾ inches for large. Insert elastic through casing and stitch across ends. Stitch inside leg seams of each piece. Trim seam allowance to ¼ inch; zigzag-stitch along edges. See Diagram 6. Stitch bloomers along center seam, matching inside leg seams. Trim seam allowance to ¼ inch; zigzag-finish edges. Turn under ¼ inch, then ⅜ inch along top edge. Stitch in place, leaving an opening at center back. Cut a piece of elastic, 17 inches for small, 18 inches for medium, or 19 inches for large. Insert elastic into casing. Overlap ends ½ inch and stitch together. Stitch opening in casing closed.

BONNET

For bonnet, stitch interfacing to one brim piece. Stitch brims together along curved edge. Grade and clip seam allowance. Turn right-side-out. Baste straight edges together. Topstitch ¼ inch from

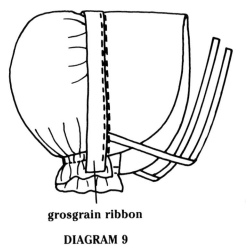

grosgrain ribbon

DIAGRAM 9

curved edge and then every 1 inch across brim. See Diagram 7. Press under ¼ inch on straight edge of bonnet back. Fold straight edge to right side along fold line. Stitch along side from fold to dot. Clip to dot. Trim seam allowance. Turn right-side-out. To make casing, stitch along top of flap and again ⅜ inch below. See Diagram 8. Cut a length of elastic 5 inches for small, 5½ inches for medium, or 6 inches for large. Insert elastic in casing so ends are even with outer edge of seam allowance; stitch across end of casing. Gather curved edge of back evenly to fit brim; stitch seam. Fold ties in half lengthwise; stitch along long edge and one end. Trim seam allowance; turn right-side-out. Baste a tie to seam of bonnet ½ inch from lower edge. Stitch 1-inch-wide ribbon over seam of bonnet. See Diagram 9. Turning under ends, fold ribbon to back; stitch ends to casing. See Diagram 10.

DOLL

For doll, stitch seams right sides together, using ¼-inch seam allowance, as follows:

Stitch shoes together in pairs, leaving straight end open. Trim and clip seam allowance; turn right-side-out. Stuff shoes; stitch straight ends together. Stitch dress pieces together, leaving an opening between dots. Clip and trim seam allowance. Turn right-side-out. Stuff dress. Insert both shoes in opening. See Diagram 11. Slipstitch edge together and to shoes. Sew lace around dress ¼ inch from lower edge.

Fold hands in half; stitch curved seam. Trim seam allowance to ⅛ inch. Turn right-side-out. Stuff hands slightly. Baste hands to lower edges of two sleeve pieces. See Diagram 12. Stitch sleeves together in pairs, leaving an opening between dots. Clip seam allowance; turn right-side-out. Stuff arms. Slipstitch edges of opening together. Sew lace around lower edge of sleeve. Sew arms to body.

Using doubled thread, turn under ¼ inch around muslin circle; make a row of gathering stitches by hand along edge. Gather edge over a ball of stuffing. Knot thread and sew edges together so head is slightly oval. See Diagram 13. Draw face on smooth side. Embroider eyes in brown satin stitch and mouth in red fly stitch. Sew head to body. See Diagram 14.

Stitch bonnet brims together along curved edge. Clip and trim seam allowance. Turn right-side-out. Place brim around head and stitch it in place along straight edge. Using doubled thread, turn under ¼ inch on bonnet back and make a row of tiny gathering stitches. Gather bonnet back over back of head. Slipstitch back to brim and dress. See Diagram 15. Make a small bow with red ribbon; tack bow to lower edge of bonnet brim.

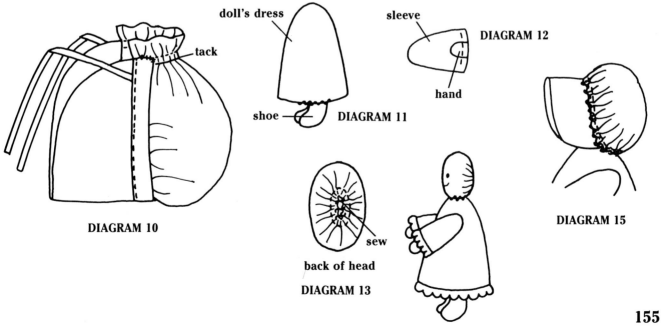

tack

DIAGRAM 10

doll's dress

shoe

DIAGRAM 11

sleeve

hand

DIAGRAM 12

back of head

DIAGRAM 13

sew

DIAGRAM 14

DIAGRAM 15

155

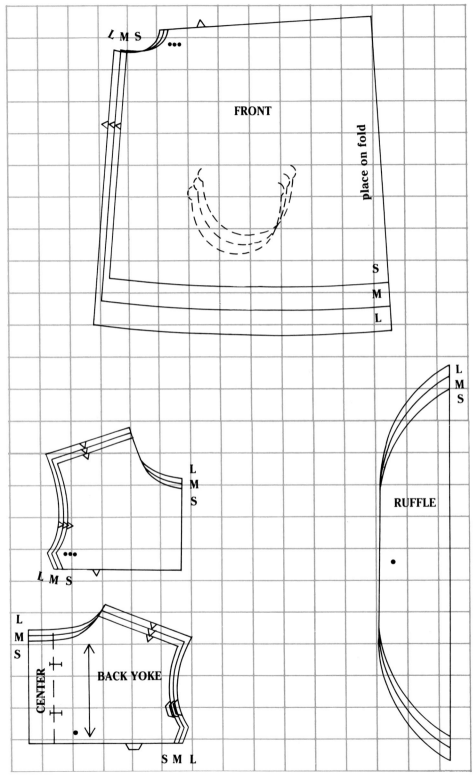

FRONT

place on fold

S
M
L

L M S
•••

RUFFLE

L
M
S

L
M
S

L M S

•••

L M S

CENTER

BACK YOKE

L
M
S

L
M
S

S M L

156   1 square = 1 inch

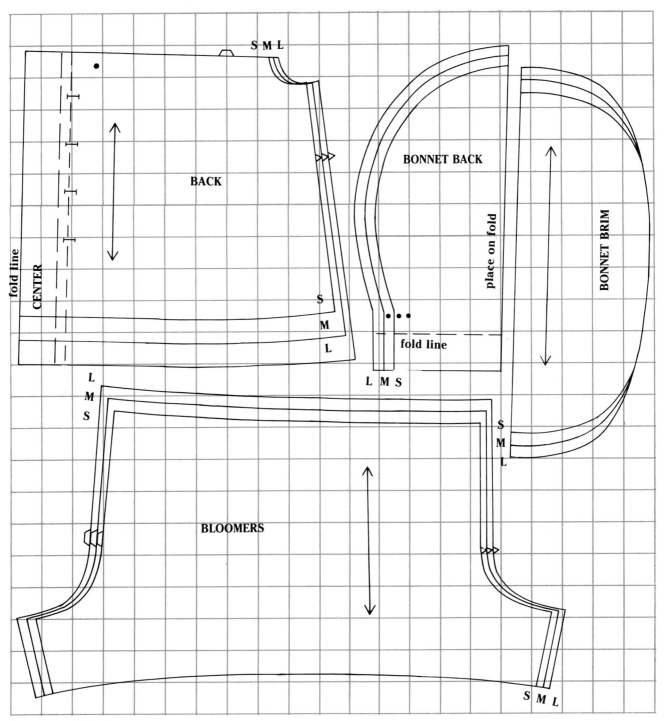

S M L

BONNET BACK

BACK

fold line

CENTER

place on fold

BONNET BRIM

S
M
L

L M S

fold line

L
M
S

S
M
L

BLOOMERS

S M L

1 square = 1 inch

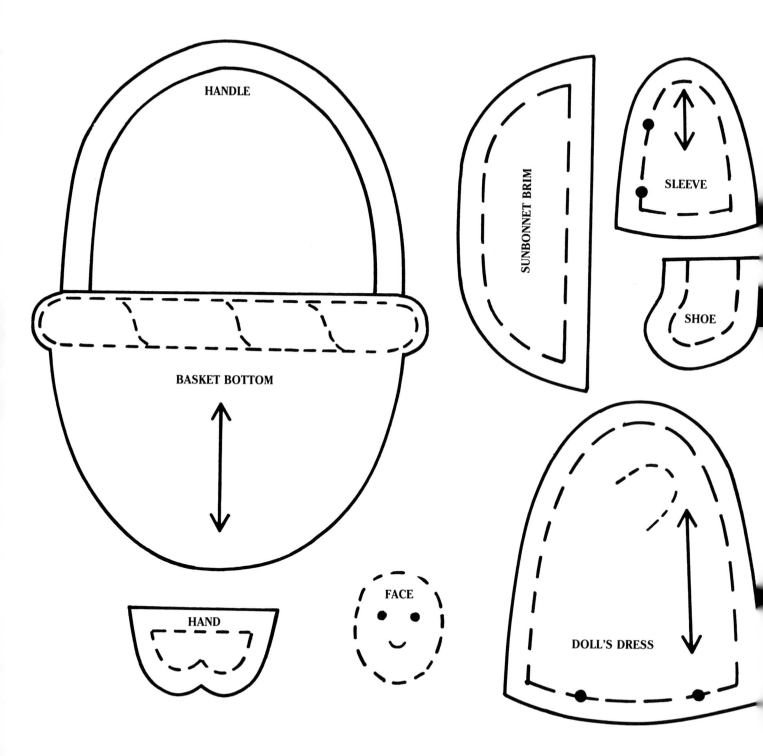

HANDLE

SUNBONNET BRIM

SLEEVE

SHOE

BASKET BOTTOM

HAND

FACE

DOLL'S DRESS

158

Sailboat Sunsuit and Hat

Here's a classic sunsuit for a picture-perfect little boy. The appliquéd sailboat pocket holds a nautical teddy bear. Made of light blue-and-white striped seersucker, the sunsuit has a snap crotch. And the white piqué hat has nautical buttons that match the sunsuit.

SIZES:

For sunsuit: small (12 months), medium (18 months), large (24 months); for hat, measure diameter of head: small (18 inches), medium (19 inches), large (20 inches)

MATERIALS:

For sunsuit:

45"-wide light blue-and-white striped seersucker or light blue poplin, cotton twill or other medium-weight fabric: ⅞ yard for small and medium and 1 yard for large

Scraps of white, blue, brown, red-and-white striped, and red print fabric

Handful of polyester stuffing

⅜ yard 21"-wide interfacing

Scraps of fusible webbing

½ yard each red and black six-strand embroidery floss

⅜ yard light blue or white bias tape

Sewing thread to match fabrics, plus bright yellow

6" piece ¼"-wide blue ribbon

Two ⅝"-diameter buttons with anchor design

3 size 16 snap fasteners

For hat:

½ yard white seersucker, piqué, or other medium-weight fabric

½ yard white medium-to-stiff woven interfacing

White thread

⅝ yard 1"-wide white grosgrain ribbon

⅜ yard ¼"-wide polyester elastic

Three ⅝" buttons with anchor design

Enlarge pattern for the size of sunsuit you wish to make, following instructions in the how-to chapter. Note that ⅝-inch seam allowances are included on patterns. With fabric folded in half, cut two fronts, two backs, one front facing, and one back facing. Cut front and back interfacing pieces. Lightly trace sailboat design in position on left front of sunsuit. Trace patterns for the flag, sail, jib, sailor bear, collar, and boat, *adding* ¼-inch seam allowance to boat only. Cut two boats from red print, flag from blue, sail and collar from white, and jib from red-and-white stripe. Trace bear to one half of brown fabric, leaving ¼-inch seam allowance around shape. With fabric folded double, cut out bears ¼ inch beyond line.

SUNSUIT

Following instructions for machine-appliqué in the how-to chapter, apply fusible webbing to wrong side of sail, flag, and jib. Fuse pieces in place on left front. Using matching thread, zigzag-stitch along edges of pieces. Zigzag along line of mast, using bright yellow thread. Right sides in, sew boat pieces together, leaving an opening for turning between dots. Trim and clip seam allowance; turn right-side-out. Slipstitch opening closed. Topstitch along upper edge of boat. Pin boat on left front. Stitch along edge of sides, bottom, and 1¼ inches of top edge at front of boat.

To make sunsuit, stitch all seams right sides together, using ⅝-inch seam allowance unless otherwise indicated, as follows: Stitch fronts together and backs together along center seam. Trim seam allowance below notches to ¼ inch; zigzag-stitch along edge. Press remaining seam allowance open and zigzag-finish edges. Baste front interfacing to wrong side of front. Trim corners of back interfacing ¼ inch inside seam allowance; baste in place on wrong side of back. Stitch fronts to backs along side seams; zigzag-finish edges.

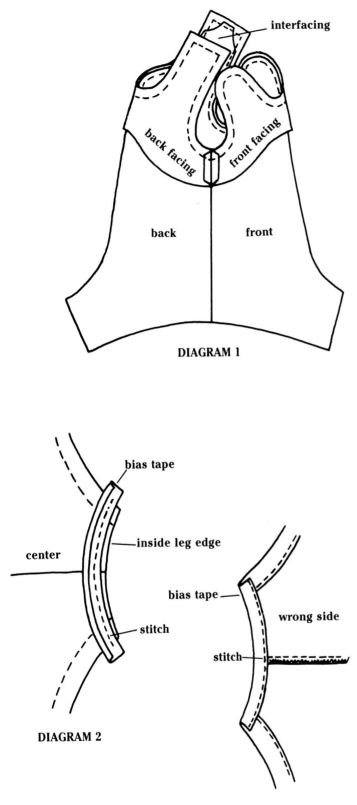

DIAGRAM 1

DIAGRAM 2

DIAGRAM 3

Stitch front facing to back facing along side seams. Finish lower edge of facing with zigzag stitch or press ¼ inch to wrong side and stitch in place.

Pin and then stitch facing to sunsuit, matching side seams and notches. See Diagram 1. Trim corners. Grade and clip seam allowance along curves, following instructions in the how-to chapter. Press facing to inside of sunsuit; topstitch ⅛ inch from edge. Tack lower edge of facing to side seams.

Press ¼ inch to wrong side on lower edge of legs. Then turn up a 1-inch hem; Press in place. Machine-stitch or slipstitch hem in place. Cut bias tape in half across width; lightly press open one fold of bias tape. Place open fold along right side of inside leg edge on both back and front. Stitch along line of fold ¼ inch from edge. See Diagram 2. Turn in ends and fold bias tape to wrong side. Stitch along inner edge of bias tape. See Diagram 3. Apply snap fasteners to center and ends of inner leg edge.

Make buttonholes along lines shown on pattern piece on front shoulders. Sew buttons to dots on back. As the child grows taller, move buttons toward end of backs to lengthen shoulder space.

SAILOR BEAR

Pin, and then stitch bear pieces together along line, leaving an opening between dots. Trim seam allowance to ⅛ inch and clip curves. Turn right-side-out. Stuff bear. Slipstitch opening closed. Using doubled brown thread, quilt along broken line between head and ears. Using three strands of floss, embroider eyes and nose in black satin stitch and mouth in red backstitch. Turn under the ⅛-inch seam allowance on collar; stitch along edge. Place collar on bear and sew pointed ends together at center front. Tie a small bow with blue ribbon and sew in place over ends of collar.

HAT

For hat, measurements are given for size 18 with sizes 19 and 20 in brackets. Stitch all seams with right sides together, using ¼-inch seam allowance (which is included in pattern and measurements).

Trace pattern for size crown you wish to make. From white fabric, cut a bias strip 4″ × 22½″

[23½″—24½″] for brim. See Diagram 4. Cut six crown pieces from white fabric. From interfacing, cut brim same size as fabric brim, and a circle 11½″ [12″—12½″] inches in diameter.

For each half of crown, stitch three crown pieces together along long edges. Then stitch halves together along center seam. On interfacing circle, mark edges about every 5¾″ [6″—6¼″] so that there are six marks evenly spaced. At each mark, make a dart-shaped pleat of a little over an inch deep, so interfacing will fit inside hat. See Diagram 5. Baste tucks in place. Place interfacing in hat so a pleat is under each seam; baste together along edges. Baste interfacing to wrong side of brim. Sew ends together. Fold in half lengthwise; baste ¼ inch from edge. Using an iron, stretch and press outer edge while easing inner edge to fit 18″ (19″—20″) hat. See Diagram 6. Topstitch around brim at ¼-inch intervals. With seam of brim at center back, sew brim to crown. Baste ends of an 11½″ [12″—12½″] piece of elastic to center of each side section for chin strap. Place grosgrain ribbon along seam allowance with edge just inside stitching. See Diagram 7. Sew in place, turning under one end of ribbon to finish neatly. Sew buttons to seams of the two front sections ¼ inch above brim.

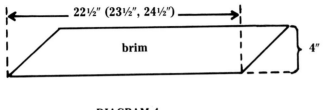

DIAGRAM 4

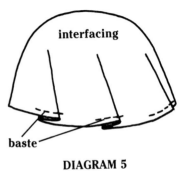

DIAGRAM 5

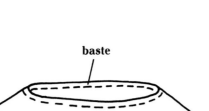

DIAGRAM 6

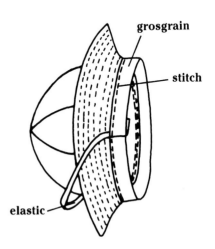

DIAGRAM 7

162

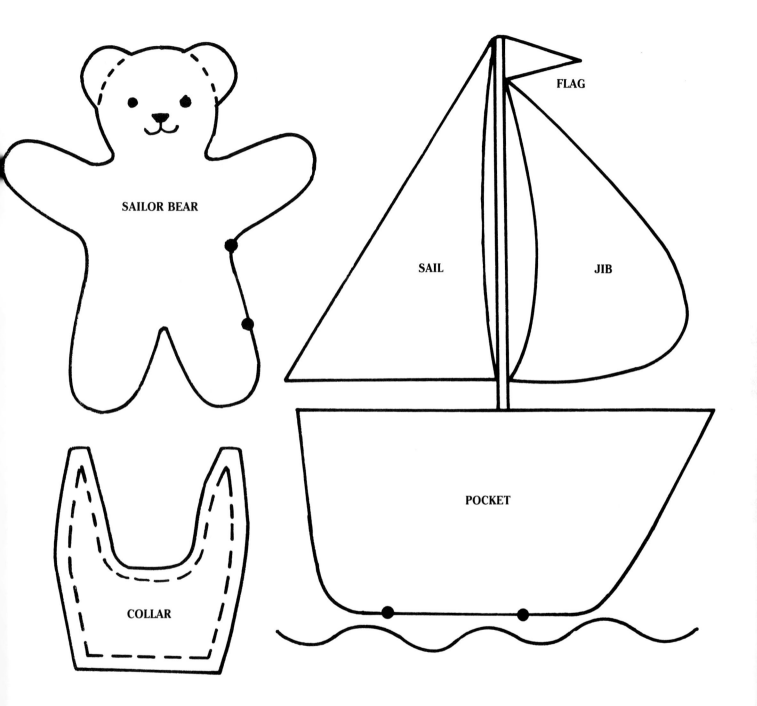

SAILOR BEAR

FLAG

SAIL

JIB

COLLAR

POCKET

163

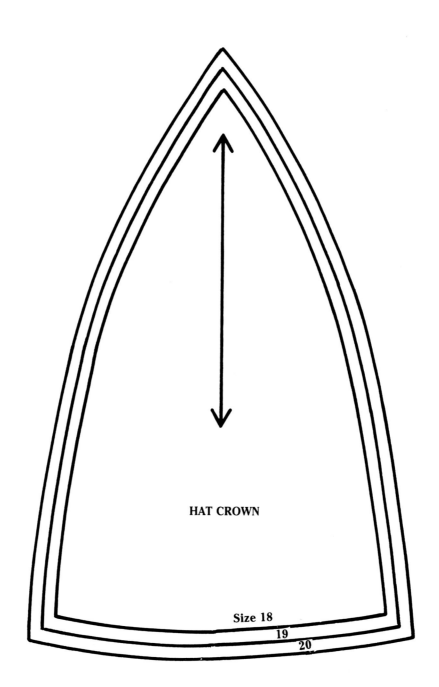

HAT CROWN

Size 18

19

20

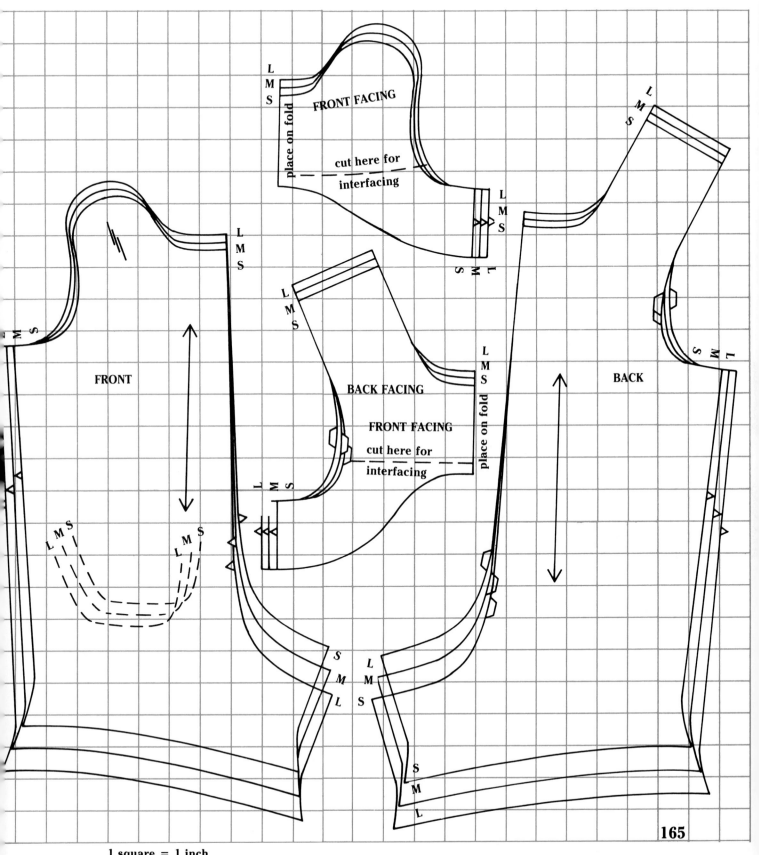

FRONT FACING

place on fold

cut here for interfacing

FRONT

BACK FACING

FRONT FACING

cut here for interfacing

place on fold

BACK

165

1 square = 1 inch

Down-On-The-Farm Overalls

These classic bib overalls in denim are decorated with favorite farm animals. A tiny appliquéd cow, pig, and duck are at home in a pasture made of bright-colored fabric. Snap fasteners along the edges of the inside leg allow for quick diaper changes.

SIZES:

Small (6–9 months), medium (12 months), large (18 months), and extra-large (24 months)

MATERIALS:

45″-wide blue denim fabric: for small size, 1 yard; medium and large sizes, 1⅛ yards; extra-large size, 1¼ yards

⅛ yard green fabric with white dots

¼ yard blue cotton fabric

Scraps of yellow, red, brown, off-white, tan, and white fabric for appliqués

6″ square fusible webbing

1½ yards blue bias tape

Sewing thread to match fabrics

⅜-yard ¾″-wide elastic

Two ⅝″-diameter white buttons

8 snap fasteners

Enlarge the pattern for the size overalls you wish to make, following instructions in the how-to chapter. Note that ⅝-inch seam allowances are included on patterns. Trace the section of the bib below the curved broken line to make pattern for hillside pasture. Following instructions for machine-appliqué in the how-to chapter, make patterns for appliqué animals.

From denim, cut two fronts, two backs, one bib, one waistband, two upper pockets, and two shoulder straps. From blue cotton, cut one bib, two pockets, and one waistband. From green, cut two leg border strips, 2¼″ × 13½″, and hillside. Cut barn from red; silo, duck's bill, and feet from yellow; cow from brown; spots from off-white; pig from tan; and duck from white. Cut fusible webbing for appliqué pieces.

Baste hillside to denim bib. Fuse appliqué pieces on bib. Stitch hillside and appliqué pieces in place with zigzag-stitch. Stitch roof and door of barn and cow's horn with white thread and all other shapes with matching thread. Stitch cow's tail in brown zigzag-stitch with straight-stitch lines at end. By hand, embroider eyes in black and white satin stitch and mouth in red backstitch.

Sew all seams right sides together, using ⅝-inch seam allowance unless otherwise indicated, as follows:

Stitch lining to bib. Trim seam allowance. Turn right-side-out. With white thread, topstitch ⅛ inch from the top and side edges and again ¼ inch from first row of stitching. Baste bib to center of one long edge of waistband. Stitch waistband to waistband lining along edge with bib. Trim seam allowance. Press waistband piece away from bib. See Diagram 1.

Right sides up, baste upper pockets to pocket pieces above curved line; zigzag-stitch along curved edge. See Diagram 2. Stitch pocket to front of overalls along curved edge. See Diagram 3. Trim and clip seam allowance. Press pocket to wrong side of fronts along curved seam line. Topstitch ⅛ inch from edge and again ¼ inch from first row of stitching. Wrong sides together, fold pocket in half and stitch lower edges together. See Diagram 4. Fold pocket to inside so upper and side edges are even with front; baste edges together. See Diagram 5.

Stitch fronts together along center seam. Trim seam allowance to ¼ inch; zigzag-finish edges. Stitch lower edge of waistband to top of joined front. Trim seam allowance. Turn under seam allowance of lining; baste edge in place along seam line. From right side, using white thread, topstitch ⅛ inch from upper and lower edge of waistband.

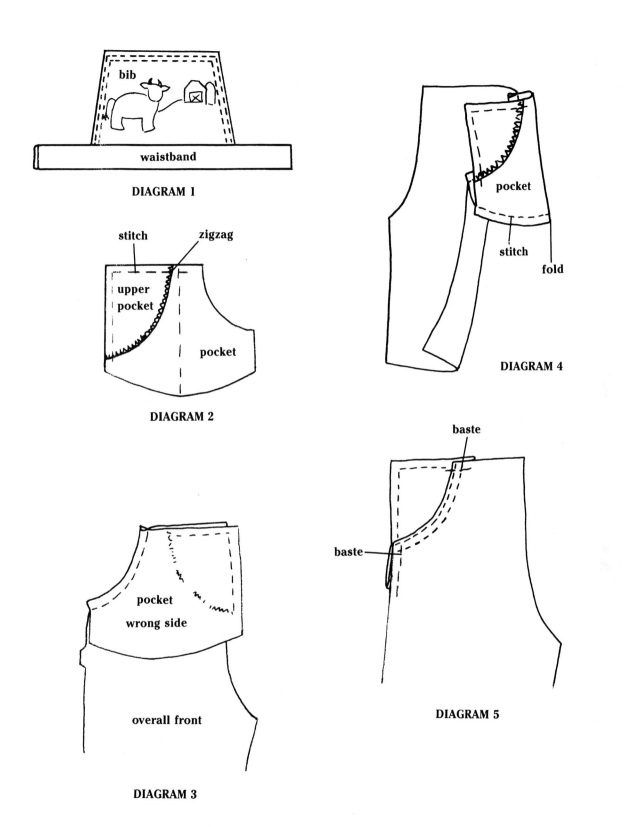

DIAGRAM 1

bib

waistband

DIAGRAM 2

stitch

zigzag

upper
pocket

pocket

DIAGRAM 3

pocket

wrong side

overall front

DIAGRAM 4

pocket

stitch

fold

DIAGRAM 5

baste

baste

Stitch backs together along center seam. Trim seam to ¼ inch; zigzag-finish edges. Press under ¼ inch, then 1 inch along top waist edge. Using white thread, stitch ⅛ inch from top and bottom to form a casing. Cut the length of elastic needed for the size you are making: small, 8½ inches; medium, 9 inches; large, 9½ inches; and extra large, 10 inches. Insert elastic into casing. Stitch to secure elastic, ¾ inch from ends of casing. Trim excess elastic from side seam allowance. Using white thread, stitch fronts and backs together at sides. Make a flat-felled seam, following instructions in the how-to chapter.

Trim leg border strips to length of lower edge of legs. Fold strips in half across width; trim top edge into a curve. See Diagram 6. Wrong side up, stitch straight edge of green border to lower edge of wrong side of legs. See Diagram 7. Trim seam allowance. Press border to right side. Baste upper edge to legs. Fuse animals in place on center front of borders. Zigzag-stitch hillside and animals in place, using matching thread. Stitch pig's tail with

tan and duck's wing with yellow. Hand-embroider pig's eye in black and white satin stitch, nose in black straight stitch, and mouth in red straight stitch. Embroider duck's eye in black satin stitch.

Press open one fold of bias tape piece 1 inch longer than inside leg seam. Beginning ½ inch from end of tape, place opened fold along inside leg seam ¼ inch from edge; stitch along crease. Fold bias tape to wrong side, turning under ends. Stitch along long inner edge. Insert four snap fasteners along each leg. See Diagram 8.

Fold shoulder straps in half lengthwise. Stitch along one end and long edge. Trim seam allowance; turn right-side-out. Zigzag-finish unfinished end. Topstitch ⅛ inch from long edges and seamed end, using white thread. Place 2 inches of straps under back edge, 1½ inches from center seam with elastic stretched. Stitch along top and bottom of casing. Make ⅝-inch-long horizontal buttonholes on bib, ½ inch from top edge and ⅜ inch in from side edge. Sew buttons to shoulder straps 1½ to 2 inches from ends.

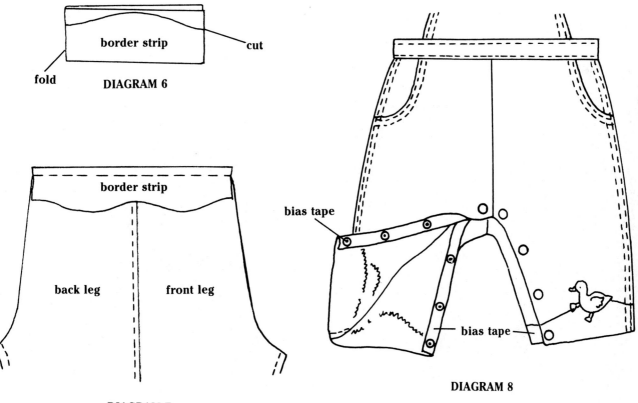

DIAGRAM 6

fold

border strip — cut

DIAGRAM 7

border strip

back leg — front leg

DIAGRAM 8

bias tape

bias tape

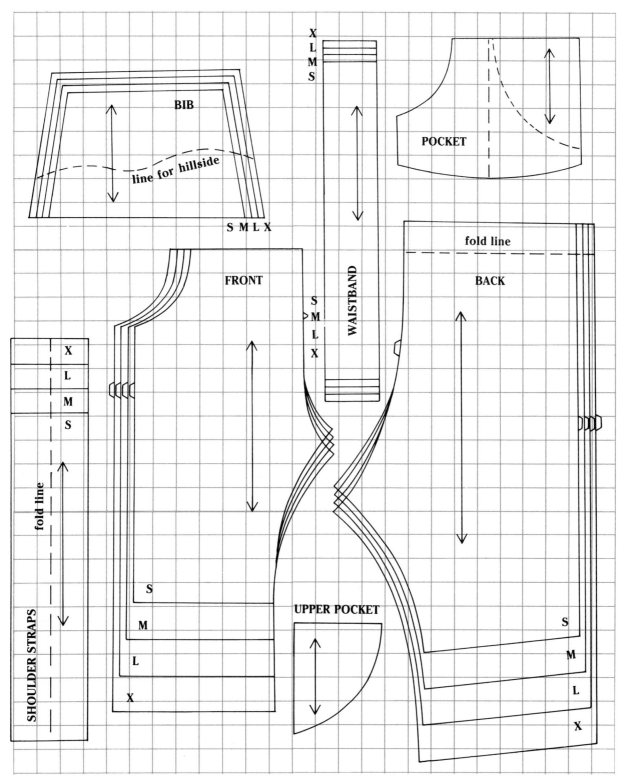

BIB

line for hillside

S M L X

X
L
M
S

POCKET

fold line

BACK

FRONT

WAISTBAND

S
M
L
X

X
L
M
S

fold line

SHOULDER STRAPS

S

M

L

X

UPPER POCKET

S

M

L

X

Striped, Hooded Sweater

Bold and bright, this sweater has a sporty style that is perfect for a stroller ride to the playground or even a trip to the grocery store on a cool, windy day. Simple shaping and basic crochet stitches make it easy for beginners.

SIZES:
6 months [12 months—18 months—24 months]
Chest measurement of finished garment: 20″ [22″—23″—24″]

MATERIALS:
Pingouin Pingofrance (acrylic and wool sport-weight) yarn, 3 [4—4—4] (50 gr—1¾ oz) skeins red (Main Color—MC); 1 skein each yellow (color A), blue (B), and green (C)
Aluminum crochet hooks, sizes E and F (3.50 and 4.00 mm) or sizes that give you the correct gauge
Three ⁹⁄₁₆″-diameter red buttons
Tapestry needle

GAUGE: 13 sc = 3″
Note: See page 214 for Crochet Abbreviations and Terms.

BACK: With smaller hook and color B, ch 8. *Row 1*: Sc in 2nd ch from hook and each remaining ch across (7 sc). Ch 1, turn. *Row 2*: Sc in front loop only of each sc. Ch 1, turn. Repeat row 2 for ribbing until piece measures 9″ [10″—10½″—11″]. Break off.

Turn ribbing sideways and, with larger hook and MC, work 44 [48—50—52] sc evenly spaced along long edge, working sts into ends of rows. Working through both loops of sc, work 4 more rows with MC. Now work stripe pattern as follows: * work 1 row A, 5 rows MC, 1 row C, 5 rows MC, 1 row B, 5 rows MC; repeat from * for stripe pattern. Work even until back measures 7″ [7½″—8″—8½″], or length desired to underarm.

Armholes: Next row: Sl st across first 4 sc, work to within last 4 sc. Ch 1, turn. Work even on 36 [40—42—44] sc, continuing stripes, until armhole measures 3¾″ [4″—4¼″—4½″]. Break off.

FRONT: Work same as back until piece measures 6½″ [7″—7½″—8″], or ½″ less than back to underarm.

Front opening: First side: Next row: Continuing stripes, sc in first 19 [21—22—23] sc. Ch 1, turn. *Next row*: Sc back to arm edge. *Next row*: Sl st across first 4 sc (armhole), work remaining 15 [17—18—19]. Work even in stripe pattern until armhole measures 2″ [2¼″—2½″—2¾″], ending at arm edge.

Neck: Next row: Sc in first 11 [12—13—13] sc. Ch 1, turn. *Next row*: Sl st in first sc, sc to end. Ch 1, turn. *Next row*: Sc in first 9 [10—11—11]. Ch 1, turn. Work even until armhole measures same as for back. Break off.

Second side: Next row: Skip center 6 sts, attach yarn and sc remaining 19 [21—22—23] sc. Ch 1, turn. *Next row*: Sc back to center front edge. Ch 1, turn. *Next row*: Sc in first 15 [17—18—19] sc. Ch 1, turn (armhole completed). Complete to correspond to first side.

SLEEVES: With smaller hook and C, ch 8. Work same as for back ribbing until piece measures 5¾″ [6″—6¼″—6½″]. Break off.

Turn ribbing sideways and, with larger hook and MC, work 26 [28—30—32] sc evenly spaced along long edge. Work 4 more rows with MC, increasing 1 sc at beg and end of last row. Continue to inc 1 sc at beg and end of row every inch 3 times more, and work stripe pattern as follows: * Work 1 row B, 5 rows MC, 1 row A, 5 rows MC, 1 row C, 5 rows MC; repeat from *. When incs are completed, work even on 34 [36—38—40] sts until sleeve measures 7½″ [8¼″—9″—9½″], or length desired to shoulder. Break off.

HOOD: With smaller hook and A, ch 7. Work ribbing of 6 sc in same manner as for back ribbing until piece measures 15″ [15½″—16″—16½″]. Break off.

Turn ribbing sideways and, with larger hook and MC, work 68 [70—72—74] sc evenly spaced along long edge. Work 4 more rows MC. Work stripe pattern as follows: * Work 1 row C, 5 rows MC, 1 row B, 5 rows MC, 1 row A, 5 rows MC; repeat from *. Work even until piece measures 4″ [4″—4¼″—4½″].

First side on back: Next row: Continuing stripes, sc in first 24 [25—26—27] sts. Ch 1, turn. Work even in stripe pattern for 2½″. Break off.

Second side: Skip center 20 sc and attach yarn. Work remaining 24 [25—26—27] sc to correspond to first side.

FINISHING: Block pieces following instructions on page 20. Sew shoulder seams. Sew sleeves to armholes. Sew sleeve and underarm seams. *Button Placket*: With smaller hook and A, ch 7. Work ribbing of 6 sc in same manner as for back ribbing until piece measures 2¾″, or length of front opening. Break off. Mark placement for 3 buttons evenly spaced on placket. *Buttonhole Placket*: Work same as for button placket, working buttonhole row opposite markers as follows: Sc in 2 sc, ch 2, skip 2 sc, sc in last 2 sc. Ch 1, turn. On next row, sc in each sc and ch (6 sc). Sew button placket to bottom and left side of opening for girl, right side for boy. With bottom end overlapping button placket, sew buttonhole placket to other side of opening. Sew on buttons.

Hood: Sew center back seam of hood. Sew top edge of back to hood, easing to fit. Sew hood to neck edge of sweater, with edge of hood ribbing ½-inch in from each front edge, easing to fit neck edge with any extra fullness on hood at center back.

BABY'S

ACCESSORIES

Bath Towel and Sponge Set

T he yellow terrycloth duck is a covered sponge that can be used for washing Baby . . . and as a bath toy. After bath time, Baby can get rub-a-dub-dubbed in this soft terrycloth hooded towel. This attractive set makes an imaginative gift for a lucky newborn.

MATERIALS:

1 yard 45″-wide white terrycloth
½ yard blue-and-white print fabric
⅛ yard yellow terrycloth
Scraps of orange and blue cotton fabric
Beige and blue six-strand embroidery floss
White, yellow, blue, and orange sewing thread
5″ × 8″ × 1″ polyurethane foam, or a bath sponge

LUCKY DUCK BATH TOWEL

From white terrycloth, cut a 36-inch square and a triangle, following Diagram 1 for hood. If you are using a velour terrycloth, one side is softer and smoother than the other: use this soft side as the wrong side of the fabric so it will be on the inside of the towel. Cut seven 1½-inch-wide bias strips from blue and white print, following instructions in the how-to chapter. Join six of them together on the straight grain. Using remaining bias strip, bind 14-inch edge of triangle, following instructions in the how-to chapter. Use ⅜-inch seam allowance for binding. Right sides out, pin the hood to one corner of the square. See Diagram 2. Trim to round the corners. Baste the hood to the square. Bind the entire edge of the towel neatly, joining the end of the binding on the straight grain.

For the appliqué, make patterns for the duck, bill, and balloons by tracing the shape outlines. Cut the duck from yellow terrycloth, two balloons from

blue fabric, and the beak from orange fabric. With the hood at the top, the appliqué will be placed on the outside corner of the right-hand side. See Diagram 3. From right corner of long edge of hood,

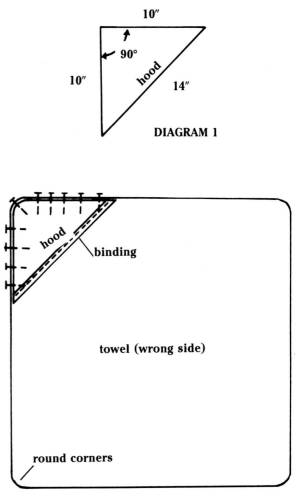

DIAGRAM 1

DIAGRAM 2

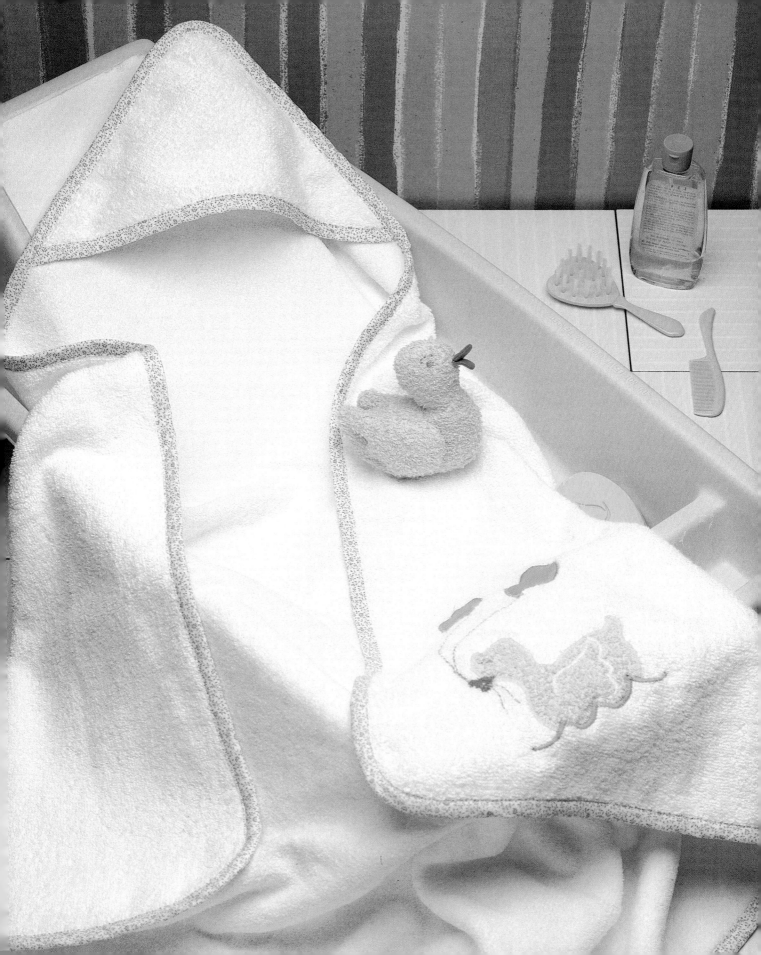

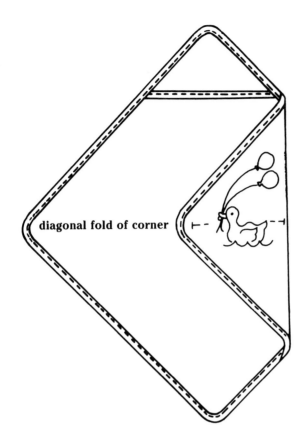

diagonal fold of corner

DIAGRAM 3

match the edges of the sides adjacent to the right-hand corner. Mark the middle of the diagonal fold for about 9 inches with a few pins. See Diagram 3. Place the appliqué pieces on the towel so the line of pins matches the broken line on the pattern and the duck is about 5 inches from the curved edge of the corner. Baste the pieces in place by hand. Mark the position of the wing with a few basting stitches. Use white thread on the bobbin for machine-appliqué and machine embroidery. Appliqué the upper edges of the duck with yellow, the balloons and the waves along the lower edge of the duck with blue, and the beak with orange. Machine-embroider the wing, using white thread. Using three strands of floss, hand-embroider the eye in blue satin stitch, and the balloon strings and the eyebrow in beige backstitch.

DUCK SPONGE

Cut two ducks, four wings, and bottom from yellow terrycloth. Cut two bills from orange cotton. Trace or transfer the seam lines to wrong side of half the pieces, if you desire. Transfer dots to wrong side. Trace along inner broken lines to make patterns for foam or sponge pieces. Cut one duck and two wings from foam or sponge.

Right sides together, stitch duck pieces together, leaving straight edge open between dots. Clip seam allowance along curves. Turn right-side-out. Insert foam inside duck, working head and tail into place. Turn under edge of bottom and lower edge of duck; baste edges in place if you desire. Matching dots, pin base to duck; slipstitch edges together securely, using doubled thread.

Stitch two sets of wings together, right sides together, leaving an opening between dots. Trim and clip seam allowance. Turn right-side-out and insert foam into wings. Slipstitch edges of opening together. Sew wings securely to body. Stitch bill pieces together, right sides together, leaving a ½-inch opening on one side. Trim and clip seam allowance. Turn right-side-out and slipstitch opening. Fold bill in half and sew fold to front of head. Tack inner layers together ⅛ inch from fold to hold the bill in place. Using three strands of floss, embroider eyes in blue satin stitch and brows in beige backstitch.

DUCK SPONGE

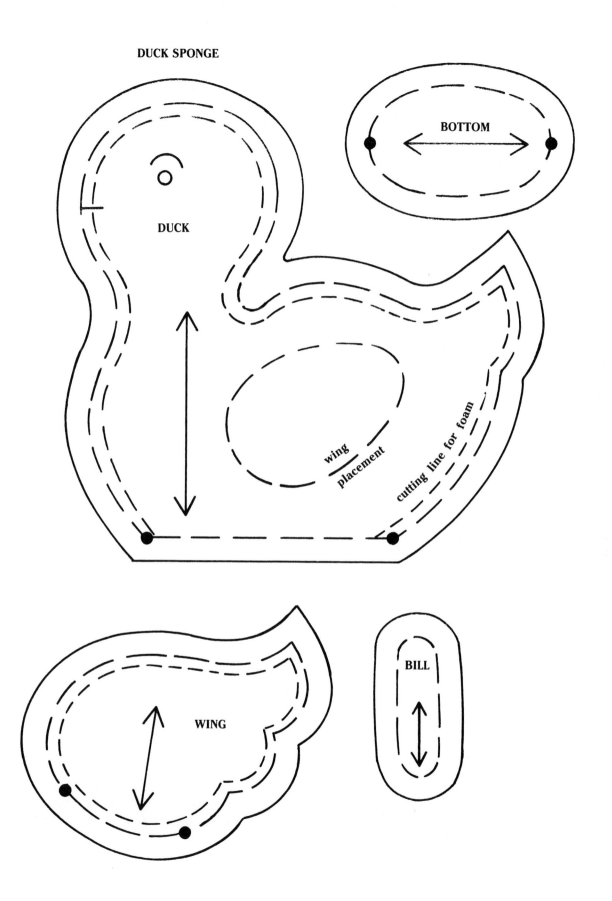

BOTTOM

DUCK

wing placement

cutting line for foam

WING

BILL

179

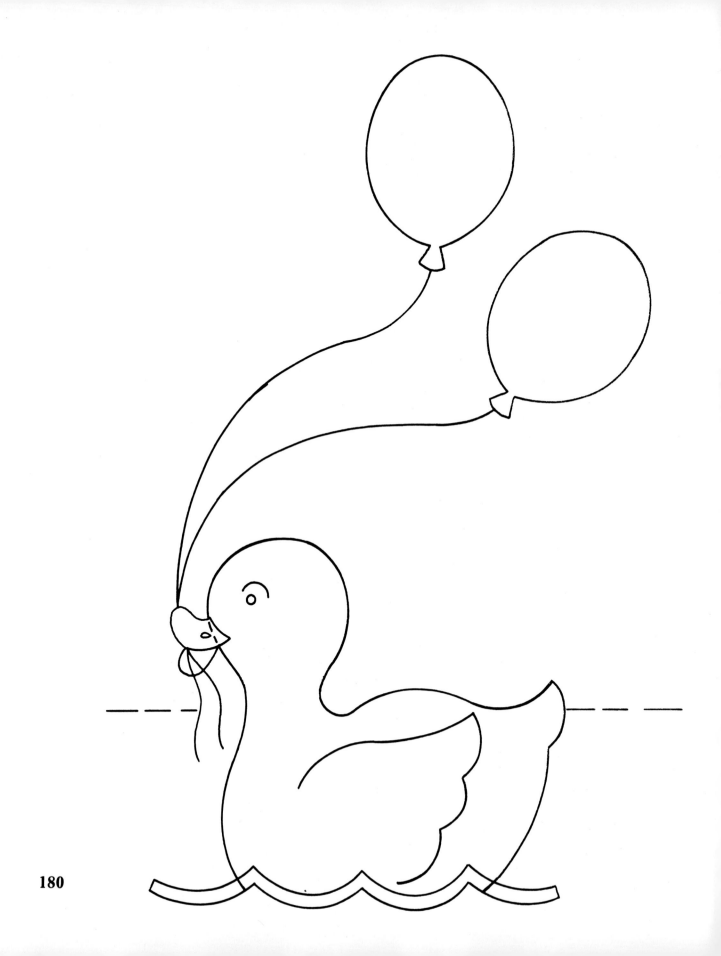

Please-Don't-Feed-the-Animals Bibs

unny, cheerful animal bibs make mealtimes friendly. Even fussy eaters will love mealtimes when the bright colors and big eyes of these bibs appear. The bibs are machine-appliquéd plain and printed cotton fabrics, and they're quilted.

BUNNY BIB

MATERIALS:
Cotton fabrics:
   ⅜ yard yellow heart-print
   5″ × 8″ scrap yellow-and-white print
   6″ square light pink
   6″ × 7″ scrap orange
   4″ × 6″ scraps green print
   Two 1¼″ × 12″ strips of green print
   2″ squares of each solid white and brown
14″ × 18″ piece quilt batting
6″ square fusible webbing
Sewing thread to match fabrics, plus bright pink

Enlarge patterns for bib, following instructions in the how-to chapter. From yellow heart print, cut two heads and four ears. Cut two muzzles from yellow-and-white print. From pink, cut two inner ears, two rosy cheeks, and one nose. Cut two carrots from orange and two leaves from green print. Cut two large eye pieces from white and small eye pieces from brown. Transfer placement markings lightly to pieces if desired. Cut fusible webbing for eyes, nose, cheeks, and inner ear pieces. From batting, cut one head, two ears, two cheeks, one muzzle, one carrot, and one leaf.

Fuse nose in position on one muzzle piece. Using matching thread, zigzag-stitch around nose. Use ¼-inch seam allowance. Baste batting to wrong side of muzzle along seam line; trim batting close to basting. Right sides facing, stitch muzzle pieces together, leaving an opening between dots. Clip seam allowance along stitching. Turn right-side-out. Slipstitch opening closed. Using bright pink thread, machine-embroider mouth with closely spaced zigzag stitches. Pin muzzle to head front; zigzag around top, using matching thread and beginning and ending ¼ inch from mouth. For cheeks, trim ³⁄₁₆ inch from batting pieces. Place them in center of cheek area on head front. Fuse cheeks to head front over batting; zigzag-stitch around cheeks. Fuse large white, then small brown eye pieces to head front. Zigzag around edges and along lines for eyelashes with brown thread. Baste head front to batting along seam line.

Fuse inner ears to right side of ear front pieces so there is both a left and a right ear. Zigzag-stitch around inner ear. Baste ear fronts to batting; trim batting close to basting. Right sides together, stitch ear fronts to backs, leaving lower edge open. Clip seam allowance along stitching; turn right-side-out. Baste along lower seam line. Machine-quilt along inner ear, using 8–10 straight machine stitches per inch.

Right sides together, baste ears to top of head front between dots. Right sides facing, with ears between layers, stitch head front to back, leaving an opening for turning between dots at lower edge. Clip seam allowance. Turn right-side-out. Slipstitch opening closed. Machine-quilt around muzzle and cheeks. Mouth edge of muzzle is not stitched to head.

Right sides facing, fold green print strips in half lengthwise for ties. Stitch across one end and along long edge. Turn right-side-out. Turn under raw edges at ends; sew in position on back of ears.

Baste carrot and leaf pieces to quilt batting; trim batting close to basting. Right sides facing, stitch carrot pieces together and then leaf pieces to-

gether, leaving openings between dots. Turn right-sides-out. Shred a little batting from scraps and stuff leaves lightly. Turn side edge of leaves under; slipstitch edges together. Topstitch along broken lines of carrot and leaves. Insert end of leaves into top of carrot; slipstitch them together securely. Slip carrot into mouth; slipstitch it in place on front.

PUPPY DOG BIB

MATERIALS:
Cotton fabrics:
   ¼ yard light brown with white dots
   8″ × 12″ piece beige with brown dots
   6″ × 7″ piece yellow heart print
   2″ square each solid white and brown
   Two 1¼″ × 12″ strips blue with white dots
12″ × 18″ piece quilt batting
2″ square fusible webbing
Sewing thread to match fabrics, plus bright pink

Enlarge pattern for bib, following instructions in the how-to chapter. From light brown fabric, cut two heads and two ears. From beige with brown dots, cut two muzzles and two ears. From yellow print, cut two bones. Cut nose from brown. Cut two large eye pieces from white and two small eye pieces from brown. From batting, cut one head, one muzzle, one bone, and two ears. Cut fusible webbing for nose and eye pieces.

Fuse nose in position on one muzzle piece. Using matching thread, zigzag-stitch around nose. Use ¼-inch seam allowance. Baste batting to wrong side of muzzle; trim batting close to basting. Right sides facing, stitch muzzle pieces together, leaving an opening between dots. Clip seam allowance along stitching. Turn right-side-out. Slipstitch opening closed. Using bright pink thread, machine-embroider mouth with closely spaced zigzag stitches.

Pin muzzle to head front; zigzag around top, beginning and ending ¼ inch from mouth. Fuse large white and then small brown eye pieces to head front. Zigzag-stitch around edges and along lines for eyelashes with brown thread. Baste head front to batting along seam line.

Baste beige ear pieces to batting; trim batting close to basting. With right sides facing, stitch beige ears to light brown ears, leaving short edge open. Clip and trim seam allowance; turn right-side-out. Baste along lower seam line. With beige side down, baste ears to head front between large and small dots. Right sides facing, with ears between layers, stitch head front to back, leaving an opening for turning along one ear between large and small dots. Clip seam allowance. Turn right-side-out. Slipstitch opening closed. Machine-quilt along edges of muzzle. Mouth is not stitched to head. Fold ears to front along fold line; slipstitch in place.

Right sides facing, fold blue fabric strips in half lengthwise for ties. Stitch across one end and along long edge. Turn right-side-out. Turn raw edges under at end; sew to inner edge of fold line of ear on back of bib.

Baste one bone to batting. Stitch bone pieces together with right sides facing, leaving an opening between dots. Clip seam allowance. Turn right-side-out. Shred a little batting from scraps and stuff bone lightly. Slipstitch opening closed. Topstitch ¼ inch from outer edge of bone. Slip bone into mouth and slipstitch it in place on front.

PANDA BIB

MATERIALS:
Cotton fabrics:
   8″ × 22″ piece solid white
   8″ × 10″ piece black with white dots
   5″ × 8″ piece green-and-white print
   1″ square solid light blue
   Two 1¼″ × 12″ strips pink print
18″ × 8″ piece quilt batting
3″ × 6″ piece fusible webbing
Sewing thread to match fabrics, plus bright pink

Enlarge pattern for bib, following instructions in the how-to chapter. From white, cut two heads, two muzzles and two large eye pieces. From black with white dots, cut four ears, two eye patches, and one nose. From light blue, cut two small eye pieces. Cut four bamboo shoots from green-and-white print. Transfer placement markings lightly to pieces, if desired. Trace seam line to wrong side of two bamboo shoot pieces. From batting, cut one head, two ears, and one muzzle. Cut fusible webbing for large and small eye pieces, eye patches and nose.

Fuse nose in position on one muzzle piece; using matching thread, zigzag-stitch around nose.

Baste batting to wrong side of muzzle along seam line; trim batting close to basting. Right sides facing, stitch muzzle pieces together, leaving an opening between dots. Clip seam allowance along stitching. Turn right-side-out. Slipstitch opening closed. Using bright pink thread, machine-embroider mouth with closely spaced zigzag stitches.

Pin muzzle to head front; zigzag-stitch around top, using matching thread and beginning and ending at mouth. Fuse eye patches and large and small eye pieces in position on head front. Zigzag-stitch around each shape, using matching thread. With black thread, zigzag-embroider pupil of eye in center of blue eye section. Baste head front to batting along seam line.

Baste two ear pieces to batting along seam line; trim batting close to basting. With right sides facing, stitch remaining ears to padded ears along outer curve. Clip seam allowance along stitching; turn right-side-out. Baste edges together along lower seam line. Machine-quilt along broken line of ear. Baste ears to head front between markings. Right sides facing, with ears between layers, stitch head front to back, leaving an opening for turning between dots of one ear. Turn right-side-out. Slipstitch opening closed.

Right sides facing, fold strips of pink print in half lengthwise for ties. Stitch across one end and along long edge. Turn right-side-out. Turn under raw edges at end; sew in position on back of ear.

Stitch bamboo shoot pieces together in pairs, leaving an opening between dots. Trim and clip seam allowance. Turn right-side-out. Shred some scraps of quilt batting and stuff shoots lightly. Slipstitch opening closed. Machine-quilt along lines of shoots. Slip bamboo shoots into mouth and sew in place.

BUNNY BIB

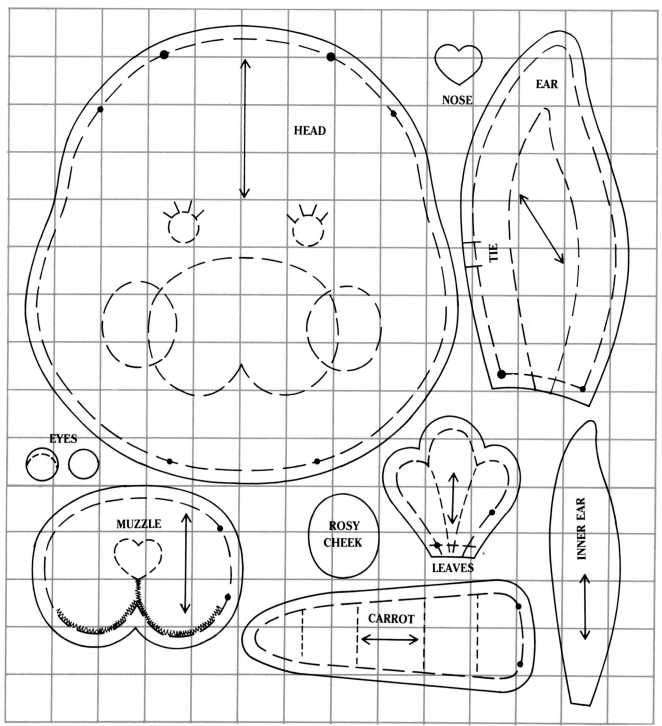

1 square = 1 inch

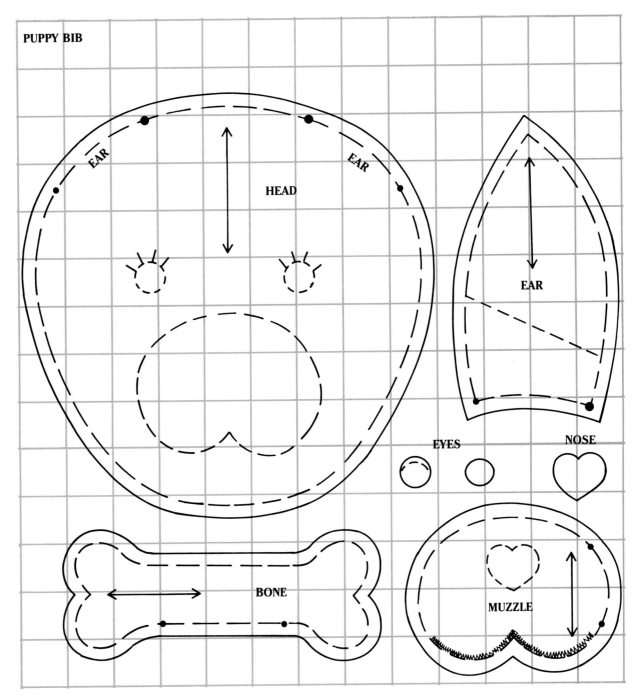

PUPPY BIB

EAR

EAR

HEAD

EAR

EYES

NOSE

BONE

MUZZLE

PANDA BIB

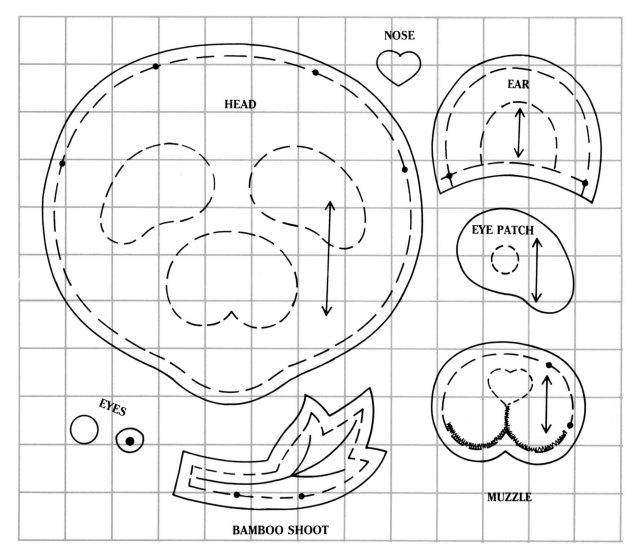

NOSE

HEAD

EAR

EYE PATCH

EYES

MUZZLE

BAMBOO SHOOT

1 square = 1 inch

Snow-Baby Bunting

T his is an extra-warm and cozy bunting. The winter snow scene is appliquéd in cotton fabrics with cool colors . . . but layers of quilt batting will keep Baby warm and happy. The bunting is an ambitious project, but well worth the time and effort.

MATERIALS:

45"-wide cotton fabrics:
1 yard light green with white hearts
1 yard solid white
¼ yard lavender-and-white print
½ yard light blue with white dots
Small pieces of solid green, pink, and light yellow
Four 29″ × 42″ pieces thick (high loft) quilt batting
8″ × 10″ piece fusible webbing
1¾ yards ½-inch wide eyelet ruffling
½ yard each light brown and pink six-strand embroidery floss
Sewing thread to match fabrics

Enlarge pattern for background pieces and appliqués, following instructions in the how-to chapter. Make patterns for each background section, *adding* ¼-inch seam allowance to the lower edges of sections A, B, and C. When cutting background sections, remember to place the center back edge on the fold. From white, cut a 29″ × 42″ piece to underline background, section B, one or two snowman pieces (if prints show through white snowman, cut two pieces and baste them together by machine along edge) and one pompon. From light green print, cut lining piece 29″ × 42″ and section C. Cut section A from light blue and section D from lavender print. From pink cut two large hearts, two small hearts, and one hat. Cut one tree from light green. Cut scarf from light yellow. Cut two 1½″ × 10½″ ties each from light blue, lavender print, and light green print. Cut fusible webbing to go behind each piece, following instructions for machine appliqué in the how-to chapter.

Pin sections A, B, C, and D on white underlining fabric with each piece overlapping the section above it. Baste along the edges of sections and ½ inch in from outer edges. Using matching thread, zigzag-stitch along top edge of sections B, C, and D. Place snowman on appliquéd background about 5 inches from lower edge and 3¼ inches from left side; fuse in place. Place hat, pompon, scarf and small hearts on snowman and fuse pieces in place. Place tree on right side of bunting 3½ inches from side with bottom of tree at top of section C. Zigzag-stitch around outer edge and inner lines of each piece, using matching thread. If desired, zigzag-stitch around lower edge of tree with white thread for more contrast with section C. Fuse a large heart to each top corner of lining 1¾ inches from edges; zigzag around edges, using pink thread.

Baste two pieces of quilt batting to wrong side of both bunting and lining. Trim batting close to stitching. Right sides up, baste eyelet ruffling to top of bunting above center dots, following curved line at corners. Make two tiny pleats at curve to add fullness. See Diagram 1. Trim seam allowance to ½ inch from stitching line at corners.

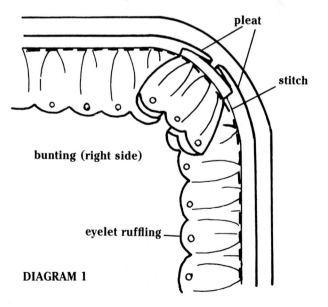

DIAGRAM 1

189

Fold ties in half lengthwise. Making ¼-inch seams, stitch along edge and across one end. Clip corner; turn right-side-out. Matching edges, baste ties to left side of bunting as follows: one light blue tie just below dot, one green tie below top of section C, and one lavender tie 2½ inches from lower edge.

Right sides together, pin and then stitch lining to bunting along top and side edges ½ inch in from edge. Turn right-side-out. Hand-baste bunting and lining together along lower edge with batting layers between them. Then hand-baste along lower edge of each appliquéd section and lower edge of snowman and tree where background is not visible.

Baste along outer edge of large hearts. Machine-quilt along basting lines, using matching thread and a stitch length of 8–10 stitches per inch.

Right sides together, fold left side (edge with ties), then right side to center back with each overlapping center back by ½ inch; pin along lower edge and curved line. Following curves at sides, stitch along lower edge. Trim and zigzag-finish seam allowance. Turn in ½ inch on raw ends of remaining ties. Sew ties to right side of bunting, matching colors and position to opposite ties on left front and sewing ends 2 inches in from center edge.

HAT

POMPON

SCARF

LARGE HEART

SMALL HEART

TREE

SNOWMAN

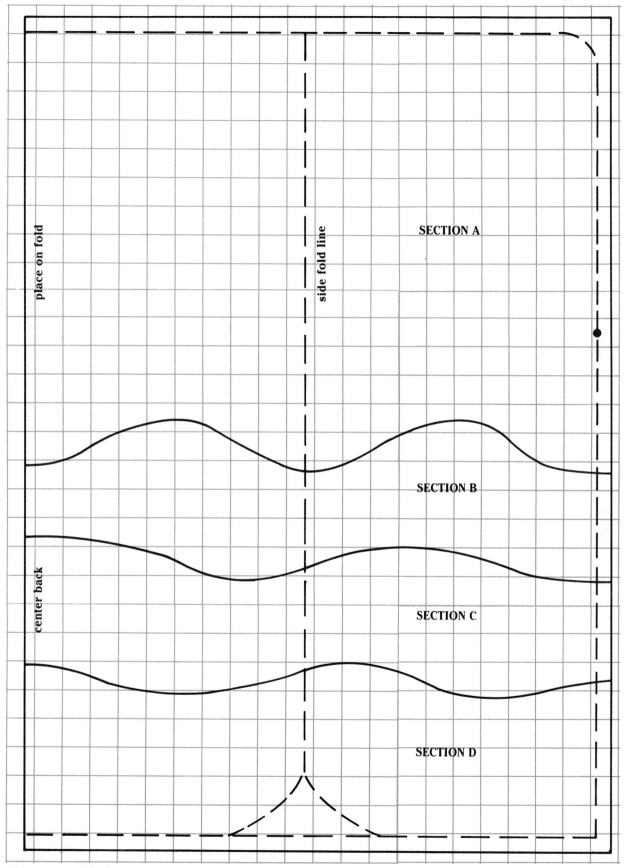

place on fold

side fold line

SECTION A

SECTION B

center back

SECTION C

SECTION D

1 square = 1 inch

Sleepy-Bear Blanket

This classic receiving blanket is doubly warm because it's made from two layers of cotton flannel. A machine-appliquéd bear decorates a corner, and the blanket is trimmed with eyelet edging. It's an easy and fun project!

MATERIALS:
1 yard each lavender and white cotton flannel
Scraps of mint green, light brown, and yellow cotton flannel or cotton fabric
7″ square fusible webbing
½ yard each pink, black, and white six-strand embroidery floss
3¾ yards 1″-wide white eyelet edging
Sewing thread to match fabric

Cut one 33″ × 33″ square each from lavender and white cotton flannel. Make patterns for appliqué pieces, following instructions for machine-appliqué in the how-to chapter. Cut one head and two paws from light brown, moon from white flannel, pajamas from mint green, and two small stars and one large star from yellow. Trace features lightly on head and trace buttons on pajamas.

Following the instructions for appliqué, fuse pieces onto upper right corner of lavender square as shown in the photograph, allowing ½ inch around edge of square for seam allowance. Clip along line between legs to fit pajama piece over moon. Zigzag-stitch around shapes and along lines of design, using matching thread.

Use two strands of floss for features. Using black, embroider long line of eyes with fly stitches and remaining lashes with tiny straight stitches. Embroider nose in black satin stitch. Using pink floss, embroider mouth with backstitch and lines on ear with straight stitch. Using three strands of white, embroider buttons with French knots.

Right sides in and beginning at corner, baste eyelet edging around lavender square ½ inch from edge, mitering remaining corners. See Diagram 1. Sew ends together along diagonal to miter corner; zigzag-finish seam allowance edges. Right sides together, sew white square to lavender square ½ inch from edge, leaving an opening for turning in center of one side. Trim seam allowance and corners; turn right-side-out. Slipstitch edges of opening together. Using white thread on bobbin and lavender thread for top thread on sewing machine, topstitch ¼ inch from edge of blanket.

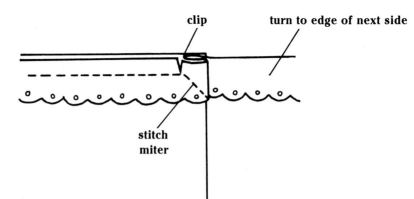

clip   turn to edge of next side

stitch
miter

DIAGRAM 1

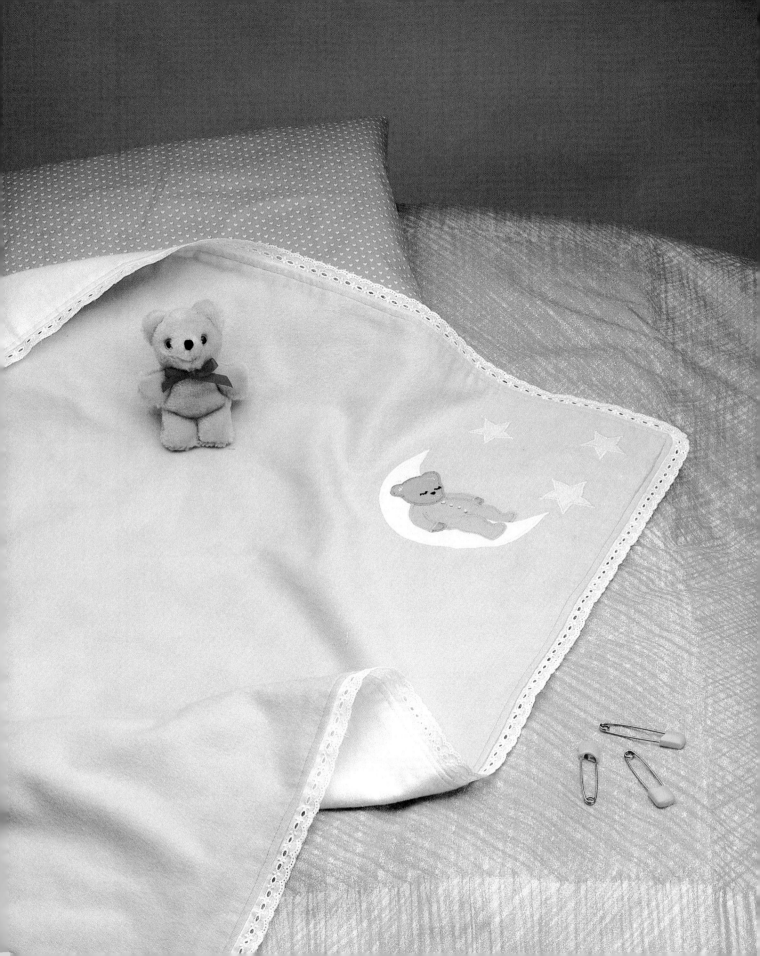

Rock-a-Bye Music Box

T his miniature rocking horse contains a music box. It's a beautiful decoration for the nursery. Although it's a bit too fragile to be a baby toy, a child over three years old can carefully play with it. Everyone will enjoy the melody . . . including Baby!

The horse is made of cotton velveteen and pearl cotton trimmed with ribbons and felt. The wooden rocker is cut from wood, then glued and painted in matching colors.

MATERIALS:

1 music box, 2″ × 2½″ × 1¼″ or smaller (available
    at craft or ceramic supply stores)
Two 15″ × 4″ pieces ³⁄₁₆″-thick pine
20″ × 4″ piece ⅛″-thick pine
¼ yard cream-colored velveteen
3″ × 6″ piece red veleveteen
5″ × 5″ square black felt
1″ × 2″ piece dusty blue felt
½ pound polyester stuffing
½ yard each black and blue six-strand embroidery
    floss
Two 15-meter skeins gold #3 pearl cotton
Off-white, black, red, and blue sewing thread
½ yard ¼″-wide red velvet ribbon
⅝ yard ¼″-wide blue satin ribbon
4 gold sequins
4″ piece ½″-diameter wooden dowel
Four ¾″-long, ⅛″-diameter screws
Dusty blue, red, and gold acrylic paint
White glue
Masking tape
TOOLS:
Drill, ¼″ and ⅛″ drill bits
Small craft saw
Screwdriver
2 small paintbrushes: one ½″-wide flat brush; one
    ⅛″-diameter brush for details
1 sheet each medium and fine sandpaper

Enlarge the pattern, following instructions in the how-to chapter. Make a pattern for the whole rocker by tracing half of rocker to each side of the center line. From cream-colored velveteen, cut two sides, four front legs, four back legs, one underbody and four ears. Transfer dots to wrong side of fabric and features to right side of fabric. Cut saddle from red velveteen. Cut four hoofs and soles from black felt. To cut wood, trace rockers onto ³⁄₁₆-inch pine. Cut out along line with craft saw. Using a pencil and ruler, draw and cut the following pieces on ⅛-inch pine: two sides, 1½″ × 3½″; two top and bottom pieces, 2¼″ × 3½″; two ends, 1½″ × 2¼″; four slats, 1¼″ × 3½″; and four braces, 1″ × 1¼″. Cut four 1″-long pieces from dowel. Transfer placement markings to inside of rocker.

Sew all seams with right sides together, using ¼-inch seam allowance unless otherwise indicated, as follows:

Stitch sides together along head and back between dots, leaving space for tail and underbody open. Stitch underbody to sides, matching dots and marks and leaving a 3-inch opening for turning between dots on one side only. See Diagram 1. Clip seam allowance along curves. Turn right-side-out. Stuff body firmly. Turn under edges along opening and slipstitch edges closed.

Stitch front legs and back legs together in pairs, leaving straight lower edges open. Clip seam allowance along curves. Turn right-side-out. Turn under ¼ inch along lower edge; baste along fold. Stuff

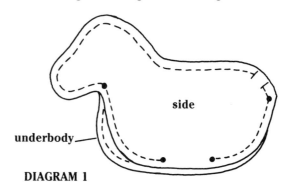

DIAGRAM 1

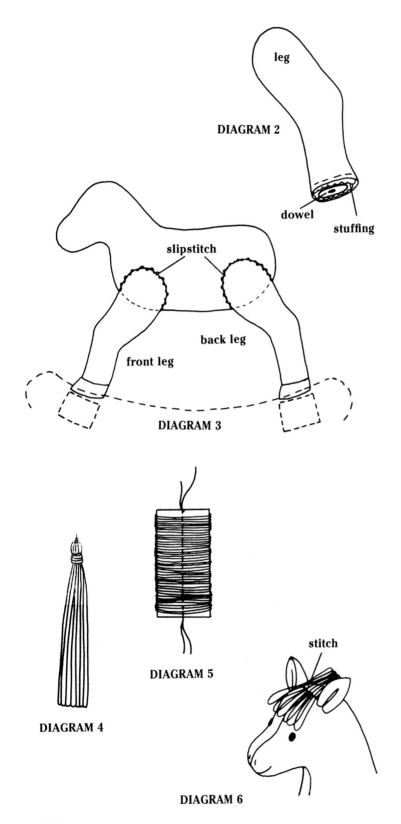

leg

DIAGRAM 2

dowel

stuffing

slipstitch

back leg

front leg

DIAGRAM 3

DIAGRAM 5

stitch

DIAGRAM 4

DIAGRAM 6

leg to 1 inch from lower edge. Drill a ⅛-inch-diameter hole in center of flat end of each dowel. Insert dowel into leg so that it is even with lower edge. Place stuffing around dowel. See Diagram 2. Whipstitch sole to bottom of leg. Place one hoof around each leg at lower edge; whipstitch to sole and leg along lower edge. Pin front and back legs on body, following placement lines. When compared to rocker pattern, legs should be in position to sit on top of small boxes indicated by broken lines. Slipstitch legs to body. See Diagram 3.

Stitch ears together in pairs, leaving straight end open. Trim seam allowance on sides to ⅛ inch and trim corner. Turn seam allowance under along lower edges; slipstitch edges together. Fold ears in half lengthwise; stitch them to head along placement lines.

Using four strands of black embroidery floss, embroider eyes with satin stitch and mouth and nostrils with straight stitch.

For tail, wrap pearl cotton around a 7-inch scrap of cardboard thirty times. Tie a short length of pearl cotton around loops at one end of cardboard. Cut loops at other end of cardboard. Wrap end of tie around tail. See Diagram 4. Insert tied end into opening on horse about ½ inch and sew it securely in place.

For mane, fold a 5″ × 11½″ piece of paper into thirds across width so that it is about 3¾ inches wide. Set aside 2 yards of pearl cotton for sewing. Beginning ½ inch from ends, wrap pearl cotton loosely around paper with loops close together. Machine-stitch along center of paper. See Diagram 5. Tear paper from each side of loops along perforations of stitching. For bangs, fold a 1½″ × 6″ piece of paper into thirds across width so that it is 2 inches wide. Wrap pearl cotton around it twelve times. Stitch across loops ½ inch from one end. Cut loops closest to stitching. Remove paper. Place bangs on head with stitching even with center of ears. Using pearl cotton, backstitch bangs to head over stitching. See Diagram 6. Place stitching line of mane along neck and backstitch to neck seam.

Stitch curved dart in center of saddle. Press or baste under ¼ inch along edges. Stitch hem in place with running stitches, using four strands of blue embroidery floss. For stirrups, cut two 3-inch pieces of blue ribbon. Fold each in half and sew

196

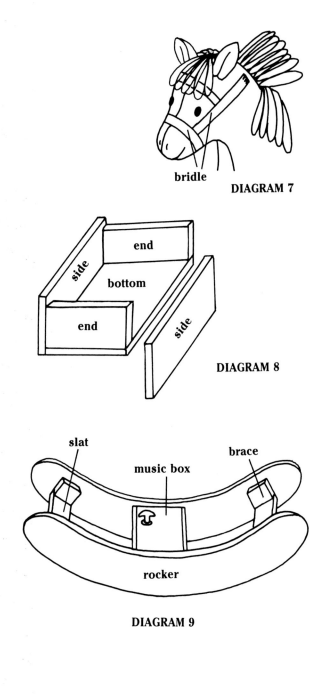

bridle

DIAGRAM 7

DIAGRAM 8

end *side* *bottom* *end* *side*

slat *brace* *music box* *rocker*

DIAGRAM 9

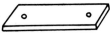

slat

DIAGRAM 10

ends to hem of saddle in center of each side. Place saddle on horse, matching dart to center seam; tack it in place along seam and lower edges. Cut two hearts from dusty blue felt; glue in place on sides of saddle.

For bridle, cut two 3¼-inch pieces of red ribbon. Beginning under mane, pin strips along side of head, ending about ⅜ inch above mouth. See Diagram 7. Tack ends in place. Cut a 4½-inch piece of red ribbon. Wrap it around head over lower ends of side strips with ends overlapping on seam under head. Sew ends together; stitch lower edge of ribbon to head with tiny running stitches. Cut a 3¼-inch length of ribbon. Place it across head about ½ inch above eyes, tucking ends under side strips; sew ends in place. Cut a 13-inch length of blue ribbon for reins. Turn under ends; sew to sides of bridle so ribbon loops back around neck. Sew a sequin to sides of bridle where strips of ribbon meet.

Sand pieces of wood so they are smooth. To make box, glue ends to bottom. Glue sides to bottom and ends. See Diagram 8. Allow glue to dry. Glue braces to position on inside of rockers indicated by broken lines; allow glue to dry. With music box in wooden box, mark position on box top where key fits in music box. Drill a ¼-inch hole or the size needed to fit around key. If necessary, place a small amount of batting around music box to fill out box. Glue top on box and screw key into music box. Sand box lightly when glue is dry. Glue box to center of rockers within broken lines. See Diagram 9. Be sure to keep rockers parallel; allow glue to dry completely. Glue two slats between rockers below braces. Drill two holes along center of remaining slats ½ inch from ends. See Diagram 10.

Paint slats and entire base with blue paint, painting two coats if necessary. Allow paint to dry completely. Using strips of masking tape, mask off a ⅛-inch-thick stripe ⅛ inch from edge all around each rocker. Cut six small hearts out of center of a piece of masking tape. Place three hearts on each rocker. Paint stripe gold and hearts red. When paint is dry, remove masking tape. Attach slats to dowel inside front and back hoofs of horse with screws. Glue slats between rockers so they sit on top of braces.

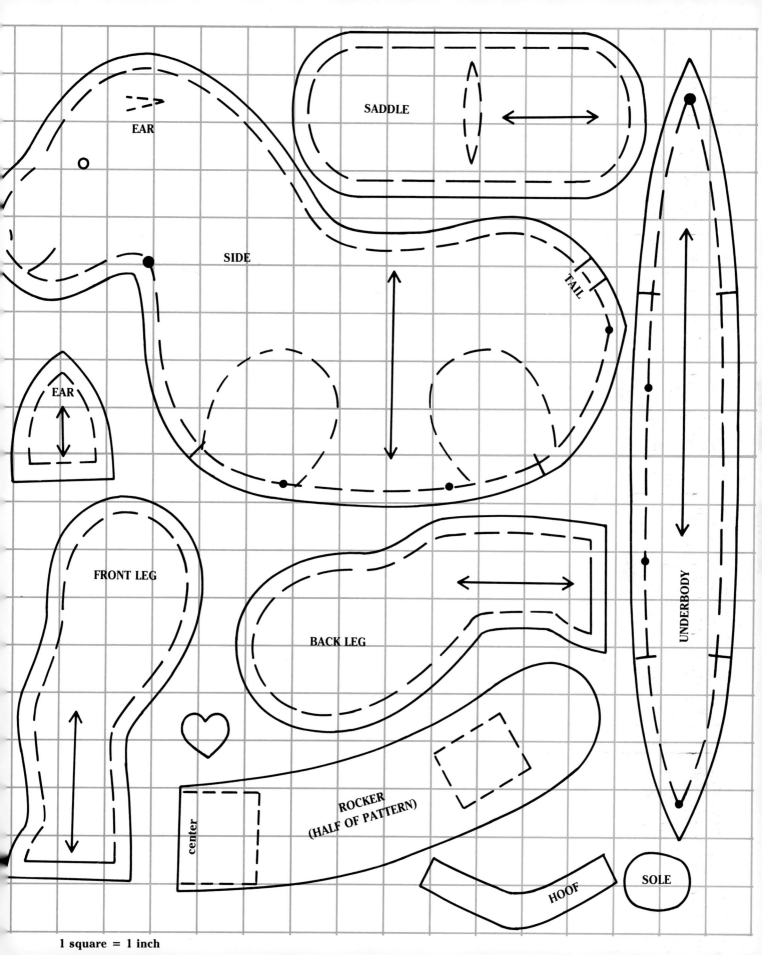

EAR

SADDLE

SIDE

TAIL

EAR

FRONT LEG

BACK LEG

UNDERBODY

center

ROCKER
(HALF OF PATTERN)

HOOF

SOLE

1 square = 1 inch

Baby's First Christmas

Celebrate Baby's first Christmas with these three counted cross-stitch projects. The angel ornament is made of stuffed fabric and felt and decorated with counted cross-stitch. The bib features holiday motifs and a festive lace edging. Baby's first Christmas stocking—personalized and decorated with an appliqué angel—is a perfect place for Santa's presents . . . and Grandma's too!

ANGEL ORNAMENT

MATERIALS:

8″ × 12″ piece white eighteen-to-the-inch Aida cloth

4″ square felt to match skin color

7″ square white satin or cotton fabric for wings

2 or 3 handfuls of polyester stuffing

Six-strand embroidery floss: 2 yards gold, 1 yard each of red and green, ½-yard color for eyes, 5 yards color for hair

½ yard ¼″-wide lace edging

White and flesh-colored sewing thread

¼ yard ¼″-wide light green satin ribbon

¼ yard ⅛″-wide white satin ribbon

4″ piece gold metallic soutache braid

Embroidery hoop

Trace patterns for angel onto tracing paper. Cut an 8″ × 7″ square of Aida cloth. Using contrasting thread, make a row of basting stitches by hand along the vertical center of the fabric. Work center row of stitches over the squares just to the right of this line. Using pencil, lightly trace gown to each side of center basting line. Cut floss into 18- to 22-inch lengths for easy handling. Use two strands for stitches. Work cross-stitch, following stitch diagram in the how-to chapter. Follow charts for design on gown and sleeves. When embroidery is completed, steam-press piece from wrong side. Trace second gown piece for back and gown bot-

tom to remaining Aida cloth, leaving room for ¼-inch seam allowance around each piece. Cut out all pieces, *adding* ¼-inch seam allowance all around. From felt, cut two heads, two feet, and two hands.

Right sides together, stitch gown front to back, leaving lower edge open. Pin gown bottom to lower edge, matching dots; stitch, leaving a 2-inch opening in center on back side of gown. Clip seam allowance around shape. Turn right-side-out. Stuff gown. Hand-quilt along line between sleeves and body. Whipstitch hands to center of sleeves. Whipstitch feet to center of lower edge of gown front about ¼ inch apart. Sew ¼-inch lace around lower edge of gown and sleeves.

For head, whipstitch top and sides of pieces together, leaving an opening between dots. Stuff slightly. Whipstitch lower edges together. Using three strands of floss, embroider eyes with satin stitch. Embroider mouth with a tiny fly stitch, using red floss.

For straight hair, cut forty-five 2-inch lengths of six-strand floss. Place each piece, one at a time, across top seam of head with about ¾ inch hanging in front. See Diagram 1. Sew in place with tiny backstitches, using three strands of floss in needle. Smooth hair down over front and back of head. Trim and glue ends in place.

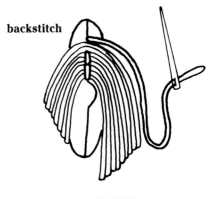

backstitch

DIAGRAM 1

200

For curly hair, work French knots on head or make loopy curls as follows: Thread a needle with a 24-inch length of three strands of floss; knot ends together. Wrap another three-strand piece of floss around a pencil several times. Cut end of floss and knot ends of floss left in needle, holding end so curls do not unwind. Slip the needle under the loops, then pass it through between the two ends; pull tightly. See Diagram 2. Slide curls off pencil and sew to head. Reknot end of thread on needle and repeat until head is covered.

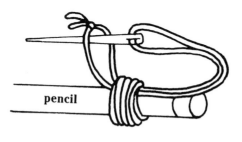

DIAGRAM 2

Trace two wings to same half of the wrong side of white fabric, leaving room for ¼-inch seam allowance around each piece. Fold fabric in half with right sides together; pin layers together along lines. Cut pieces apart, if desired; stitch along lines of wings, leaving an opening between dots. Trim seam allowance to ¼ inch; clip along curves and trim corner. Turn right-side-out. Stuff wings. Slip-stitch opening closed. Hand-quilt along broken lines on wings. Pin wings to back of gown.

Sew head over top of gown. Sew wings to back of gown sleeves and head. Sew ends of braid together in a circle to form halo; tack to back of head. Fold white ribbon in half; sew ends to back of head for hanging loop. Tie light green ribbon in a small bow; sew to gown just below chin.

CHRISTMAS STOCKING

MATERIALS:
6″ × 20″ piece white eighteen-to-the-inch Aida cloth
7″ × 15″ piece of red cotton fabric with white dots.
10″ × 15″ piece of white cotton lining fabric

2″ square piece of felt to match skin color
Scrap of white satin, optional for wings
10″ × 15″ piece of thin quilt batting
Six-strand embroidery floss: 2 yards each gold, light green, and red; 1 yard light brown, 1 yard color for hair; ½ yard color for eyes
½ yard ⅜″-wide lace edging
5″ piece ¼″-wide lace edging
Red, white, gold and flesh-colored sewing thread
⅜ yard ¼″-wide light-green satin ribbon
Embroidery hoop
3″ piece of thin gold metallic cord

To personalize stocking, write Baby's name in cross-stitch on graph paper, choosing the letters from the cross-stitch alphabet chart. If you wish to make a stocking that can be passed down through the family for any baby, write the word *Baby's* in place of the name. Center the name horizontally on the stocking top so that it rests on the broken line on the chart. If you do not wish to include the year, respace the lines vertically.

Cut a 6″ × 8″ piece of Aida cloth for front of stocking top. Mark the horizontal center and vertical center, by hand with basting stitches, using contrasting thread. Work the center stitches to the right of the vertical line and just above the horizontal line. Cut the floss into 18- to 22-inch lengths. Use two strands of floss for stitching. Work cross-stitches, following instructions in the how-to chapter. Stitch front of stocking top, following chart. When embroidery is complete, steam-press from wrong side. Count out from embroidery and mark stitching line indicated by outer solid line on chart using basting stitches. Trim fabric, adding ½ inch outside stitching line.

If desired, mark and stitch border design on another 6″ × 8″ piece of Aida cloth for back of stocking top, or else simply cut a 4″ × 6″ piece of Aida cloth for a plain white back.

Enlarge pattern for stocking and appliqué angel, following instructions in the how-to chapter. Make patterns for gown, hands, feet, head, and wings, following instructions for machine-appliqué, also in the how-to chapter. Lightly trace angel's gown onto remaining Aida cloth; mark vertical center with basting thread. Stitch heart and holly design on skirt, following chart. Cut out gown. From felt, cut head, two hands, and two feet. Cut two wings from white satin or corner of lining fabric. Cut two stockings from red fabric with white dots.

Right sides together, sew a stocking top to each stocking piece. Using these pieces as patterns, cut two whole stockings from batting and two from lining. Baste wings and gown in place on stocking front, slipping hands and feet under edge. Whipstitch hands and feet in place, using matching thread. Zigzag-stitch around gown and wings with white. Whipstitch head on angel. Sew pieces of ¼-inch-wide lace to lower edge of gown and sleeves. Embroider eyes and mouth, using two strands of floss. Embroider straight hair with satin stitch, or curly hair with French knots. Baste quilt batting to wrong side of stocking pieces. Trim batting close to basting. Right sides together, stitch linings to stocking pieces along top edge. Trim seam allowance. Fold lining to batting side of stocking pieces; baste edges together along seam line. With red sides together, stitch stocking fronts to back along raw edges. Trim seam allowance to ¼ inch and zigzag-stitch over raw edges. Turn stocking right-side-out. Sew ½-inch-wide lace to lower edge of stocking top. Fold a 5-inch piece of ribbon in half for hanger; sew to upper right corner inside stocking. Make a small bow with remaining ribbon; sew to neck edge of gown.

CHRISTMAS BIB

MATERIALS:
10″ × 14″ piece eighteen-to-the-inch Aida cloth
9″ × 11″ piece white cotton fabric
Six-strand embroidery floss: 5 yards light green, 3 yards each red and brown, 2 yards gold, ½ yard black
1 yard ⅜″-wide lace edging
White sewing thread, plus 1 yard contrasting-color thread
1 yard ⅜″-wide light-green satin ribbon
Embroidery hoop and needle

Using contrasting thread, make a row of basting stitches by hand along the vertical center of Aida cloth. Work center row of stitches as indicated on chart over the squares to the right of this line. Begin bottom border about 2½ inches from lower edge. Cut floss into 18- to 22-inch lengths for easy handling. Use two strands for stitching. Work cross-stitch following instructions in the how-to chapter. Work right half of bib, following chart. Work left half of border, stars, and reindeer in same manner, reversing chart from center to side. Using straight stitch, work reindeer's eye in black and mouth in red.

When embroidery is completed, steam-press piece from wrong side. Following instructions in the how-to chapter, enlarge bib pattern on one half of an 8½″ × 11″ piece of tracing paper with centers matching. Fold paper in half along center and trace other half of bib to paper. Center pattern over embroidery, making sure seam line is ¼ inch outside border. Make adjustments in pattern, if necessary. Pin pattern in place and cut out bib. Cut lining from white fabric.

Right sides together, stitch front to lining, leaving a 3-inch opening on one side. Clip seam along curves. Turn right-side-out. Slipstitch edges of opening together along seam line. Stitch lace around edge of bib, turning under ends at center back and sewing them in place. Cut ribbon in half on the diagonal. On straight ends, turn ¼ inch to right side twice. With wrong sides up, sew hemmed edge of ribbon to lining side of bib at top edges of back.

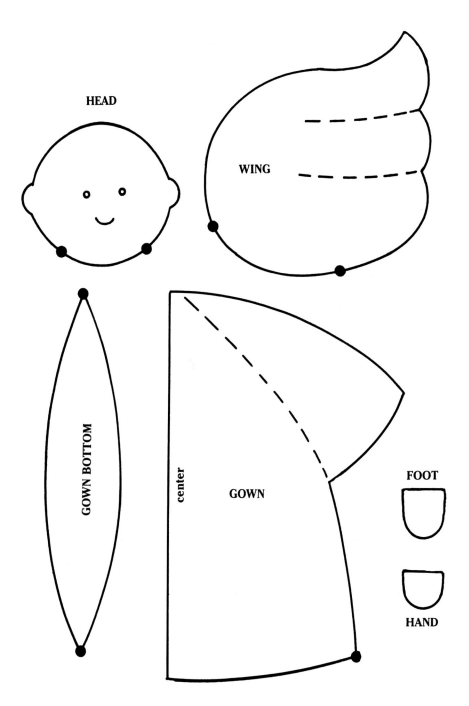

HEAD

WING

GOWN BOTTOM

center

GOWN

FOOT

HAND

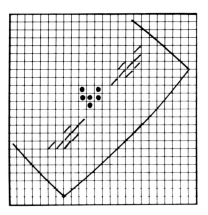

RIGHT SLEEVE
(work in reverse for left sleeve)

KEY

•	GOLD
╱	LIGHT GREEN
X	RED

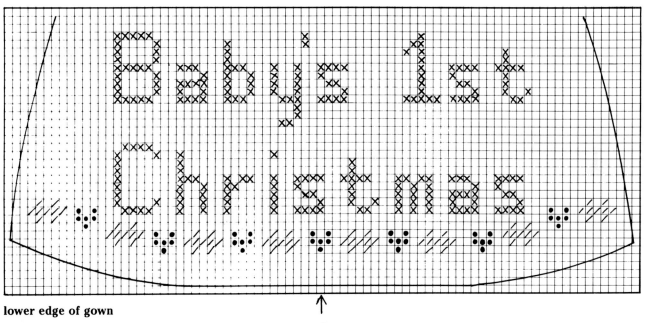

lower edge of gown

↑
center

1 square = 1 inch

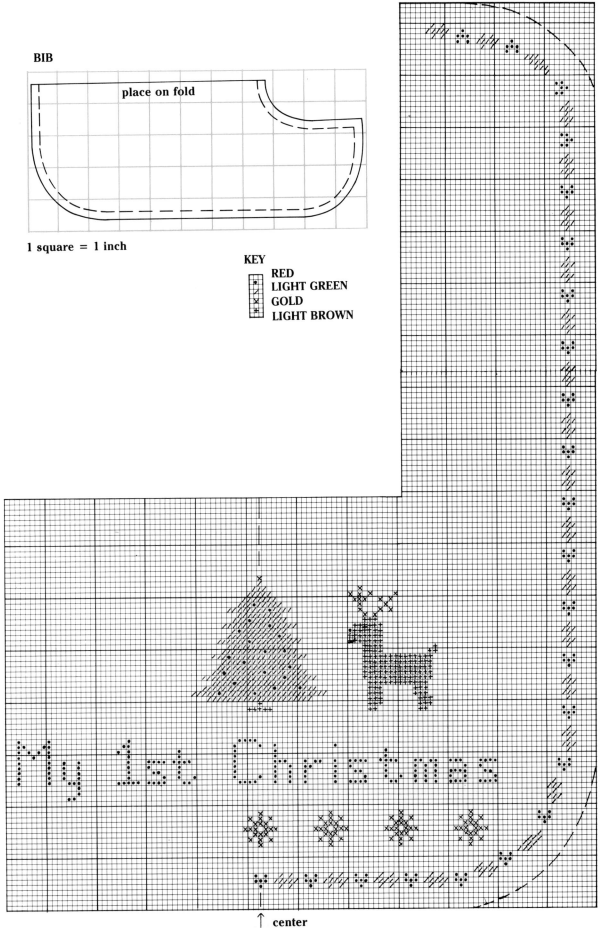

BIB

place on fold

1 square = 1 inch

KEY

RED
LIGHT GREEN
GOLD
LIGHT BROWN

My 1st Christmas

↑ center

STOCKING TOP

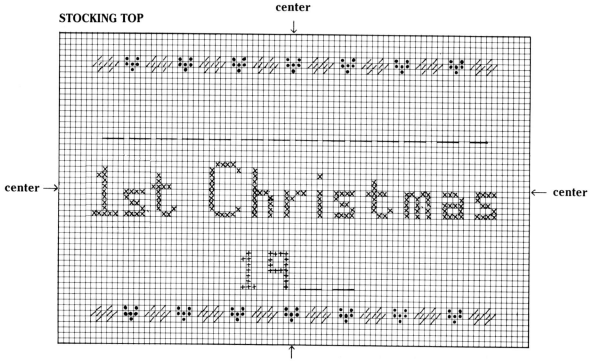

center ↓

center → ← center

center ↑

ANGEL'S GOWN

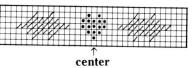

center ↑
(begin six spaces from lower edge)

ALPHABET CHART

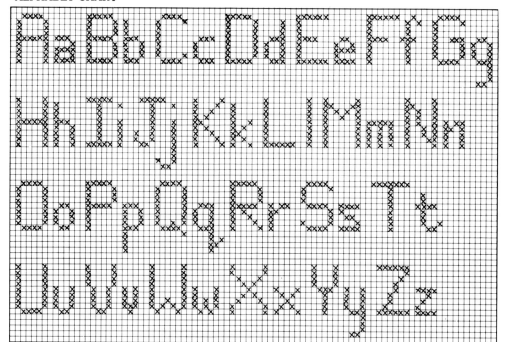

KEY
·	RED
/	LIGHT GREEN
×	GOLD
+	LIGHT BROWN

Sampler Picture Frame

hat a wonderful way to commemorate Baby's birth! Personalize this sampler with name, birthdate, and weight—then add a photo of the new arrival to complete the record.

MATERIALS:

13″ × 14″ piece fourteen-to-the-inch Aida cloth

⅜ yard off-white cotton fabric

9″ × 9¼″ quilt batting

8″ × 10″ piece fusible webbing

Two 9″ × 9¼″ pieces heavy cardboard

Six-strand embroidery floss: 6 yards light brown; 5 yards each light blue, blue, peach, light green, and yellow; 1 yard each lavender, white, and black. (If you wish to use another color to embroider the name, date, and weight, you will need about 4 yards of that color.)

Off-white sewing thread, plus 1 yard of contrasting-color thread

20″ piece of string

Embroidery hoop and needle

White glue

Use the cross-stitch alphabet chart to graph the baby's name, placing first and middle names on one line and last name below. Leave a blank space between each letter. Graph the birth date and weight. Mark the center of each line. When stitching the sampler, line up the center of each line with the center of the cross-stitch chart, and place the lower line of the words in the squares above the broken lines indicated on the chart.

Finish the edges of the Aida cloth with zigzag or overcast stitch. Using a contrasting-color thread, mark the vertical center and horizontal center, by hand, with a row of basting stitches. Mark the center opening for the photograph on both halves of the center with a row of basting stitches. Work the center stitches to the right of the vertical center line and just above the horizontal center line. Cut floss into 18- to 22-inch lengths for easy handling; use three strands for stitching. Work cross-stitch

following instructions in the how-to chapter. Work the left half of picture frame, following the chart. Work the right half of the frame, reversing the chart from center to side. When working the right bear, place his heart on your right-hand side. See photograph. Stitch the name, birthdate, and weight in position as planned. Embroider antennae of butterfly in light brown backstitch. Stitch bird's wing and beak in peach backstitch. Embroider the bunny's eye in black satin stitch, nose in peach satin stitch, mouth in peach straight stitch, and tail in white French knots. When the embroidery is completed, steam-press the sampler from the wrong side.

From off-white fabric, cut frame facing, 8¼″ × 8½″; frame back, 11″ × 10½″, and inner fabric, 8¾″ × 8½″. Cut a 3½″-wide × 3¾″-long rectangular opening in the center of batting and one cardboard piece. Place sampler front on frame facing with right sides together and centers matching. Pin around center opening indicated by basting line. Machine-stitch around opening, using a short stitch-length (at least 12 stitches per inch). Trim fabrics to ¼ inch inside stitching and clip to stitching at corners. See Diagram 1.

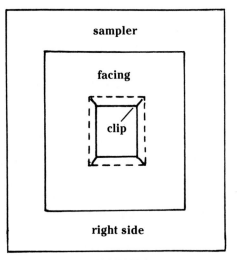

DIAGRAM 1

Turn facing to wrong side and press. Place cardboard between front and facing, matching center openings. Attach facing to cardboard along opening with 1-inch wide strips of fusible webbing. See Diagram 2.

Slip batting over front so it is between front and cardboard. Fold edges of sampler front to back of cardboard, mitering corners; fuse or glue edges in place. Fuse or glue remaining facing over edges of front. See Diagram 3.

Place backing right side down under remaining piece of cardboard. Fold edges of fabric over edge of cardboard, mitering corners; glue or fuse edges in place. Glue inner fabric on cardboard over edges of backing. Allow glue to set on both frame pieces.

Using a small nail or the point of a pair of scissors, punch a tiny hole through frame back 2 inches from top and 1 inch from sides. See Diagram 4. Make a second hole ¼-inch below first on each side. From back, using string, stitch through holes on one side then on the other, so there are two horizontal strings across backing. Tie ends in back so string is taut.

On back of frame front, place a line of glue around top bottom and one side. See Diagram 5. Place another line 1½ inches from first. One side of frame will be open to insert the photograph. Center back on front and press them together. Hold edges together with T-pins and allow the glue to dry completely.

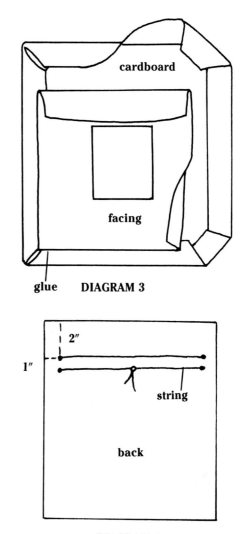

DIAGRAM 3

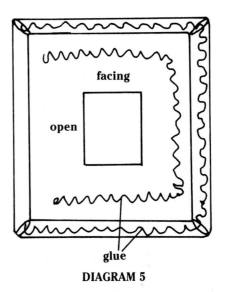

DIAGRAM 4

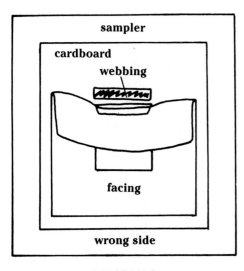

DIAGRAM 2

DIAGRAM 5

211

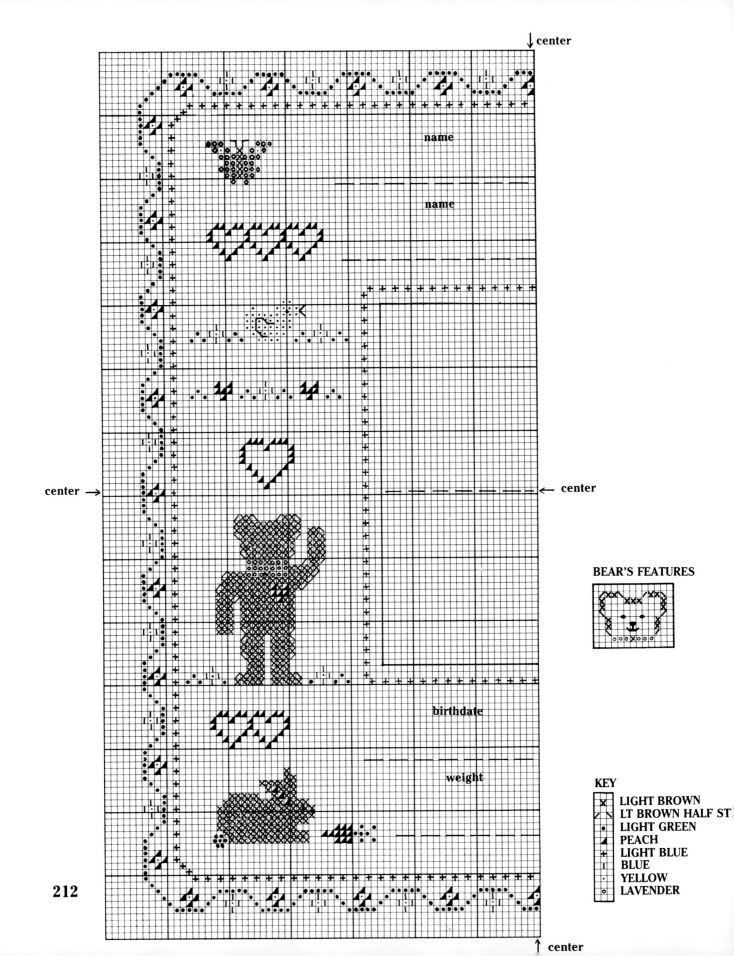

center

name

name

center → ← center

BEAR'S FEATURES

birthdate

weight

212

KEY

✕	LIGHT BROWN
◪	LT BROWN HALF ST
•	LIGHT GREEN
◣	PEACH
+	LIGHT BLUE
‖	BLUE
∙	YELLOW
⊙	LAVENDER

center

CROSS-STITCH ALPHABET

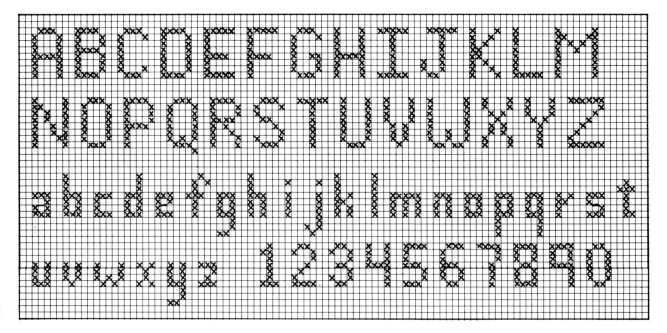

Abbreviations and Terms

KNITTING

beg — beginning

dec — decrease

dp — double-pointed

inc — increase

k — knit

p — purl

rnd(s) — round(s)

st(s) — stitch(es)

tog — together

yo — yarn over (see below)

[ ] — denotes size changes. Number before brackets indicates sts or measurement for smallest size; each following number within brackets indicates sts for each successively larger size. Use only number for size you are making.

( ) — means to repeat the directions within the parentheses as many times as indicated.

Repeat from * — means to repeat all directions following * as many more times as indicated, in addition to the first time.

k 2 tog — Knit two stitches at the same time as if they were one stitch, by inserting right needle point through front loops of both stitches.

stockinette st — K 1 row, p 1 row.

yarn over — Wrap yarn once over needle to make loop on needle. On following row, work yarn-over loop as a stitch.

CROCHET

beg — beginning

ch — chain

inc — increase

sc — single crochet

sl st — slip stitch

st(s) — stitch(es)

[ ] — denotes size changes. Number before brackets indicates sts or measurement for smallest size; each following number within brackets indicates sts for each successively larger size. Use only number for size you are making.

( ) — means to repeat the directions within the parentheses as many times as indicated.

Repeat from * — means to repeat all directions following * as many more times as indicated, in addition to the first time.

Index

For information on how you can have
Better Homes and Gardens
delivered to your door, write to:
Mr. Robert Austin,
P.O. Box 4536, Des Moines, IA 50336.